FINDING
MEANING and BEAUTY in
an IDIOTIC WORLD

Wei-Ching Chang, PhD

 FriesenPress

Suite 300 - 990 Fort St
Victoria, BC, V8V 3K2
Canada

www.friesenpress.com

Front cover image: "Wonders of sun dogs" by Who-Ching Chang, Acrylic on canvas, 16 x 20 inches, 2015.

ISBN
978-1-5255-3749-3 (Hardcover)
978-1-5255-3750-9 (Paperback)
978-1-5255-3751-6 (eBook)

1. PHILOSOPHY, METAPHYSICS

Distributed to the trade by The Ingram Book Company

To my family, friends, and all who care about the future of humanity.

Acknowledgements

MY DEEPEST THANKS TO MY FAMILY: MY FATHER, SYMONDS TUNG-LAN, and my mother, Grace Hung-huei, my brother, William, and my sisters, Sophia and Jean, for their devotion to lifelong learning and role modelling, and for providing vital support in numerous ways; my daughter, Solene, for embodying artistic and environmentalist ways of life, and my son, Jason, for sharing most enjoyable times playing tennis and engaging in intellectual musings, and their mother, Linda, for learning from all our trials and tribulations, including marriage/unmarriage, parenting, and caregiving to our parents.

I am indebted to the education systems in Taiwan, the United States, and Canada: the National Taiwan University and the University of Minnesota for philosophical thoughts, the University of Oregon and University of Toronto for training in mathematics and statistics, and the University of Alberta, not only for teaching and research, but also for allowing me to audit numerous thought-provoking courses after my retirement. I am truly grateful to all the teachers and many bright students in all these classes, some of them I have mentioned in the book although there are too many to name here. In the last ten years of my working life, I did cardiovascular research at the Canadian VIGOUR Centre (CVC), University of Alberta, and I would like to thank Dr. Paul Armstrong for his facilitation of high-quality research, and for one of his generous year end presents: Thomas Friedman's *The World is Flat*, from which I learned about the modern version of the just war theory. I am also indebted to many courses offered at the Edmonton City Arts Centre, especially Jade O'Riley's "The Poet Within." By repeatedly taking her classes, I was forced to learn many poetry forms. Jade has been a great teacher, and it is through her guidance that all the poems in this book are created.

Naturally, I am also thankful to many friends, among them Marie-Laure Baudet. She came to the University of Alberta from Brittany, France, to do a doctoral degree in physiology. We became good friends, taking yoga, aikido, and qigong classes together, plus organizing a philosophy circle to discuss many interesting issues, including feminism (as mentioned in Section 7.2 of this book). Next, I would like to thank my Russian friend, Nina Krakovna, who exemplifies the philosophy of "work hard and play hard"—including a trip with me to climb China's famed Yellow Mountain and informing me about *The Longevity Puzzle* mentioned in Section 8.1. I am also grateful to Joy Fraser, a nursing-health administration professor, with whom I have exchanged ideas and developed our paper, "Cooperate! A Paradigm Shift for Health Equity." My sincere thanks are also to my dear friend Jenny Tsai, with whom I have taken many art courses, attended art shows, and gone on bike rides to city parks. Her childlike curiosity is contagious, and she is always looking for challenges in life. Although officially retired as a professor in toxicology before she immigrated to Canada from Taiwan, she went back to Taiwan recently to undertake stem cell research and therapy. I should also thank Jack Tuszynski, a super-bright physics professor turned medical researcher, who has been my tennis partner for decades, for his lasting and stimulating friendship and support. Last but not least, I would like to thank Linda Duncan, our NDP member of parliament, for her inspiring political activism. She used to come to my daughter's yoga class and to my year-end "Age of Aquarius" party. When I got hurt recently, she came to the hospital to cheer me up and brought me Steven Pinker's *Enlightenment Now*. I find it inspiring, making the case for reason, science, humanism, etc., as I have been doing in my work.

If I am allowed to go all the way back to Taiwan, my indebtedness to my former philosophy teacher, Yin Hai-kuang, is obvious. He was the one who introduced me to Bertrand Russell, Karl Popper, Alfred Jules Ayer, the Vienna Circle, Wittgenstein, and the whole field of the philosophy of science. His fearless criticism of authoritarianism has a lasting impression on me and is reflected in this manuscript.

I would also like to thank FriesenPress. All the staff members are extremely helpful, and the editor in particular has made numerous valuable suggestions for improving the manuscript, its organization and presentation. As a result, I hope that the quality of this book will meet the approval and even exceed the expectations of its readers.

Table of Contents

Preface

What now matters most is that we rich people give up some of our luxuries, ceasing to overheat the Earth's atmosphere, and taking care of this planet in other ways, so that it continues to support intelligent life. (Parfit & Scheffler, 2011, p. 419)

WHAT ARE THE MOST IMPORTANT THINGS IN ONE'S LIFE? WHAT WOULD I like to share the most with my loved ones? What would be my most valuable gifts to my family, my friends, and the world? How would I like to be remembered by those who care about me?

I am a dreamer, always dreaming about a better world. Perhaps what I can and should do is to share my thoughts and experiences with my loved ones and with any like-minded people anywhere in the world. Therefore, after my seventy-third birthday on December 28, 2010, I resolved to start jotting down some of my thoughts in hopes of leaving something memorable behind. I have been preparing myself for more than a decade, especially since my retirement in the mid-2000s. I have been reviving my interests in philosophy and literature, and researching issues such as equity in relation to health and gender, the Taoist philosophy of yin and yang and its applications in the form of acupuncture, feminist theory and philosophy, political philosophy, contemporary Canadian and global literature, and the art of photography, drawing and painting. So, on New Year's Day 2011, I felt inspired and confident enough to face my computer, gather my thoughts, and start pounding the keyboard. I thought I had something interesting, profound, and insightful to say about life in general and personal experiences in particular, which may resonate with people around me. My efforts wouldn't be in vain if I could inspire and touch the hearts of just a few individuals.

A brief personal history may help the reader to understand where I'm coming from. I was born on December 28, 1937, in Taiwan, which was under Japanese rule until 1945, when, after fifty years, Japan ceded Taiwan back to China at the end of the Second World War. In 1947, however, there was a popular protest against police brutality in Taipei, which escalated into an island-wide uprising. Chiang Kai-Shek's Nationalist government reacted by sending its army from Mainland China and violently suppressed the uprising, executing or imprisoning its leaders, participants, and sympathizers. An estimated 18,000–28,000 people died during this period (*Shattuck 2017*). This was followed by the imposition of martial law in 1949, and the so-called "white terror" lasted until 1987. Anyone critical of the Nationalist government during that period was branded as a communist or communist sympathizer, and as many as 140,000 people were summarily imprisoned and three to four thousand executed (*Yang 2017*). There was no freedom of speech, and during my university years, many prominent intellectuals—including one of my philosophy professors, and later some of my classmates—were persecuted for speaking out against government policies, or simply for advocating human rights and democratic ideals.

I loved literature during my formative years, spending much of my leisure time indulging in all the Chinese and world literature I could lay my hands on. Without a second thought, I went on to study Chinese literature at the National Taiwan University in 1956. Unfortunately, almost the entire Chinese Literature Program was devoted to studying Chinese classics, since much of the contemporary literary works were banned in Taiwan as being left-leaning and subversive. Since there was no freedom of expression, I figured it was not possible to be a writer under such an oppressive regime, so I switched my major to philosophy. Like thousands of new university graduates who were disillusioned with the political atmosphere at the time, I got the help of my family to do a master's degree in philosophy at the University of Minnesota. However, I found it much too difficult to master the subtlety and nuances of the English language to further pursue a career in academic philosophy, so I turned to mathematics and statistics at the University of Oregon and completed a PhD at the University of Toronto. That's how I settled on a long research career in Alberta, Canada, the land of opportunity, first in tourism, followed by hospital care and health care policy, and finally in public health and cardiovascular research at the University of Alberta.

I missed philosophy and literature, however. So when the International Society for Equity in Health was formed, and an inaugurating conference was held in Cuba in 2000, I seized the opportunity and wrote and presented a paper on the meaning of equity in health, which was subsequently published in an academic journal. The concept of equity inspired me, so I continued my research into gender and socioeconomic influences through my work in cardiology, but also as a hobby in my leisure time through reviewing literature in feminism and Taoism. Eventually, I decided to explore the concrete applications of the philosophy of yin and yang to the practice of acupuncture, so, as a retirement project, I enrolled myself in a three-year acupuncture program and obtained a diploma in acupuncture from MacEwan University. Since I had the luxury to live on my pensions instead of acupuncture practice, I decided to devote myself to full-time learning and writing—by auditing courses in philosophy, women's studies, political science, English literature, East Asian Studies, etc., in addition to writing poetry, exploring the art of photography, and drawing and painting.

I didn't know or remember anything about poetry in English except, somehow, for the opening stanza of Longfellow's "A Psalm of Life" from my high school English: "Tell me not, in mournful numbers, / Life is but an empty dream! / For the soul is dead that slumbers, / And things are not what they seem." So, I thought it would be neat to learn something about English poems, since poems tend to be short and sweet, versatile, and easier to compose and finish than essays and novels. They constituted an excellent medium of learning and expressing myself in English, organizing my thoughts, and putting them on paper. It really complemented all my other studies, since some of the ideas I learned from these courses inspired me to compose my poems, which I sent to my poetry instructor, Jade O'Riley, for comment, criticism, and suggestions. I have benefited greatly from all such instruction, reading, writing, and interactions. Since my poetry tends to be philosophical in nature, I thought the combination of my poetry with the prose here would enhance and illuminate my viewpoints better and more clearly. If they complement each other, why not experiment with this new literary form, an expanded version of Japanese *haibun*?

Well, what would I like to write about? I am not entirely sure, although I have some pretty good ideas. In the back of my mind, I want to write something philosophical: What are the most valuable things in life? How do we live a good life? What are the sound (rational, ethical, and aesthetical) and faulty (irrational, unethical, and unappealing) ways of thinking and behaving? Why do we think the way we do, and how can we do better? I think the world is in such a mess because most of us don't think clearly, rationally, ethically, compassionately, and charmingly all the time with the big picture—including everyone in the world—in our minds. So the least I can do is to sort out this mess not only for myself but also for others around me. Having witnessed the horrors of wars and atrocities at home and all over the world—WWII, the White Terror in Taiwan, the Korean War, the Cold War, the Vietnam War, the two Gulf Wars, the war on terror, and the conflicts, mass murders, and genocides that occurred in many countries in Africa, Eastern Europe, Asia, South and Central America, the Middle East, etc., and even in the United States and Canada—I have to ask myself about the intelligence and sanity of human race and where we are heading. Are aggression and a warlike mentality inevitable? What would it take to change the self-destructive course of our past and present? What can I do to make a difference so that we have a future for us individually and collectively, especially for generations to come?

Unless we think and act rationally and ethically with the welfare and the future of the entire human race utmost in our mind, we may be doomed and heading for continued conflicts, miseries, and even extinction. That's what motivates me to write—in English—since my family and loved ones are mostly in North America now. We really need further rounds of cultural renaissance or revolution to liberate us from irrational, superstitious, narrow-minded, egoistic, nationalistic, and sub-global ways of thinking about the world. Such a concern is global and universal despite local variations and differences. Nothing short of the ethics of global citizenship would save humankind. That's the message—such as Parfit's idea of sustaining intelligent life—I would like to explore and develop, justify, and convey in this manuscript, so as to inspire myself and share with others. The whole exercise, of course, is idealistic, but as Judith Butler says, and I will elaborate in Section 7.4, one of philosophy's jobs is to tackle what seems impossible but worth doing—lest our world becomes impoverished.

The French philosopher Gilles Deleuze thought it premature to ask serious philosophical questions such as: "What was it all about, what have I been doing all my life?" until one reaches old age. Perhaps my timing, now at eighty years of age, is just about right for my musing of some of the most significant and yet controversial issues in epistemology (How do we know?), ontology (What exists? What's reality? What's the world really like?), ethics (What's good or bad, and how should we live?), and aesthetics (What's beauty? What's art?), and their intersections, among others. The issues I'll be addressing in the following sections, although philosophical in nature, have practical implications on how we deal with the world. Since these issues are confusing even to the best minds in the past and the present, I'll try to elucidate them as best as I can and take sides/stands when I see fit. So here goes . . .

Wei-Ching Chang, 2018,
Edmonton, Alberta, Canada

1.
The Meaning of Life

"I realize that mortals are only tiny drops lost in an ocean of time." (Helen Keller, 1936; as quoted in Belck 1967, p. 55)

THERE IS NO QUESTION THAT OUR LIVES ARE JUST MINUTE SPECKS IN THE vast universe of space and time if viewed from the "point of view of the universe," to use the English philosopher Henry Sidgwick's phrase. That much is certain, and also humbling. Do our lives of less than 100 years (for most of us) matter much when considering the billions of years since the existence of our universe, with trillions of stars in our universe? We all like to think, or wish, our lives have some meaning—not only to ourselves, but also to others. The worst thing that could happen to any of us is the feeling of total insignificance and worthlessness, that our lives do not count and that they mean nothing. I'd like to start, therefore, by addressing this crucial issue, to affirm and justify life's meaning.

Many prominent thinkers have denied that life has any meaning. Friedrich Nietzsche, for instance, didn't see any meaning to be had in this or any other life, and he viewed Christianity, which claimed true meaning to be found only in a supernatural world, as a big mistake. Sigmund Freud also thought meaning to be an illusion, a product of the vicissitudes of early childhood. Both thought that only a small group of "strong" or "mature" elites could transcend such nihilism or illusion, while others couldn't live peacefully and productively in a state of life's meaningfulness. Albert Camus, of course, is famous for expressing a nihilistic view, denying the possibility of meaning due to the lack of after life and of a rational, divinely ordered universe. Viktor Frankl (1963), in his fascinating book *Man's Search for Meaning*, advises us:

> Ultimately, man should not ask what the meaning of his life is, but rather must recognize that it is he who is asked. In a word, each man is questioned by life and he can only answer to life by answering for his own life; to life he can only respond by being responsible. (p. 172)

All we can and should do, according to Frankl, is to live responsibly. True—we have to live in the present as best as we can. The question of meaning, I maintain, emerges only when we reflect, interpret, and pass judgement on our lives. Hence, it's a second-order reflection after we have lived, responsibly or not. We can't change the past, but we can assess and learn from it. We could ask: are we condemned to performing an endless and senseless work all our lives, as depicted in Camus' *The Myth of Sisyphus*? If we find our lives in the past have been somewhat meaningless, can we do something to make them more meaningful in the future?

I firmly believe that it's not pointless to ask the question of life's meaning. Jean-Paul Sartre (2007/1945) famously states, however, that "life has no meaning *a priori*. Life itself is nothing until it is lived, it is we who give it meaning, and value is nothing more than the meaning that we give it." (p. 51) It's true that we can and should do our best to make it more meaningful, but I don't think his existential view that life has no meaning *a priori* is correct. In response to Dawkins' and other neo-Darwinists' view of nature as having "no design, no purpose, no evil and no good, nothing but blind, pitiless indifference," the British philosopher Mary Midgley (2012) states:

> It is an objective fact that all living things behave purposively: that is, they all strive and struggle to live in the way that their particular nature requires. They do not, of course, need to be conscious to do this. (p. 110)

Thus, there is no question that life behaves purposively. It is in our genes and DNA. The meaning of life is already embedded in the mysterious process of evolution of the world, from the inanimate to the animate; and in the case of living beings, to acquire "knowledge," consciously or unconsciously, for survival and flourishing in whatever environments they happen to be in. For humans, in particular, life also developed through what Dawkins called "memes" (units of culture), and life is individually as well as culturally diverse and conflicting at times. The meaning of life also evolves over time in response to the changing natural and cultural environment. However, the overriding purpose of all creatures is "survival and flourishing," to have "the good life." The meaning of life, therefore, is in the natural (conscious or unconscious) drive to achieve the idealized good and healthy life. When we say our lives aren't meaningful (enough), what we are saying is that we aren't satisfied with our lives, which aren't as good as they could be. It's a reality check relative to the ideal of what the particular lives could be. Such an Aristotelian ideal has also been enunciated, for example, in Confucius' image of an ideal gentleman who understands and does what's right, unwavering in the face of hardships—in contrast to the "small" or "inferior" man who understands what's profitable and sees what's right, but does not do it. Taoism, which is more egalitarian, propounds the spontaneous ways of being, working with the natural flow of energy—in harmony with nature and with our true selves. These ways of thinking help us elucidate the meaning of our lives.

A meaningful life, however, is not the same as a happy life, although they may overlap considerably. Many great artists and writers—such as Vincent Van Gogh, Paul Gauguin, Friedrich Nietzsche, Ernest Hemingway, John Keats, Akira Kurosawa, Virginia Woolf, and Sylvia Plath, for example—suffered severe depression in their lives and some of them even committed suicide, and yet few would question the meaningfulness of their lives. Happiness, though, cannot be pursued; it must ensue—as proffered by Frankl. The same advice may apply to meaningfulness, although it can be pursued to some extent by reflecting and renewing one's self and environment, so as to actualize one's dreams. In my case, I was not totally satisfied with my life after over thirty years of research in tourism, health care, hospital care, and clinical medicine. Although I've authored many papers in peer-reviewed academic journals and attained some degree of satisfaction and meaningfulness of life, a sense of emptiness surfaced in my consciousness when I approached retirement age: I haven't accomplished my youthful dream of becoming a writer! And I have not explored the mystery of life to my satisfaction! I was truly blessed because I was able to consciously pursue my writer's dreams after retirement in hopes that a more meaningful life would ensue. It's never too late in life to try! Even if nothing is going to come out of it, at least I have the satisfaction that I have tried.

So I embarked on intellectual expeditions, studied acupuncture at McEwan University, followed by auditing courses in literature, philosophy, cultural and political theories, art histories, and fine art, etc. at the University of Alberta. Retirement turned out to be a tremendous blessing, giving me all the freedom to consciously seek meaning in life, to cultivate self-discovery and self-renewal. For most of my adult life, I have been developing and utilizing the left side of my brain, and under-developing the right side. So it was time to seek a rebalancing in me, and in the world, the Tao or the Way of nature: to harmonize the left and the right, the reason/rationality and the emotion/intuition, the quantitative and the qualitative, the masculine and the feminine, and the yang and the yin. This transformation is the theme of my following poems:

Awakening / Aubade / 2012

It's a long time coming and yet it has to come
I wonder what happens to my writer's dream
I feel queasy and ponder what I've become
A mundane researcher with an altered scheme
I resolve to lift myself out of the ho-hum

I want to change course but see only darkness
There must be a ray of hope if I keep researching
Thirty-five years is a long time to suppress

My passion and yearning for creative writing
I make amend to prevent my dream's regress

A Cuban conference on health equity
Finally brings light and illuminates my way
I jump on this golden opportunity
I write and present a paper far away
To enact my renaissance without delay

That's the dawning of my awakening
There's no turning back, I can no longer await
Fulfilling my destiny as a writer in waiting
I've exerted my will, and the rest is fate
To carry on my life's most sacred mandate

I Have A Dream World / Haiku / 2015

I have a dream world
Where truth, beauty, goodness reign
And harmony rules

Since we are social creatures, we also crave for connecting with others in various ways for mutual support—to love and be loved. So I'll turn to the topic of love, which I consider to be the most fundamental and essential ingredient of a meaningful life.

2.

Love: A Many-Splendoured Thing

Love is the ultimate and highest goal to which man can aspire. (Viktor Frankl, 1946, 1992)

Love makes the world go around. Love is blind. All you need is love . . . (Jeanette Winterson, 1992)

To love a thing means wanting it to live. (Confucius)

THERE IS NO QUESTION THAT LOVE SUSTAINS LIFE AND RENDERS IT meaningful—or not, if abused. The depiction of love as "a many-splendoured thing" in the popular 1955 movie, based on the 1952 autobiographical novel *A Many-Splendoured Thing* by Han Suyin, is very apt. The more I delve into this concept, the more splendid it presents to me while cognizant of its devastating effects when associated with dark and less rosy emotions. For life to flourish, there is nothing more important than positive, mature, and altruistic love, in contrast to negative, immature, and possessive love, to value and cherish it. Biology teaches us that all living creatures strive to survive, flourish, and propagate their genes. It is, indeed, a biological imperative to value life as a living being, and humans are no exception. I have never questioned my will to live. Yes, my life has ups and downs. I experienced many failures and some successes, but never in my life, not even when I lost my jobs or went through a divorce, for instance, did I experience any inkling of giving up my life.

Love gives more meaning to life. When I audited courses in English literature in recent years, however, I was struck by the prevalence of anxieties, depression, and even suicides among the most gifted and accomplished writers—among them were Charlotte Perkins Gilman (1860–1935) who was diagnosed with incurable breast cancer and committed suicide, Virginia Woolf (1882–1941) who drowned herself due to chronic bipolar disorder, Elizabeth Bishop (1911–1979) who was afflicted with depression and alcoholism, Dylan Thomas (1914–1953) who died of chronic alcoholism, Anne Sexton (1928–1974) who killed herself by idling her car in a closed garage after bouts of depression and substance abuse, Sylvia Plath (1932–1963) who had a history of depression and committed suicide after the separation from her poet husband Ted Hughes, and the accomplished Taiwanese writer Qiu Miaojin (1969–1995) who committed suicide in Paris at age twenty-six. For whatever reason—often haunted by their experiences of early childhood abuse or psychosocial taboos of being gay, for instance—they no longer valued and loved their lives enough to willingly, or compulsively, forego the biological imperative of the will to live, which is clearly influenced by one's culture and life experience. The French philosopher-writer Albert Camus (1991/1955) begins his *The Myth of Sisyphus and Other Essays* with the statement: "There is but one truly serious philosophical problem, and that is suicide." (p. 3)

I'm also struck by this nagging philosophical question: is human life worth preserving? Indeed, life emerged and perished throughout the Earth's four billion or so years of history, and new species came and went, so why should we be concerned if human beings do not survive and prosper in the future? This is a theme explored in some recent science fiction (SF) novels such as *Calculating God* by Robert Sawyer (2000) and *Watchmen* by Alan Moore (2005/1987). The threat of human extinction is there through, for example, an explosion of a supernova in *Calculating God* and a nuclear holocaust in *Watchmen*. Jon, a superhero in *Watchmen*, has to wrestle with this question and weigh the pros and cons of their implications. Most of us take the value of life for granted, but why should we? Crooked Finger, a tortured Schopenhauerian philosopher-recluse in the fascinating 1995 Dutch feminist film *Antonia's Line*, rejects life and regards it as a source of unending agony and misery according to the so-called male principle, and is driven to suicide; whereas Antonia, who upholds the life-affirming female principle, enjoys life to the very end, rejoices in death as a natural event when the time comes, and shares it with her loved ones.

Rather than viewing the world as a joke or an illusion, and life as painful and aimless as Schopenhauer would want us to believe, I cherish the life-affirming feminine principle in view of the wonders of the evolution of life, consciousness, emotion, and intelligence, and of the universe that sustains them. Anyone who has watched David Suzuki's documentary series *The Nature of Things*, or the amazing film *March of The Penguins*, for instance, would be awe-struck about life's miracles. Our lives are indeed miraculous and precious, dazzling and beautiful beyond all imagination, although we often fail to notice and appreciate them. This failure to appreciate and love our lives leads us to devalue our lives. On the other hand, we would naturally value our lives and find them meaningful if we love ourselves and cherish the world around us. There is so much to love, adore, explore, grasp, know, appreciate, experience, imagine, rejoice, etc. in this world. As Antonia puts it poetically, it is the only dance we dance. The choice is ours: love of life, although inherent in our biological design, needs to be constantly nurtured and cherished in a world full of hostilities and apathies in order for it to manifest itself and become universal.

The above thoughts inspired me to write the following poem:

Love Is Life's Most Important Thing / Shakespearean sonnet / 2011

I'd say love is life's most important thing
Through love we gain true appreciation
That life is a miraculous wellspring
Dazzling beyond all imagination

Loveless, we may despair, commit suicide
Give up our precious lives prematurely
Our depression draws us to life's downside
Unable to see the upside clearly

Should we care if we have a death instinct
Or if *Homo sapiens* do not survive?
It's common that creatures become extinct
So, why should we care whether humans thrive?
We love and care because life's fantastical
Despite its ups and downs, it's magical

2.1. Selfish and Blind Love

LOVE IS SUBLIME. LIFE WITHERS WHEN DEPRIVED OF LOVE. HOWEVER, love can also be selfish or blind. This message was brought home when I watched a 2006 Spanish-American movie, *Goya's Ghosts*, directed by Milos Forman.

It was a haunting, fictitious story of a wealthy merchant's daughter, Ines, whom the famous painter Francisco Goya used as a model for his paintings. She was falsely accused of practising Judaism and "put to the question" (a euphemism for torture) by the Spanish Inquisition. Upon obtaining her confession, she was imprisoned. To secure her release, her father Tomas Bilbatua approached, through Goya, Brother Lorenzo, a monk who vowed to restore the power and authority of the church through harsh means such as "the question." While visiting Ines in prison, Lorenzo raped her. However, Lorenzo himself was put to the question by Tomas and confessed to being a monkey. Lorenzo was subsequently promised to burn his confession upon Ines' release, and was given a large sum of gold for the Church to plead leniency, but the Inquisitor General Father Gregorio, while accepting money, refused to release Ines.

Ines stayed in prison for fifteen years and gave birth to a baby girl, Alicia, who was taken away from her. Then the French army under Napoleon invaded Spain, abolished the Inquisition, and set the prisoners free. The disgraced Lorenzo became Napoleon's chief prosecutor, lived in luxury, sent Ines to an asylum upon learning that he fathered Alicia, and did everything possible to prevent Goya's attempt to unite the mother and the daughter, by trying to send Alicia to America. Eventually, however, the British defeated the French troops, the Spanish Inquisition was restored, and Lorenzo was arrested and sentenced to death if he did not repent. Ines was there at the site of the execution, frantically calling Lorenzo, believing in her confused state of mind that the baby she found a while ago was their daughter, while Alicia was in the arm of a British officer scoffing at Lorenzo. Refusing to repent, Lorenzo was garrotted, and his dead body was taken away on a cart while escorted by Ines holding his hand.

Why did Ines love despicable Lorenzo to the very end? Because he was the only man she knew and was intimate with, and whom she trusted and put all her hope in for her salvation. She was grateful to him and didn't know he had taken advantage of his position and power for his sexual gratification. How could she have known what a mean character he was? Ines' love of Lorenzo sustained her to the very end. The film was open-ended, however. Would Goya continue his efforts to bring the mother and the daughter together after Lorenzo's death? Would that benefit the mother and the daughter? What would happen to them?

Indeed, why do we love? Love is an important ingredient of the will to live. When love ceases, life dims. Love may be conditional upon knowledge: our knowledge of the object of love may alter our perception of love, but we may not really know the object enough to change our perception. Love can be blind. It's not Ines' fault she loved Lorenzo with all her heart. Ignorance can be bliss, although I can't help feeling a bit sad after watching the movie.

So, what's love? Many poets have written about it. The Cento is a poetic form made up of lines from poems by other authors. It's kind of fun to see what other poets have written about love, and how I can compose my own poem about love based on other poets' works. So, here it is, my poem, borrowing the lines from other poets, about love:

What Is Love? / The Cento / 2012

"How does Love speak?" (Ella Wheeler Wilcox, "Love's Language")

"Speak earth and bless me with what is richest." (Audre Lorde, "Love Poem")

"Love calls us to the things of this world." (Richard Wilbur, "Love Calls Us . . .")

"Love set[s] you going like a fat gold watch." (Sylvia Plath, "Morning Song")

"What is love, but a beacon, to guide the wayward heart." (Matt Dubois, "Love Defined")

"Like wings of a hummingbird, my heart flutters feverishly." (Elisha Bancer, "Beautiful Dream")

"I crave your mouth, your voice, your hair." (Pablo Neruda, "Love Sonnet XI")

"I love thee with the breath, smiles, tears, of all my life! (Elizabeth Barrett Browning, "Sonnet 43")

"I carry your heart with me." (E. E. Cummings, "I Carry Your Heart With Me")

"I count no more my wasted tears." (Elizabeth Akers Allen, "At Last")

"I love you without knowing how, or when, or from where." (Pablo Neruda, "Love Sonnet XVII")

"Love, it was good to talk to you tonight." (Marilyn Hacker, "Rondeau . . .")

2.2. Love and Jealousy

LOVE IS UBIQUITOUS. IT'S EVERYBODY'S "IMPERATIVE NEED"; IT'S "UNION with somebody, or something," (p. 30) and our sanity depends on it, as stated in Eric Fromm's (1955) *The Sane Society*. It also has many faces: self-love, parental love, brotherly/sisterly love, friendship and romantic love, love for work, love of nature, etc. Love, however, can be distorted by unequal power relations—as in the case of Ines' love of Lorenzo—and is often destroyed by negative emotions such as jealousy. Indeed, according to Hara Estroff Marano (2009), "Jealousy is not just the main motivation for spouse battering. Sexual jealousy is the leading cause of spousal murder worldwide."

Jealousy, moreover, entails a sense of insecurity and inadequacy, and that's what happened in the haunting 2014 German movie, *Cloud 9: A Story of New Love in Old Age*. In that movie, a sixty-seven-year-old woman, Inge, who was married to Werner for thirty years, unexpectedly fell in love with seventy-six-year-old Karl. Despite her blissful love and perhaps out of guilt, she eventually confided her love of Karl to Werner—against the advice of her daughter, Petra. Inge kept saying sorry to Werner, adding, "I didn't want this. It just happened." Werner, on the other hand, started blaming himself, asking her, "What did I do wrong?" To which Inge replied, "You didn't do anything wrong. Otherwise we couldn't have lived together for 30 years." These words failed to console Werner, who, after Inge moves out, commits suicide. Inge, of course, was devastated: "I didn't want this . . . It can't be true . . . It's my fault ..."

Love between Inge and Karl was beautiful, except that it devastated Werner. Why couldn't love be shared? Why should Werner feel jealous and insecure, rather than being happy for Inge? Doesn't loving someone mean wanting the best, and happiness, for the one we love? Earp (2012) has framed this issue in terms of the clash of drives and ideals. While conceding that the practice of "open marriages" isn't ethically problematic on the surface and may, in fact, work for some since the human species didn't evolve as monogamous, he nevertheless maintains that "it simply wouldn't work on a wide scale" because of jealousy (in addition to inequality): "Jealousy is as much a part of our nature as is the impulse to cheat, and few open marriage resolutions are likely to erase the pain caused by a philandering spouse." (pp. 15-16) According to Hara Estroff Marano (2009), however, jealousy "isn't quite as inevitable as it's been made to appear," since those who are more cooperative, agreeable and compassion-ate are less likely to be jealous as compared to those who are neurotic and suspicious—as shown by the University of Texas psychologist David Buss' work.

Robert S. Griffin, in his review, "On 'Cloud 9,'" states: "John Lennon wrote a song called 'Nobody Loves You' that includes the lines: Nobody loves you when you're old and gray. Nobody sees you when you're on cloud nine." Then he reflects:

> It's true, as I can attest, that far fewer people love you when you are old and grey, and far fewer see you when you are on cloud nine, or in any other state of being, for that matter. But, contrary to Lennon's lyrics, someone might love you when you are old and grey, it's possible, and really, it only takes one person to love you if it is the right person. And someone might see you, you can't be sure no one will. However it turns out, though, the exis-tential challenge, to call it that, for me and someday for you, is to live fully and with honor anyway; to affirm our lives, not end them. (p. 5)

Right on, Robert! How true! In addition to jealousy, another mortal sin in life is guilt. Love is everywhere in this wonderful world if we look for it. It's possible, and indeed imperative, for us to cultivate altruistic, inspiring love and live fully and serenely, by letting go of such negative feelings associ-ated with immature, possessive love. In fact, a meta-analysis of twenty-five relevant studies (Acevedo & Aron, 2009) found that in long- and short-term relationships, romantic love without obsession was strongly associ-ated with relationship satisfaction, but obsession was negatively correlated with it in long-term relationships. Although love is beautiful, perhaps Petra was right: Inge should not have felt guilty and confided in Werner, since Werner is not the type who can handle it. Ignorance is bliss at times!

Werner's love of Inge, moreover, is not based on friendship, "the best kind of love"; and for Aristotle, it bears "good will to each other and wish good things for each other, without this escaping their notice" (Burton, 2017). The best kind of love, therefore, is to empathize, and share both the joy and sorrow with each other. That is the kind of love I admire the most; always wish for the best for your loved ones, as expressed in my poem below:

On Friendship / Free Verse / 2012

Is that Albert Camus who says
Don't walk in front of me
Nor behind me
Just walk beside me
And be my friend?

I'm so grateful that
You risk being vulnerable
Willing to open your heart and mind
Your inspiration for human excellence
Also inspires me to soar to my limits

I'm so fortunate that
You are committed
To sharing and further exploring our dreams
You just join in, in search of
Promising ideas and possibilities

I'm so happy that
You have been gentle with me
When I'm slow and fail to follow you
You just smiled and waited
And let me take my time to catch up with you

I'm so thankful that
You make time for us
To go for walks and share talks
We treat ourselves with laughs and plays
Art galleries, cozy restaurants, and all

I'm so mindful that
You are precious for our mutual flourishing
That you make me who I am
Though our friendship may or may not last
I always treasure my fond memory of you

2.3. Love and Euthanasia

LOVE, HOWEVER, MAY MOTIVATE ONE TO END THE LIFE OF A LOVED ONE. That is the message of a remarkable 2008 French film, *I've Loved You So Long*, written and directed by Philippe Claudel. The lead character, Juliette, a physician, is released from prison after fifteen years for ending the life of her son through lethal injection, because of her son Pierre's incurable disease and uncontrollable pain. Her parents disowned her, forbidding her much younger sister Lea to mention Juliette or visit her in prison. However, Lea has always loved her sister, and welcomes Juliette into her family, which consists of her husband Luc, her mute father-in-law, and two daughters adopted from Vietnam. The movie is about the daunting process of Juliette's reintegration into the family and their social circles. The issue of mercy killing serves as a backgrounder and is never directly debated and discussed.

What is one to do when a loved one is undergoing unbearable suffering, and yet there is nothing one can do to improve the situation? Who should make the final, irreversible decision to end that life . . . or not? Isn't it Juliette's right as the mother in this film to end Pierre's life out of love, if that is what she is compelled to do? What right do her parents have to condemn Juliette and treat her as a non-person? The debate on euthanasia has gone on for ages, but the general thrust of the debate is clear: is the decision based on love and the well-being of the person in question or not? We value life as well as the will to live, but it's time to welcome death when life is withering and not worth living. Few people know when to give up power, and even fewer people know when to give up life. Sadly, most wait until the bitter end . . . and too often act ungracefully and unethically . . . and condemn those who wish to act wisely and proactively. What a farce!

Pierre is fortunate to have Juliette as a loving mother, who as a physician ends his life with a lethal injection. Many others were not as fortunate. In 1995, Gilles Deleuze, a noted French philosopher, leapt to death from his flat in Paris at age seventy; and in 2012, Tony Scott, a well-known Hollywood director, jumped off the Vincent Thomas Bridge in the Los Angeles Harbour at age sixty-eight. Why is our society so cruel and not loving enough to provide more humane ways to exit from this world? Don't they deserve more love from us than what they have received? True, certain safeguards should be in place to prevent premature end-of-life decisions, but it's unconscionable not to provide such options. Love! Yes, we need to extend love to the very end of our life. I'd be honoured if my children would act on my behalf to make life-and-death decisions for me if I am not in a position to do so. To that end, I'd quote Qiong Yao's convictions about the end-of-life decisions, which resonate in me. She is well known as "queen of romance novels" in Taiwan, although I've hardly read her novels. This is an excerpt from an article about Chiung Yao (2017) as reported in *The Straits Times* on March 14:

> On Sunday, she [Chiung Yao] posted what she called "the most important letter she has ever written," in which she rejected life-prolonging measures and requested a simple send-off after death.
>
> "I'm 79 and will be 80 next year. I have not left Earth earlier because of reasons such as war, poverty, an accident, a disaster or illness. Attaining this age is by heaven's grace.

So, from now, I will face death with a smile," she wrote in a letter addressed to her son and daughter-in-law.

She exhorted them that, should she be unable to decide for herself, never to send her for any major operation or into intensive care, reported Apple Daily. She also objected to tube-feeding—"or any type of nameless tubes"—and emergency life-saving measures such as intubation or defibrillation.

She also asked for a family-only final farewell, asking that there be no religious rites, obituaries, public memorials, wake and funeral, opting instead for an eco-friendly burial in a flower garden following cremation—all to be over within a week.

Pointing to the problem of global warming, she also spurned incense-burning and prayers during the annual Qing Ming tomb-sweeping festival.

The beloved author also said she was making public her wishes in case her son becomes too overcome by love or pressure and tries to keep alive the shell of her body.

She said she was now at peace to start on her next book or script and work with a grandchild on a book.

3.

Truth: Authenticity

THE QUEST FOR MEANING IS INSEPARABLE FROM THAT FOR AUTHENTICITY: a lifelong process to discover our true selves and the world around us, and to find fulfilment in life according to our dreams. The concept of authenticity, like that of truth, is a human construct to characterize the relationship between our perception and reality. The reality of how we actually live is just a fact, which may or may not correspond well with how we wish, or ought, to live. Authenticity is about how we ought to live in the present and future, which presupposes true self-knowledge and knowledge of the world around us. Unfortunately, few of us are able to live an authentic life because most of us have no clear idea about our true self, what we should aim for in life, or how to achieve it. After the lifetime of chasing after something we thought was worthwhile, such as fame, wealth, or power, some of us may come to realize that we have wittingly or unwittingly barked up the wrong tree, willingly or unwillingly lived an inauthentic life.

To live authentically or truthfully, the concept of truth is the next most important thing in life: to understand what life is about, to distinguish between myth and reality, and between fiction and nonfiction. It is about the harmony between mind and matter, and between "epistemology" (or how we know) and "ontology" (or what exists). Freud, in his *Beyond the Pleasure Principle*, develops a theory of the personality structure in terms of the id (the drive and passion), ego (the concept of self and reason), and superego (the morality and conscience). To obtain a clear and realistic concept of ourselves and of the world around us, we need to develop a healthy ego internally and a superego externally from the id, individually, collectively, and culturally, throughout our lives.

The development of a healthy ego—to differentiate and gain a realistic understanding of ourselves and of the world around us—is essential to our survival and flourishing. A good starting point is a common-sense picture of reality as outlined by the distinguished philosopher Karl Popper (Figure 1) in a lecture delivered at the University of Michigan in 1978. This picture consists of an ontology of three different but interacting "Worlds": (a) the "physical" world (e.g., stars, trees and flowers, animals, and human bodies); (b) the "mental" or "psychological" world (e.g., senses, perceptions, emotions, mental images, and thoughts); and (c) the "artificial" world (e.g., the products of the human mind, such as languages, tales and stories, religious myths, scientific theories, songs and symphonies, paintings and sculptures, airplanes, and buildings). The artificial world is roughly equivalent to our so-called culture, which includes religions and moral teachings derived from the superego. Supernatural beings, according to this ontology, are nothing but artificial, human creations and imaginations.

Figure 1. Sir Karl Popper (1902–1994), Austrian-born British philosopher. Generally regarded as one of the greatest philosophers of science in the 20th century, Popper was also a social and political philosopher of considerable statue, being a staunch defender of the "open society".

We should further refine Popper's three-world theory, however. The Cartesian dualism of mind versus matter is a good starting point because the mind (e.g., consciousness) is distinct from matter (e.g., the structure and activities of the brain). Modern physics shows us, however, that particles and waves are different manifestations of the same underlying entities, and that mass and energy are interchangeable. Hence, mind and body may also be conceived as different manifestations of the same underlying reality: energy or "Qi" in Chinese cosmology. Like the blind men and the elephant, idealists only see everything in the world as the mind whereas materialists only see everything as matter. The fact is that epistemologically our images of reality are all mental constructs or simulations, through which we infer and (re)construct the world ontologically to figure out what entities are physical, mental, or artificial, and exist out there or in here. Postmodernists tend to be idealists who conflate and confound epistemology with ontology and refuse to go beyond mental constructs and their human products (e.g., texts and discourses) to infer the existence of the physical world; materialists and behaviourists, on the other hand, refuse to acknowledge the reality of the mind in others because they are so dazzled by the scientific dogma of "objectivity" that anything "private" and "not public"—and therefore not directly observable—is deemed inadmissible and banished from their ontological views of reality.

What, then, is reality? How can we distinguish it from fiction? At present, 3D printing can already do amazing things (such as printing toys and tools), and the healing of wounds and creation of human organs (such as kidneys and livers) for transplantation are already in sight. But we shouldn't get too carried away. Jon, a superhero in Alan Moore's (1986-1987) graphic novel *Watchmen*, is said to have disintegrated into pieces in a test chamber by accident and is put back together again with a supernatural power. This, of course, is possible only in science fiction like *Watchmen*, in which Jon states, "a live body and dead body contain the same number of particles. Structurally there is no discernible difference. Life and death are unquantifiable abstractions." (p. 21) This, of course, is nonsense, since there is a world of difference between life and death, between a functioning live body and a non-functioning dead body; and such distinctions are far from mere human "abstractions," since they are real and not the creations of human minds. The same goes for tele-transportation in *Watchmen* and other SF novels and movies, telekinesis in Japanese manga (comics) and anime Akira, and also in animal (or possible human) cloning. It is empirically impossible to: (a) reassemble our bodies instantaneously into live ones after disintegrating into atoms and molecules, or (b) reconstruct (clone) an exact replica of an animal or person instantaneously using the DNA information and the materials in a distant location such as Mars, because it takes years of growth for embryos to mature into adult bodies. Jon and tele-transportation/cloning, therefore, cannot possibly be real. Life remains a mystery, but it is a misrepresentation to depict it only as a human abstraction.

Like my father, I have never been religious. I can still distinctively remember, when I first studied the history of Western philosophy in Taiwan, that my professor's opening statement was "Man created gods, not the other way round." Following Popper, moreover, I would classify anything supernatural as a product of the human mind. Hence, it puzzles me to no end why so many people are still fascinated with the supernatural in this day and age. Didn't we go through the Age of Reason and the Age of Enlightenment, the scientific, technological, and information revolutions, and all that? Why can't we free ourselves from the yoke of irrational beliefs—the supernatural, non-realistic, distorted images of the world? To me, any belief in the supernatural is against an "enlightened rationality," which supposedly would lead us out of the superstition and tyranny that characterize the long cultural histories of the bygone era. Why on earth would so many intelligent people—among them are talented artists, writers, philosophers, and even scientists—continue to believe in the supernatural, such as gods, angels, devils, ghosts, souls, reincarnation, etc.? Is it because such beliefs serve to reassure them, to allay their pain, anxiety, and uncertainty, and to give their lives a sense of purpose and hope? Research shows that believers are "happier" than non-believers, but this apparent happiness comes at a cost since there is no shred of evidence of the existence of the supernatural. They are clearly conjured up by us since different cultures have created their own religious myths and tales of creation. The concept of intelligent design, moreover, is self-contradictory, because the image of an intelligent designer varies by culture: Greek, Nordic and Teutonic, Hindi, Christian, Muslim, Chinese, Japanese, etc. The concept of creation also entails an infinite regression: who created the creator, the creator of the creator, etc. Thus, it is best to do away with the myths of creation and embrace a naturalistic belief that the universe has always existed and evolved: no beginning and no end.

Once I got into a debate with my Philosophy of Biology instructor about whether methodological naturalism logically entails metaphysical naturalism. I think Barbara Forrest (2000) got it right when she stated that "given the procedurally necessary exclusivity of methodological naturalism in science and the unavailability of any other workable method for grounding any claims with existential import, any metaphysical view of the cosmos other than the naturalistic one is epistemologically unjustifiable." (p. 13) I also made use of Occam's razor (that entities should not be multiplied beyond necessity) by quoting Wittgenstein (1961/1921), who states: "Occam's razor is, of course, not an arbitrary rule nor one justified by its practical success. It simply says that unnecessary elements in a symbolism mean nothing." (p. 97) I think the best use of this common-sense criterion is to prove (show) that "supernatural entities" are unnecessary: it is irrational or meaningless to assume their existence beyond natural entities. Since supernatural entities can never be meaningfully known ontologically, I'd favour an atheist than agnostic stance—according to Wittgenstein's (1961/1921) famous aphorism, "What we cannot speak of we must consign to silence." (p. 151)

My instructor, Professor Ingo Brigandt, disagreed, stating in the class blog: "My position is that methodological naturalism commits one to being an agnostic – not an agnosticism where one is shy to make a judgement about transcendent matters, but where one categorically asserts that nothing can be known about transcendent matters, neither their presence nor their absence." Strictly speaking, of course, he is right, and he is not alone in advocating agnosticism. The British philosopher-Broadcaster-parliamentarian Bryan Magee (2016), in his book, *Ultimate Questions*, argues that there are countless aspects of reality that we can't experience because we don't have the proper sense organs, such as echolocation in bats. As a result, our knowledge is extremely limited, and we are faced with the reality consisting of vastly "unknowable unknowables." Understandably, Magee advocates "active agnosticism," which is "a positive principle of procedure, an openness to the fact that we do not know, followed by intellectually honest enquiry in full receptivity of mind." (p. 26)

My position is that, since there is no credible rational evidence for the existence of a supernatural realm, we are justified to reject its existence until proven otherwise—based on the logical empiricist position that no empirical proposition, unlike an analytic statement (e.g., a statement in logic and mathematics), is absolutely true. Unlike the agnostic, the atheist has the conviction and advantage of not having to endlessly wonder and anxiously doubt whether to expend their precious energy on "unproductive activities" such as attending religious preaching and ceremonies, which often contradict with scientific teachings. To the agnostic, as Magee puts it, "There is a world of difference between being lost in the daylight and being lost in the dark." To the atheist, there is a world of difference between being lost and not being lost—while keeping a degree of open-mindedness.

I also think John Lennon got it right when he composed "Imagine" and sang: "Imagine there's no countries / It isn't hard to do / Nothing to kill or die for / And no religion too / Imagine all the people / Living life in peace." Religion served its purpose in the past to help relieve human suffering, but it is time for us to forsake it due to its irrationality and irreconcilable differences with science and common sense, not to mention the violence associated with religious extremism of our time. It is a fitting tribute to my sister, Sophia, when my daughter, Solene, chose "Imagine" and we sang it together at her seventieth birthday celebration in 2005.

Truth is an essential virtue in our lives. If we have a distorted concept about ourselves and about the world, we will have no inner or outer peace and harmony; hence, we cannot act wisely and be happy. It's our lifelong quest to know ourselves and be authentic, because it's unsatisfying and even painful to be inauthentic, to be a poseur. This way of thinking motivated me to write the following poem,

Be True to Thyself / Carpe Diem / 2011

It's never too early nor too late
To be just right
Not too big nor too small
Neither inflated nor shrunken
Seize the moment, now is the time
Not tomorrow nor the day after
To shape and reshape our egos

Inflated egos lead to hubris
Shrunken egos to agoraphobia
They betray our true selves
Engender unrealistic expectations
And lead us down the garden path
So seize the moment now
Initiate a fresh reality check
Rid ourselves of all delusion
Let go of oversized selves
Pump up undersized egos
And be, and feel, just right
In peace and harmony with the world

3.1. Language and Self

LANGUAGE IS OF UTMOST IMPORTANCE TO ALL OF US. THIS IS PARTICU-
larly the case if we are to narrate unique experiences, ideas, or insights
not previously verbalized and expressed by others. Therefore, I find Peter
Adamson's (2018) article "Wittgenstein & the War" extremely infor-
mative, as I, too, like Gottlob Frege and Bertrand Russell, had a hard
time getting the ideas of Wittgenstein's early work, *Tractatus Logico-
Philosophicus*, straight. As summarized by Adamson, Wittgenstein argued

that underlying our everyday language is a set of propositions that describe reality. The simplest propositions express "facts"—e.g., the proposition "the giraffe is tall" represents the fact that the giraffe is tall. Hence, these basic propositions are like "logical pictures" of reality, and such facts always deal with physical reality. However, this means that abstractions such as morality and beauty cannot be shown in language, thus forcing him to end it in a kind of mysticism—dismissing the *Tractatus* itself as a ladder that must be thrown away once one has climbed up it.

Wittgenstein, of course, wasn't able to go beyond the then dominant philosophy of physicalism, to extend his analysis to human abstractions such as morality and beauty—which were deemed "cognitively meaningless"—as also proclaimed by writers such as Alfred Jules Ayer. Wittgenstein in his later writings, *Philosophical Investigations*, critiques, modifies, and transforms his "picture theory," regarding language as a practical ability to use words according to the norms that constitute these language games, which cannot be explained or justified by anything else. It is wrong, according to him, to engage in epidemiology and metaphysics, because it is cognitively misguided and pointless, a symptom of the disease of intellect; and more importantly, because it turns away from discourses of a healthy, flourishing human life.

While I can appreciate his reasoning, I still think traditional epistemological and ontological reflections are inevitable and of crucial importance to all of us—to be cognitively clear about what is real and what is not, and what is "out there" or "in us"—to enable us to act appropriately in the world. Take, for instance, some of the prevailing postmodernist and social constructionist ideas, which tend to negate the existence of an external reality. While I admire the dazzling display of verbal virtuosity in the Canadian author Nino Ricci's *The Origin of Species*, which won the 2008 Governor General's Literary Award for Fiction, I have to question the book's philosophical underpinnings as shown, for example, in the protagonist, Alex's following reflections:

> Maybe the postmoderns were right, and there was nothing
> there: it was all just a blaze of synapses, one of whose little

> jobs was to make up this thing, this person-ness. He was
> starting to think that consciousness wasn't some light-
> house of self-knowledge but merely a little cave where you
> made up stories about yourself, whatever it took to hide
> the shit and the slime, the utter mollusc you were in your
> deepest nature. He wondered what was down there, under
> the shit, what kind of bedrock he might strike. (p. 383)

Of course, there is something down there. Alex's failing was not to know who he was, and what to do with his life. He needed to find himself. The reality and importance of language in shaping our self-concept is brought home by Pauline O'Flynn (2011), who quotes Dennett: "Our fundamental tactic of . . . self-definition is . . . telling stories—and more particularly concocting and controlling the story we tell others, and our selves, about who we are . . ." (p. 15) Isn't this exactly what I am doing? Telling my story, trying to define and convey who I am? As Alex realized later when he put his thesis together, "Narrative, like everything else, was a strategy. Get it right, and, like Scheherazade [in the Arabian Nights], you survived" (Ricci, 2012, p. 401). We all need to get the narratives right.

O'Flynn also refers to Kenyan writer Wa Thiong'O Ngugi's *Decolonising the Mind* (1986), which states that "any language is a carrier of culture as well as a means of communication, and maintains that mental control of the colonized was attained through the domination of their language." (p. 15) Since English is not my first language and my knowledge of English-language literature is still limited, I have to continually train myself if I am to better define, verbalize, weave, and communicate my story to others. I am fortunate that I can do it here in Canada, but that opportunity was denied to my father. He wanted to be a writer and studied English lit-erature in Japan in the early twentieth century. Although he was most proficient in Japanese—more so than Chinese Mandarin which he had to (re)learn in 1945 when Japan ceded Taiwan back to China—he refused to write in Japanese because of Japan's ruthless colonial policies against Taiwanese people. Since he didn't immerse himself in an English-speaking culture, his English was never good enough to narrate his rich and colourful life-stories, which took place in Taiwan, Japan, Southeast Asia, and Canada—he was drafted as an interpreter in the Japanese Imperial Army to liaise with the local ethnic Chinese, and also with the British prisoners of war during WWII. He simply did not have the medium that was suitable for composing and conveying his message to the world. His dream of becoming a writer was dashed under Taiwan's colonial past. In the end, he let his story be told as fiction, written by my writer-friend, Dr. Wendar Lin, in Chinese and published in Taiwan. Although that novel won literary awards in Taiwan—and there have been controversies surrounding the authenticity of the stories involved, even as a fiction!—it was regrettably never translated into English and is inaccessible to the younger generations of non-Chinese-speaking audience, including those in my family. So I wrote a poem in his memory:

My Father / Elegy / 2010

It's with a tinge of sadness that I remember my father. He was
Among the most gifted and accomplished in his generation,
And his story has been told in a prize-winning novel in Taiwan.
Yet, the stories he wrote gather dusts in my filing cabinets.

He could have been a great writer in another time and place,
Unencumbered by the cultural and language barriers of his day.
His English, which he learned in pre-WWII Japan, was iffy, despite
Seventeen years of teaching English at his hometown middle school.

Then my father had to learn Chinese again after Taiwan re-joined China
At the end of WWII when he became a middle school principal.
At age 56 he boldly resigned to become an English professor
In keeping with his youthful dreams of teaching and writing.

Sadly, his persistence and love didn't make him a successful writer
For want of opportunities to immerse in English-speaking cultures.
Given such opportunities to stand on the shoulders of the giants
Many of us could reach for the stars and actualize our dreams.

3.2. Realism and Mind-Body Identity Theory

I HAVE LONG BELIEVED IN THE IDENTITY OF THE MIND AND THE BODY. My master's thesis in philosophy in 1964 propounded this theory, since it appeared absurd to think in any other way. There simply was no mind without a body, which, of course, was real. Our minds couldn't be separated from our bodies, especially our brains. They had to be identical, exactly the same processes with distinct manifestations. I don't have a copy of my master's thesis anymore, and I don't recall whether I made a reference to JJC (Jack) Smart's 1959 article, "Sensations and Brain Processes" or not. It's interesting, therefore, to read Graham Nerlich's (2013) article about Smart, that Smart advocated the points of view very similar to mine, including: mind-body identity, scientific realism, atheism, and "act utilitarianism" (i.e., not to follow moral rules but to consider the moral utility of each act as best as we can). It's amazing to read about someone with whom we share a great many ideas in common!

Consciousness, of course, is a mystery, and the mind-body problem has intrigued philosophers for centuries. My theory of mind-body identity upholds the thesis that consciousness is an attribute of the brain process. There is no additional entity of consciousness over and above such brain processes, which have both physical and phenomenological components. That much is certain: ontologically, there are only brain processes. Epistemologically, though, we acquire knowledge through subjective-private means inaccessible to other individuals, and through inter-subjective means indirectly observable by different individuals. Cartesian dualism, therefore, is a characteristic of epistemology. A sound ontology, however, has to transcend this dualism and acknowledge the unity and identity of the two phenomenological processes. Hence, physicalism is correct onto-logically to equate human consciousness with the human brain, although it's impossible to epistemologically escape Cartesian dualism. The key to clear thinking on the question of mind-body dualism, therefore, is to avoid conflating ontology with epistemology. Within this identity theory, the mind-body interaction is no longer a philosophical puzzle because mind is body and bodies naturally interact with each other.

It is, therefore, gratifying to read Kat McGowan's (2014) article, "The Second Coming of Sigmund Freud", in which she narrates how neuro-psychoanalysis has evolved since the 1980s to integrate psychoanalysis with neuroscience. According to her, Antonio Damasio, a neurologist and neuroscientist at the University of Southern California, found in the 1990s that when a brain tumour damaged regions of Elliot's frontal lobes responsible for emotional processing, the affected person could no longer make good decisions—which led Damasio to conclude that "emotions are not irrational intrusions into reason. They are intrinsic to rational thought. " McGowan also features the South African neuropsychologist and psychoanalyst Mark Solms in the article, and concludes by quoting him as saying:

> What is most significant about the brain, in comparison
> to other bodily organs, is that it's not just an object but a
> subject . . . We must embrace the fact that a brain is also
> a mind, that it thinks, it experiences, it suffers. In a word,
> that it is us.

But, isn't Solms stating the obvious (although not to many neuroscientists)? The mind-body identity theory, although Solms does not use the term, remains alive and well, and may remain a mystery forever!

Is it possible that I am also obsessed with uncovering the mystery of the mind-body conundrum—through the tools of philosophy and now also through scientific investigations? Is such curiosity justified? I have my doubts, as expressed in the following poem:

What's Science Doing? / Spenserian Stanza / 2012

Science adores nature whole-heartedly
Enticed by her candour, beauty, and goodness

He studies all about her obsessively
Using all tricks to break down her coyness

Scrutinizing her with excess eagerness
He keeps watching, asking, guessing, and cajoling

To know her secrets with single-mindedness
He resorts to teasing and prodding

By dissecting her, does he know she might be weeping?

3.3. Taoism, Naturalism, and Acupuncture

TAOISM IS A FASCINATING PHILOSOPHY, SIMPLE AND YET COMPREHEN-
sive, commonsensical and yet profound. It also provides a sound conceptual framework (epistemology) for understanding the way of nature, which
is totally compatible with scientific and rational ways of thinking. At the
same time, its cosmology (ontology) is completely naturalistic and, simul-
taneously, it embraces rational wonders and mysticism by acknowledging
our knowledge to be too limited to comprehend the world in all its splen-
diferous aspects as well as in its totality. The opening statement of Laozi's
immortal *Tao Te Ching* is: "The way [of nature] that can be said is not the
true [eternal] way, the name that can be named is not the true [eternal]
name." No one should be so conceited as to profess of knowing everything.
Nature is so grand that it is beyond the grasp of the human mind. Only a
fool proclaims the death of science, because he thinks we might someday
come to know what is all there is to know. It is reassuring, moreover, as

Fritjof Capra (1999) elucidated in *The Tao of Physics*, that there is a close parallel between modern physics and Taoism (and other Eastern philosophies such as Buddhism and Hinduism). Thus, modern physics, like Chinese medicine, may be viewed as a refinement of Taoist philosophy.

Indeed, Taoism fascinates me as a philosophy, not as a religion, because of its thoroughgoing naturalism. It is compatible with Bruce Hauptli's (1995) more analytically oriented "explanatory naturalism" to defend reason as the best guide to reliable belief, as I shall discuss and explain later in Section 3.5. Taoism can embrace Hauptli's naturalism as it relates to rationality, extend it to all aspects of human nature, thinking, and conduct, and be in total harmony with nature. That's the Taoist ideal, to revere and nurture our human and ecological living space, and to justify it by appealing to human goals and purposes.

Taoist wisdom, moreover, is uplifting, and has been a primary source of Chinese popular maxims and proverbs as Helen Wu (2004) aptly explains. According to her, "truth is often contained in ordinary things", and "[i]t was the Daode Jing which first brought this general knowledge to light and made it a philosophical maxim." For example, everyone knows the saying, "A journey of a thousand li begins with the first step," which is from chapter 64 of *Daode Jing*. What I appreciate the most, though, is its profound insight about soft power: "Nothing under the Heaven is softer and weaker than water / But in attacking the hard and strong, no force can compare with it" (chapter 78). This has been condensed into popular maxims such as: "The soft can overcome the hard," which has been adopted, at least rhetorically if not in practice, by many scholars and politicians in both the East and the West.

Similarly, the popular proverb, "Wealth and honour are like dew on flowers" may have been derived from *Daode Jing*: "To be proud with honour and wealth will bring misfortune" (chapter 9). While many of us take pride in our technological achievements and levels of income and wealth, Taoism cautions us about the unintended and yet inevitable misfortune as a result of such blind, conceited pursuits beyond reason. Laozi (or Li Er), to whom this remarkable book had been attributed, had no illusion about the popularity of his wisdom: "I alone differ from others, essentially because I have acquired Tao."

Taoism is also intriguing. A fine application of this philosophy is Chinese medicine, which views our body as a dynamic and mutual transformation of its yin (negative) and yang (positive) components. The quantity and quality, as well as the flows of these two constituents in our body, determine our health and illness. The yin aspect is associated with deficient, internal, and cold manifestations of Qi (vital energy) that constitutes our mind-body unity, whereas the yang aspect is associated with full, external, and hot manifestations of our Qi. The aim of Chinese medicine is to achieve or restore optimal health, a dynamic balance of the yin and the yang, in terms of its Qi composition and flow. This is done through various treatment modalities, such as acupuncture, moxibustion, cupping, gua sha, herbal medicine, tui na, qigong, and tai chi. The efficacy of acupuncture, for example, has been demonstrated through rigorous scientific studies for a variety of health conditions, such as fibromyalgia, sciatic pain, dysmenorrhoea, and allergy. As a student of acupuncture, I treated some patients in our MacEwan University Acupuncture Teaching Clinic. Almost invariably, those who came for pain relief got better, and the effects lasted for a couple days to a whole week and beyond. Many were pain-free after several weeks of treatment. Weight reductions were more difficult to achieve, although some of my patients claimed to have reduced appetite as a result of acupuncture treatment. One of the most amazing outcomes of the treatments I administered was a case of a nurse whose body was bloated for over a year because of fluid retention. She could not get any relief from Western medicine and came for acupuncture treatment as a last resort. After the second session of her treatment, she reported that she profusely urinated and her oedema was gone. It was one of the most gratifying experiences I had in my life!

Unfortunately, it would take years of practice under the guidance of an expert teacher to become a competent clinician. Plus, I resolved to be a writer instead, so I decided against practising acupuncture upon my graduation from the three-year program. Do I regret my decision? Sure, it would be neat if I could maintain and improve my knowledge and skills and help others overcome their health problems. However, life is a series of trade-offs, and the naturalistic, Taoist philosophy of *wu-wei*—meaning "non-action," or "to act according to the way of nature, without effort"— comes to my mind. The key here is to know when to act and when not to act, so as not to act foolishly and in vain, with wasted effort. Were I to practise acupuncture to earn my living (which I don't have to as a pensioner), I would have less time to study to become a better writer. On the other hand, I am grateful that I had a rare hands-on experience to actually peel off some of the mystery of the art and science of acupuncture. I have learned and grown intellectually and emotionally in the process. To celebrate, I wrote a poem to commemorate my achievement.

The Riddle of Acupuncture / Villanelle / 2009

What is the meaning of life? I wondered
It's about the love of challenge, I'd say
To have Nature's mystery uncovered

What is Nature's secret I desired?
The riddle of acupuncture, if I may
What is the meaning of life? I wondered

How to become wiser and be a wizard?
By studying and needling night and day
To have Nature's mystery uncovered

It's the knowledge of yin and yang I dared
To learn all about the Tao, Nature's Way
What is the meaning of life? I wondered

Be daring to have my worldview altered
Acupuncture can do wonders by the way
To have Nature's mystery uncovered!

Years of hard work must be wildly cheered
Who cares about my hair turned more grey?
What is the meaning of life? I wondered
To have Nature's mystery uncovered!

3.4. The Origin of the Universe and the Purposiveness of Life

FOR CENTURIES, PHILOSOPHERS AND SCIENTISTS HAVE PONDERED THE nature of our world: its origin and its characteristics. Our concepts of the universe have changed over time, from geocentric to heliocentric, from the creation myths to the Big Bang and the speculative multiverse. Our concept of life is, of course, largely shaped by Darwin's and Wallace's theories of evolution. However, the Big Bang, commonly viewed as the origin of our universe, is never convincing to me. Like any creation myth, I have to question what went on before the Big Bang if there was one, and if so, what caused it to happen. There must be something preceding it for it to happen, although there is no way for us to know: the theories of the multiverse are by and large speculative, based on scanty empirical evidence. So I agree with Joel Marks (2013) that such a theory is "poppycock." The Big Bang itself was based on our educated assumption that the universe has constantly been expanding, but what if it has been alternatingly expanding and shrinking? We just don't know, and it's preposterous to pretend we do. My best guess, as stated earlier, is that our universe has always existed and evolved, with no beginning and no end.

As mentioned earlier, the British philosopher Mary Midgley (2012) presented a convincing argument about the existence of purpose in life. According to her, Dawkins and other neo-Darwinists misinterpret Darwin's theory of evolution and depict nature as having "no design, no purpose, no evil and no good, nothing but blind, pitiless indifference" (Dawkins 1995, p. 133). She wrote:

> It is an objective fact that all living things behave pur-
> posively: that is, they all strive and struggle to live in the
> way that their particular nature requires. They do not, of
> course, need to be conscious to do this. (2012, p. 110)

Midgley is surely correct to say that life behaves purposively. It is in our
genes and DNA. The interesting question, then, is: where does that purposiveness in life come from? Can we extend that purposiveness beyond
life to the entire universe? This is an open question for scientists and philosophers to investigate in the years to come, since it has bearings on our
worldview as well as on moral theory.

It should be noted, however, that the meaninglessness of life is a
widely held view with a long history. As Maria Popova (2014) narrated,
of particular interest in this regard is Leo Tolstoy, who had probably
meditated on the meaning of life more than anyone else and wrote in *A
Confession* (1879–1880):

> I, my reason, have acknowledged that life is senseless.
> If there is nothing higher than reason (and there is not:
> nothing can prove that there is), then reason is the creator
> of life for me. If reason did not exist there would be for
> me no life. How can reason deny life when it is the creator
> of life? Or to put it the other way: were there no life, my
> reason would not exist; therefore reason is life's son. Life
> is all. Reason is its fruit yet reason rejects life itself! I felt
> that there was something wrong here . . .
>
> My position was terrible. I knew I could find nothing
> along the path of reasonable knowledge except a denial
> of life; and there—in faith—was nothing but a denial
> of reason, which was yet more impossible for me than a
> denial of life. From rational knowledge it appeared that
> life is an evil, people know this and it is in their power
> to end life; yet they lived and still live, and I myself live,
> though I have long known that life is senseless and an

evil. By faith it appears that in order to understand the meaning of life I must renounce my reason, the very thing for which alone a meaning is required.

A contradiction arose from which there were two exits. Either that which I called reason was not so rational as I supposed, or that which seemed to me irrational was not so irrational as I supposed . . .

So that besides rational knowledge, which had seemed to me the only knowledge, I was inevitably brought to acknowledge that all live humanity has another irrational knowledge—faith which makes it possible to live. Faith still remained to me as irrational as it was before, but I could not but admit that it alone gives mankind a reply to the questions of life, and that consequently it makes life possible. (pp. 18–20)

Due to his doubts about reason and rationality in explaining the meaning of life, Tolstoy succumbed to a profound spiritual crisis shortly after he turned fifty, sinking into a state of deep depression and melancholia despite his literary fame, wealth, good health, and a large family: a wife and fourteen children. In this remarkable masterpiece, Tolstoy searches in vain for the meaning of life through reason. In the end, he turns to "irrational knowledge" of faith, because "it alone gives mankind a reply to the question of life, and . . . makes life possible." However, the more he examines faith, the more he finds it disconnecting with religion. So he returns to the peasants as a paragon of spiritual salvation, of accepting life without questioning it.

In contrast with what I had seen in our circle, where the whole of life is passed in idleness, amusement, and dis-satisfaction, I saw that the whole life of these people was passed in heavy labour, and that they were content with life. (Tolstoy, 1879-1880, p. 23)

The key to resolving Tolstoy's contradiction, however, is to scrutinize and clarify more closely the relationship between reason and faith, and rationality and irrationality. That is the task I am going to address in the next section. In the meantime, the best policy is always to make life as beautiful and dazzling as we can.

Life Is a Great Big Canvas / Sijo / 2010

Life is a great big canvas
Paint it and it comes alive
The future's wide open
Fathom it and it becomes beautiful
Make life as dazzling as it can be
And cherish it while it lasts

3.5. The Reasonableness of Reason

ONE OF THE MOST PUZZLING QUESTIONS IN PHILOSOPHY RELATES TO OUR quest for certainty, as epitomized in Rene Descartes' famous dictum, "I think, therefore I am." However, as Chinese philosopher Chuang Tzi (c. 369 BC–c. 286 BC) mused, how do I know that I'm not a butterfly dreaming to be a human, rather than a human dreaming to be a butterfly?

The sceptics, such as postmodernists who denigrate truth and reason, may dismiss reason on the ground that there is no conclusive proof of its supremacy over other modes of thinking, and therefore we should only suspend our belief and admit that we just do not know . . . or might as well rely on alternative modes such as faith, intuition, imaginations, etc. Even the eminent philosopher like Descartes maintained that faith is the basis of both knowledge and life. It is critically important and satisfying, therefore, to read Raymond Pfeiffer's (2014) review of Bruce Hauptli's (1995) book, *The Reasonableness of Reason.*

How can we justify reason if not with reason? Will it inevitably involve a circular argument? Is it possible to avoid it? Based on the argument of the purposiveness of human life, Hauptli maintains that all humans in all societies share some general goals such as meeting basic physiological and safety needs, love, meaning, and understanding of the world. As a naturalist, he further argues that the best way to achieve such goals is to resort to reason—including inductive and deductive logic, scientific methods, empirical observation and experimentation, etc., and not by other modes of thinking, such as faith, as the fideist would do. Thus, Hauptli concludes: "If we seek optimum goal-fulfillment, the use of reason will promote this best in the long run" (Pfeiffer, 2014, p.41). Although this is still a "weakly independent" vindication of the reasonableness of reason, perhaps this is the best we could do epistemologically due to the limitations of our intelligence in this natural world.

In reality, though, we don't always reason rationally all the time, as we rely on a "dual process" model of thought. As Scott McGreal (2012) explained, the first mode, the experiential system, is intuitive, emotional, and immediate, without a prolonged thinking process. The second mode, the rational system, is reflective, logical, and takes more time to acquire and process relevant information than the intuitive system. There are individual differences in how well these two systems interact with each other, and in the degree to which either of these systems is used. Studies have revealed that those who rely more on intuitive thinking tend to believe in supernatural phenomena more, and those who rely on rational analytic thinking tend to disbelieve supernatural phenomena. This explains why the majority of scientists, who are vocationally committed to empirical and analytic, rational decision-making, are not religious. However, the intuitive and rational modes of reasoning can operate in a parallel and non-interactive, rather than in a conflicting, manner for some people— thus enabling some scientists to be religious in their private lives while engaging in evidence-based analytic work.

I have always found it amazing for any scientists to believe in the supernatural and have half-jokingly labelled them as having split personalities. Do they really believe in the supernatural, or are they just being polite and kind—not wishing to offend the sensibilities of their loved ones who are believers? To me, it's much simpler and psychologically healthier to integrate the two modes of thinking so that, as much as possible, intuition becomes an extension of prior rational thinking. Intuition and creative thinking are important, as Albert Einstein famously stated: "Imagination is more important than knowledge." However, confusing fiction with reality is not. So I wrote the following poem:

The Supernatural is Merely Fictional / Triolet / 2012

The supernatural is merely fictional
Occam's razor entails the verdict
That paranormal beliefs are irrational
The supernatural is merely fictional
We are desperate to be immortal
Clinging to the fantasies that are derelict
The supernatural is merely fictional
Occam's razor entails the verdict

3.6. Truth, Knowledge, and Consequences

TRUTH, OF COURSE, IS BASED ON KNOWLEDGE. TO TELL THE TRUTH OF anything, we have to have a thorough knowledge of the thing under consideration. Oftentimes, we think we know and confidently explain complex arguments to others, and yet ending up making misleading statements. There is a Japanese saying: "Even monkeys fall from the tree." Experts can be wrong at times, and we need to be vigilant all the time. That's why peer review is of critical importance to minimize false or misleading claims in any scientific or philosophical publications. Moreover, truth may have serious consequences, so it is imperative to be just right and pay attention to the issue of precision when required.

Pertinent examples are contained in the 2016 book, *When Breath Becomes Air* by Paul Kalanithi. The author is a brilliant neurosurgeon, and he tries to explain the chance of survival to a patient with a glioblastoma, the tumour of the brain. According to the Kaplan-Meier curve—which measures the number of patients surviving over time—the curve drops sharply until only 5% of patients are alive at two years. Rather than saying, "Median survival is eleven months" or "You have a 95% chance of being dead in two years," Kalanithi would say, "Most patients live many months to a couple of years." (p. 95)

Now, this is a false statement, since the Kaplan-Meier curve shows only 5% of patients survive beyond two years. Kalanithi recognizes the importance of being accurate, yet in order to "always leave some room for hope," he makes a false statement—unwittingly, I presume, because he is not a statistician. I'd simply say, "You have a 50% chance of surviving beyond 1 year." If pressed for a longer-term prognosis, I would add: "You have a one in twenty chance of surviving more than two years, although you'd have a much better chance once you've survived one year," which is an accurate statement as well as leaving some room for hope.

Kalanithi also provides examples of how 1–2 millimetres of difference make enormous differences between tragedy and triumph: (a) as a result of a slight damage to hypothalamus of Matthew, a previously admitted, adorable eight-year-old boy, he became a twelve-year-old monster; and (b) for a patient with Parkinson tremors, as Kalanithi placed the electrode deep in the brain aiming for the target, the tremor improved but the patient became "overwhelmingly sad," which persisted even with an adjustment; after pulling the electrode and reposition it 2 millimetres to the right, the tremor went away and the patient felt fine.

Thus, the truth has consequences, and we should try to train ourselves to be right the first time—and every time—lest we suffer the consequences, especially when the consequences are damaging and irreversible. This means that truth is intimately related to goodness and we need a new age of enlightenment to bind them together, which is the topic I shall discuss next.

For a New Age of Enlightenment / Aubade / 2010

My youthful days were memorable: blue skies,
green fields, clear rivers, butterflies, and dragon flies . . .
Our high-tech era is amazing: video games,
The internet, iPods, Facebook, cell phones, sci-fi's . . .
I dream of those carefree days of the '60s, when
Politics was intoxicating, and love was free.
I am thrilled with our virtual information age, when
Everything's accessible at the stroke of a key.
Civil rights, women's rights, animal rights, you name it,
We have come a long way, surpassing many limits.
Anyone, anywhere, can get on the bandwagon,
Be a high-tech wizard, reap economic benefits.

Yet, my dreams of an idyllic world are shattered
By power, greed, and lust that result in endless strife.
The great democratizing cyberspace is ravaged
By viruses and addictions to Second Life.
We have brought the next generations a parlous future
By raping the Earth, ignoring global warming.
Self-interest reigns supreme, and might is always right
In power politics, which only honour winning.
Empires, multinationals, and religions flourish;
So do wars, terrors, illusions, and discontent.
Addicted to the blind faith in science and high-tech,
We fail to live in harmony and for the present.

As the ethos of relentless competition
Marches on, voices of despair are heard every day.
Half of the children in the world live in poverty,
And four-fifths of us live on less than ten dollars a day.
Millions die each year from lack of access to
Adequate sanitation or immunization.
A billion can't read or write, but trillions
Of dollars are wasted on militarization.
We'd put every child in school with less than 1%
Of our total military expenditure.
Why should some be better off than others, if we really
Are born equal despite our nature and nurture?

No. We must hope for the dawning of a new era,
when love, harmony, and prosperity rule;
When all conflicts are resolved cooperatively,
And total disarmament isn't ridiculed;
Needed resources are willingly shared by all,
To safeguard and enhance our common resources;
Rational and open discussions are the norm,
So are the pursuits of creative arts and sciences;
To bring peace, vitality, and freedom to all,
Opportunities abound to self-actualize.
Keep dreaming, my friend, because dreams may come true,
It happened before, and it may again realize.

4.

Goodness

MOST PEOPLE, I THINK, CAN ACCEPT THE ARISTOTELIAN IDEAL OF "HUMAN flourishing" or Maslow's concept of self-actualization to be at the core of what we mean by "a meaningful life." But what do human flourishing and self-actualization mean? Humans have all sorts of biological and cultural potential, both constructive and destructive. It would be absurd to indiscriminately valorize all human potential, including acts of terror, genocide, bullying, sadism, etc. This is where the concept of life's meaningfulness intersects with that of goodness, sharpens it so that ultimately, the meaning of "a meaningful life" is confined to "a good life." And this is where Ayn Rand's objectivism has gone astray, with her ideal of unconstrained human freedom in thinking and doing. Since she opposes any tampering of individual freedom, she sees in capitalism an ideal form to capitalize on human talent and doing what's best for themselves as rational beings. All we need, according to her, is to pursue our rational self-interest and actualize our potential. Ayn Rand, as I recall, was very popular in the 1970s. Everybody was talking about her, although I paid scarce attention to her at that time. Now that I know a bit more about her work after reading *Atlas Shrugged* (1957), I'm totally convinced that she's dead wrong: our self-interests are bound to come into conflict with each other, and it's imperative to place proper moral constraints on our thinking and doing. In this interdependent world, our welfare is bound together. We must transcendent the juvenile, egoistic ethics of individualism.

As I started to write this section on January 8, 2011, there was breaking news from Tucson, Arizona, announcing that a gunman, twenty-two-year-old Jared Lee Loughner, had targeted and shot Congresswoman Gabrielle Giffords in the head, killing six other people and injuring a dozen more. A massacre like this—similar to the one in 1989, when a twenty-five-year-old misogynist gunman, Marc Lepine, killed fourteen women after separating them from men at Montreal's École Polytechnique—prompts us to re-examine the ethics of human behaviour. Why is aggression against others—in the forms of violence, wars, exploitations, oppression, and atrocities—so common throughout human history even to this day? What should we do to make the world a better and safer place to live? Indeed, how should we live? Does it matter whether we live "ethically" or not? What does it mean to live ethically, i.e., to be a good person? What is goodness? As I'm now reviewing this manuscript in March 2018, a fresh memory of a mass shooting on February 14, 2018, in Parkland, Florida, where a nineteen-year-old Nikolas Jacob Cruz killed seventeen people and wounded seventeen others at his high school, still lingers in my mind.

I've always understood ethics to be about human conduct, which may or may not be good, right, or appropriate. How should we pass such judgements? When I was studying philosophy in Taiwan in the late 1950s, I was greatly influenced by the emotive theory of the logical positivist Alfred Jules Ayer, who held ethical statements to be cognitively meaningless in his influential book, *Language, Truth and Logic* (1952). This anti-cognitive theory refined views expressed earlier by David Hume (1711–1776), and also by the cognitivist, G. E. Moore, who famously labelled the derivation of a moral statement from a factual statement(s) a "naturalistic fallacy." By the time I revisited philosophy in the 2000s, this emotive, "hurrah-boo theory" of ethics—together with its philosophy of logical positivism—was largely forgotten, supplanted by other schools of analytic philosophy and was no longer in vogue.

But then I was attracted to communitarian ethics, that ethical values must be understood not in terms of the individuals' behaviour, but always with reference to a specific community—and hence they can vary from community to community. While this theory explains the plurality of existing moral values, I think it is essential that we transcend moral and cultural relativism by broadening our moral frameworks until they all reach entire humanity. The communitarian approach helps us realize that morality is a shared value among people in a community, and when values clash between/among individuals and communities, their resolution lies in finding a common ground by extending and creating a larger reference community that encompasses all the communities in question. That is how shared values are created: by considering the interests of everyone and every community so that no one becomes an outsider in our frame of reference. If we want to have certain rights and responsibilities for ourselves, we must accord the same to everyone else. Hence, ethical principles must be cognitive, rational and universal rather than emotional, whimsical, and partial. "Othering," i.e., excluding some other people from our moral reference community—by sex (sexism), race (racism), age (ageism), nationality (nationalism), etc.—is at the root of exploitation, aggression, oppression, brutality, atrocity, war, etc. If humanity is to survive and flourish, we need a global ethics that treats all humanity as one big family.

What, then, is ethics? As noted earlier, ethics is about how we should or ought to conduct ourselves. The talks of "the death of morality," for example, in the January/February 2011 issue of *Philosophy Now*, a magazine I enjoy reading regularly, are plainly nonsensical. We are always concerned with morality, wrestling with the question of how we should live and behave. What these "moral fictionists" and "moral abolitionists" maintain is that there is no objective, absolute truth in any moral claims. While I agree with their claim that morality is a social construct specific to a given culture and environment, I also recognize its biological and evolutionary basis for survival and flourishing, which, of course, is a form of objectivism. There is, indeed, a close relationship between reason and emotion in morality, as Mary Midgley (1991/2010) astutely reminds us. It is this cultural awareness of our interdependencies that requires us to develop global ethics to promote human survival and flourishing. By abandoning morality all together, therefore, these moral fictionists and abolitionists "throw the baby out with the bathwater," although they are right in warning us of the perils of excessive moralizing. Indeed, it is the art of compromising and finding common ground that enables us to go beyond our narrow cultural boundaries and include others as our own—through empathy, which Iain King (2014) calls "the bedrock of human ethics," a "moral instinct" that has "evolved like other aspects of morality and to all but the psychopathic 1% of people in the world who lack this capacity, it is a feature of the world as real as gravity." (p. 21) King's concepts of empathy and its ramification in terms of the help principle ("help someone if your time and effort is worth more to them than it is to you") (p. 21), like Carol Gilligan's (1993) feminist care perspective, explains the evolution of moral sentiments, but it does not follow, as King claims, that "we are trapped within evolution. We cannot escape it." (p. 20) Evolution can lead us to a blind alley, to extinction. Moral instincts can be good or bad. Ultimately, morality is based on cognitive judgement. If we care about human survival, we need global ethics to reinforce empathy and the help principle and reject David Hume's (1888) warning: "Reason is, and ought only to be the slave of the passions." (T 2.3.3 p. 415) So I express my dream in the following poem:

I Have A Dream . . . / The Villanelle / 2011

I have a dream to make our lives ever more wonderful,
To constantly unleash our untapped creativity.
Let's relish the journey that renders life beautiful.

I wish we'd all be less greedy and wasteful,
And always engage in earth-friendly activity.
I have a dream to make our lives ever more wonderful.

I want to know why we are sometimes so vengeful,
And how to rid ourselves of mindless insensitivity.
Let's relish the journey that renders life beautiful.

I hope we stop worshipping the rich and powerful,
And instead value and cherish more of our civility.
I have a dream to make our lives ever more wonderful.

I long for the day when we are truly mindful
Of each other's needs and shared connectivity.
Let's relish the journey that renders life beautiful.

I do what I can to write and remain hopeful,
Setting free all my power of expressivity.
I have a dream to make our lives ever more wonderful.
Let's relish the journey that renders life beautiful.

4.1. The Just War Theory and Peace

> Abolishing war in the 21st century is not only . . . possible, but also realistically necessary for human survival and well-being. (Douglas Fry, 2006, p. 263)

THERE IS NOTHING MORE MORALLY IMPORTANT TODAY THAN TO renounce the use of force as a legitimate means of conflict resolution. Although other urgent needs also clamour for our attention, our first priority should be to change our long-lasting culture of violence and war because it is a modifiable factor totally within our control. Resorting to a violent means to settle disputes would cause immediate and lasting destructions and miseries, compound existing problems, and usurp the energies and resources that should be devoted to urgent human needs such as poverty reduction, socioeconomic and cultural development, environmental protection, disease prevention and treatment, etc. Militarization and war are totally wasteful, and their human costs are mind-boggling. In the case of the 2003–2008 Iraq War, it has been estimated that 1 million people died, 4.5 million were displaced, 1–2 million were widowed, and

5 million were orphaned (Tirman, 2009). Its economic cost to the US, as estimated by Joseph Stiglitz and Linda Bilmes (2010), was between $4 and $6 trillion USD; they also found that the US (and the world's) financial crisis was due, at least in part, to the war:

> The Iraq war didn't just contribute to the severity of the financial crisis, though; it also kept us from responding to it effectively. Increased indebtedness meant that the government had far less room to manoeuvre than it otherwise would have had . . . The result is that the recession will be longer, output lower, unemployment higher and deficits larger than they would have been absent the war.

So, why did the US decide to invade Iraq? An important official excuse was that Iraq had "weapons of mass destruction" that must be destroyed. As shown in a Canadian Broadcasting Corporation (CBC) May 3, 2014, documentary, *Passionate Eye: Secrets of Modern Spies*, however, it was Rafid Ahmed Alwan al-Janabi, codenamed "Curveball," who fabricated the story of mobile biological weapons laboratories because he was fed up with Saddam Hussein. Although British, German, and American Intelligence officers had doubts about elements of this story, they believed in a significant part of this reporting. US Secretary of State Colin Powell, as well as US President George Bush, used such failed intelligence to justify their invasion of Iraq.

The Iraq war, based on a dramatic link between untruth and immorality, was a colossal mistake. Nobody won, not even the victors. It's almost always immoral to start a war in this day and age, as confirmed by most traditions in both the East and the West, and also by the United Nations, which regards war to be permissible only for reasons of self-defence or by a binding resolution from the Security Council (Hayatli, 2018; Imamkhodjaeva, 2018). As I see it, it's unconscionable that war remains glorified, and that many of the conflicts between peoples and nations today have lasted for many years, and even many decades. They have been fighting over every inch of the land/territory: no empathy, no recognition of the rights of others. I think we could learn a lot from the Chinese philosopher Mozi, a contemporary of Mencius during the Warring States Period in the fourth century BCE, who advocated a doctrine of universal love for all human beings. (de Bary & Bloom, 1999) He focused first and foremost on satisfying their material needs—such as food, clothing, and housing—and condemned the Confucians for their "ritual and music, extravagant entertainment, and above all, offensive warfare" (p. 65). Thus, according to Mozi,

It is the business of the humane person to try to promote what is beneficial to the world and to eliminate what is harmful. Now at the present time, what brings the greatest harm to the world? Great states attacking small ones, great families overthrowing small ones, the strong oppressing the week, the many harrying the few, the cunning deceiving the stupid, the eminent lording it over the humble—these are harmful to the world. So too are rulers who are not generous, ministers who are not loyal, fathers who are without kindness, and sons who are unfilial, as well as those mean men who, with weapons and knives, poison, fire, and water, seek to injure and undo each other. (pp. 69–70)

Figure 2. Mozi, also spelled Mo-tze, Motze or Micius, originally named
Mo Di (470 BCE–391 BCE), Chinese philosopher whose doctrine of
"universal or undifferentiated love." (*jian ai*) challenged Confucianism and
became the basis of a socio-religious movement known as Mohism.

It may be of interest to note that Mozi (see Figure 2) practised what he
preached. He tirelessly preached his gospel to anyone who would listen,
including the rulers who planned to start a war:

> On one of these peace missions, it is said, he walked ten
> days and ten nights, tearing off pieces of his garments

to bind up his sore feet as he went. Often Mozi and his followers, failing in their efforts at conciliation, would rush to aid in the defence of the state attacked, gaining a reputation for their skill in siege operations. In this way they became a tightly knit and highly disciplined group, leading an ascetic life and, even after Mozi's death, obediently following the directions of their "elders." (p. 65)

Confucianism, which rivalled Mohism during the Warring States Period (479–221 BCE), also regarded a war launched for purposes other than peace and humanity as unjust. This point of view was examined and discussed in a book by a Canadian scholar Daniel Bell (2010). Since it has been the position of the State Council of the People's Republic of China that "Taiwan independence" absolutely will not mean peace but a war between the two sides of the straits," and since China is now promoting Confucianism internationally through the Confucius Institutes, it surely is pertinent to interrogate what this moral, political philosophy, as narrated mainly by Mencius, has to say about war and peace. Applying this to the Taiwan-China conflict, Bell writes:

> It is obvious, for example, that war against Taiwan if it declares formal independence would not meet the Confucian criteria for justifiable punitive expeditions: so long as the Taiwanese government does not kill or starve its people, only moral power could be justifiably employed to bring Taiwan back into the Chinese orbit. (p. 34)

In promoting Confucianism, would the Chinese government adhere to this just war theory? It's hardly likely in view of China's steadfast refusal to renounce the use of force against Taiwan. Thus, Bell continues:

> But it seems just as obvious that Confucian objections are not likely to cause the Chinese government to hold back in such an eventuality.

Despite this, Bell maintains that Confucian theorizing on the just war could provide moral guidance as to when to undertake military interventions abroad.

It's unlikely, however, that China would wage a war against Taiwan, according to Thomas Friedman's (2005) Dell Theory, as proposed in his book *The World Is Flat*: "No two countries that are both a part of a major global supply chain, like Dell's, will ever fight a war against each other as long as they are both part of the same global supply chain." He explains:

> For a country with no natural resources, being part of a global supply chain is like striking oil—oil that never runs out. And therefore, getting dropped from such a chain because you start a war is like having your oil wells go dry or having someone pour cement down them. They will not come back anytime soon. (pp. 522–523)

The cost implications of a war would be astronomical, as industries and economies around the world would be disrupted, and China and Taiwan would risk the loss of their place in that supply chain for a long time. Such a war, Friedman further asserts, could lead American tech companies to move their R&D operations out of China, and trigger a widespread American boycott of Chinese goods, which could lead to serious economic turmoil inside China.

Despite its economic implications, Friedman too does not have illusions about the Dell Theory: "It does not make wars obsolete: It guarantees only that government whose countries are enmeshed in global supply chains will have to think three times, not just twice, about engaging in anything but a war of self-defence" (2005, pp. 590–591).

I find the Dell Theory pretty insightful when looking at war and peace from a globalization perspective. Although Friedman pronounced it "with tongue slightly in cheek," it really is a modern version of the just war theory, that war is justifiable only in the case of self-defence. It's a truism that peace is much more preferable to war, except when power, national pride, etc. get in the way.

And that seems to be the case, unfortunately. Zhang Zhijun, the head of China's Taiwan Affairs Office, warned a visiting Taiwanese business delegation in May 2016, just weeks after Tsai Ing-wen took office as president, "There is no future in Taiwan independence, and this cannot become an option for Taiwan's future. This is the conclusion of history." Brushing aside the concern that "some people say you must pay attention to broad public opinion in Taiwan," Zhang retorted, "Taiwan society ought to understand and attach great importance to the feelings of the 1.37 billion residents of the mainland" (Carpenter, 2018). Now, I can't find better examples than the above statements, which exemplify the errors of thinking that characterize "historicism (historical determinism)" and "totalitarianism"—that Karl Popper vigorously criticized (see Section 10.2)—as if there were historical laws dictating the course of history, and that the only aspirations that matter are your own, so that you can impose your will on others. This kind of deterministic and undemocratic thinking should, of course, be rejected, as it contributes to the ethics of "might is right," using force and violence to settle disputes. It would be particularly sad for the 1.37 billion Chinese if they forgot the history of humiliation in the hands of Western powers and Japan and become the oppressors themselves of 23.6 million people in Taiwan.

Let's be peace-lovers, not warmongers!

On War and Peace / Elegy / 2010

I mourn the death of Michelle Lang
The first Canadian journalist
To have died from the current war
In faraway Afghanistan

They say this war is a just war
'Cause so many innocent ones
Died a senseless death on 9/11
And they deserve retribution

So do those on the other side
They want retribution also
And the vicious cycle goes on
For Michelle to pay the price

War entails death and misery
Hence can any war be called just?
Who in the right mind would start one
Since action invites reaction?

Peoples of Israel and Palestine
Don't you know what your conflict means?
A crime against humanity
A root of the Mid-East conflicts

4.2. Democracy and Taiwan's Sunflower Student Movement

THE CONFUCIAN THEORY OF JUST WAR, IN FACT, ISN'T THAT DIFFERENT from the modern theory, as expressed, for example, in 1993 by the US Catholic Conference: "Force may be used only to correct a grave, public evil, i.e., aggression or massive violation of the basic human rights of whole populations" (United States Conference of Catholic Bishops, 1993; B.2). China, therefore, is well advised to stay on a moral high ground and denounce the use of force as a means to settle any political dispute. The military threat against Taiwan only antagonizes the Taiwanese, and hence is highly counterproductive. This is demonstrated in a 2011 poll in Taiwan, reporting that only 1.4% favoured swift unification with China, 23% wanted full independence, and 60% wanted to maintain the status quo indefinitely. Moreover, 54% of the respondents (up from 17% in 1992) identified themselves as Taiwanese rather than Chinese, and only 4% (down from 25% in 1992) identified themselves as Chinese.

What moral power could China justifiably employ, then, in view of the fact that so few Taiwanese now identify themselves as Chinese, and four out of five Taiwanese are happy with a "Goldilocks solution" of keeping a warm and friendly relation with China, but not so close as to lose their sovereignty and independence? Since a war across the Taiwan Strait is unthinkable in view of its economic fallout and the continued US military support of Taiwan, the most likely, if not the only, way for China to work towards her unification dream is to democratize her political system in an exemplary way to the point that the Taiwanese would one day voluntarily share the same dream. Interestingly, Bruce Gilley (2008) of Portland State University advanced a thesis that "being a democracy was nearly a necessity" for a country with the GDP per capita above $10,000 (purchasing power parities, 2002 USD), and "China will likely enter this zone around the year 2020." (p. 275) Instead of the failed "strike hard" policy, therefore, China is well advised to put the rhetoric of "peaceful rise" into practice, get rid of the thousands of missiles, fighters, and bombers ostensibly for use against Taiwan, and renounce the use of force once and for all.

China, of course, has also been practising Sun Tzu's art of warfare to further its goal of taking over Taiwan—through economic rather than military means. Having signed the controversial Cross-Straight Services Trade Agreement (CSSTA) with China in June 2013, Taiwan's Nationalist (KMT) government tried in March 2014 to unilaterally ram it through in the Legislature Yuan (LY) to ratify it—reneging on the earlier agreement with the opposition Democratic Progressive Party (DPP) to conduct an item-by-item review of the pact—after months of delay and wrangling. Thousands of students and academics, together with the members of the DPP, gathered at the LY to protest. This was followed by an unprecedented occupation of the LY floor, lasting for twenty-three days, by hundreds of students to prevent the hasty ratification of this agreement, which would ensure further economic (and perhaps political) integration with China. A huge rally was organized, numbering half a million according to the organizer and the media, although the National Police Agency put the estimate at 116,000. Eventually, the government partially caved in, promised the item-by-item review with the opposition DPP, and the enactment of an oversight bill before lawmakers reviewed the trade pact.

Taiwan's then-president, Ma Ying-jeou, had rejected the students' third demand to withdraw and renegotiate this deal, however, on the ground that its rejection "would threaten Taiwan's ability to sign trade accords with other countries. Taiwan faces higher average duties on its exports than regional competitors like South Korea, Japan and Singapore" (Ramzy, 2014). I think this rationale may be convincing IF China, like South Korea, Japan and Singapore, does not pose any threat to Taiwan's sovereignty. It's China's military, political, and economic threat against Taiwan that underlies this unprecedented student protest, dubbed as the Sunflower Movement (in reference to the light and transparency they want to bring to the government).

March of 2014 was also the month when a Ukrainian region of Crimea become part of the Russian Federation. At least Russia initiated a perfunctory motion of letting Crimea hold a referendum to show that an overwhelming majority of voters there supported joining Russia. However, it would have been better if Russia were to have taken time to negotiate with the Ukrainian government and the West, inviting rather than turning away international observers to supervise that referendum, instead of totally alienating the West by flexing its military muscle to occupy Crimea before hurriedly holding a referendum to annex it. Why the rush? What was to be gained by taking such a hardline measure? When confronted with a subsequent UN Security Council draft resolution that would have condemned the referendum in Crimea as illegal, Russia vetoed and China abstained, as expected. Emboldened by Russia's annexation of Crimea, moreover, the political strife in Eastern Ukraine escalated as pro-Russian separatists took up arms and occupied public buildings, demanding that they be annexed by Russia. Clashes between the Ukrainian riot police/ army and the separatists ensued, and many lives were lost. The relation between Russia and the Western powers remained tense over the crisis in Ukraine.

China, of course, did not take sides on the Ukraine crisis. Contrary to her rhetoric of peace and harmony, China tends to take a hardline against its racial and cultural minorities and with its neighbours. The massacre on March 1, 2014, at the Kunming railway station of at least thirty-three and the wounding of 143 people by at least ten Muslim Uighurs from the far Western region of Xinjiang is a stark reminder of the abysmal failure of the Chinese "strike hard" policy. To put its rhetoric of peace and harmony into practice, China should seriously reconsider and spell out the conditions under which the principle of self-determination would be recognized and practised. The same can be said for solving the ongoing impasse of Catalan sovereignty in Spain—it would be much better for all parties involved to negotiate and work out the conditions and procedures for peacefully resolving the conflict rather than resorting to extreme unilateral measures. It's a truism that action invites reaction, so if you strike hard, others will retaliate. The news of Russia's annexation of Crimea, as FlorCruz's (2014) article in *International Business Times* pointed out, might have deepened the anxiety of many Taiwanese about the service sector trade deal with China, i.e., playing into China's unification goals.

China's intransigence mirrors that of all other great powers, like Russia, the US, Japan, Germany, France, and Great Britain, among others. Isn't it true that power corrupts, and absolute power corrupts absolutely? Perhaps my Polish-born tennis partner, Jack has a point—that all big countries should be broken up into small ones based on the principle of self-determination, so that no country can dictate the terms of sovereignty for others. All this reminds me of E. F. Schumacher's philosophy of "small is beautiful," which should ride supreme in politics as well as in our daily lives in order to steer away from the destructive course of power politics and dysfunctional human relations! Are we capable of going beyond the death instinct?

Beyond the Death Instinct / Blank Verse / 2010

Our world is beautiful but also ugly
We don't value life and know ourselves enough
We are plagued by the unconscious death instinct
Causing havoc to ourselves and to the earth

We live, but not in touch with our selves
In seeking pleasure we forget disciplines
We eat junk food and drive everywhere
We drink too much and watch too much TV

We are ashamed when looking in the mirror
For not measuring up to Top Models
We search the internet for solutions
But no diet plan or pill does the trick.

We know plant-based diet is best for us
The ecology of the environment
We admire vegetarianism
But we'd rather eat meat than fruits and veggies

It's easier to be a couch potato
Drinking beer, munching popcorn or pizza
Than go biking or walking in a park
We even drive to nearby corner stores

Little wonder we are afflicted by
The "diseases of civilization"
Which take many decades to develop
By abusing our body and our psyche

And we have been abusing each other
Our everlasting violence and wars
Do not abate and have no end in sight
Through our blind worship of the naked power

Witness the change in our environment
Which is so much worse just in my lifetime.
Pollution, toxic waste, global warming
You name it—the list is long and endless

We all know life and death go hand in hand
Where there is life there is will to live
But I wonder from whence comes the death instinct
Can't we just accept death and not wish it?

Life-and-death instincts come from the same source
But aggression can be sublimated
Civil wars have been averted for years
In countries with fair and democratic rules

But we have a long way to go to settle
Internal and external aggressions
And turn them into positive forces
That's our task if we are to have a future

4.3. Conflict Resolution

CONFLICT IS A FACT OF LIFE. HOW SHOULD IT BE RESOLVED? ARE VIOLENCE and war ingrained in human nature and hence inevitable? The American anthropologist Douglas Fry, in his book *The Human Potential for Peace* (2005), challenges that commonly held assumption based on anthropological evidence: it's possible and necessary to abolish war and promote peaceful ways to resolve human conflicts. However, the dominant approach adopted by most countries, such as the US, Russia, Israel, and China, fails to manage conflict cooperatively, e.g., the US War on Terror, the Russia-Ukrainian confrontations, Israeli-Palestinian conflicts, and China's hardline policy against the Uighur militants. We really need to re-examine our own biases and blind spots and work toward a global culture of peace. I was therefore impressed when I read two articles for peace by peaceful means: "Building Peace Through Harmonious Diversity: The Security Approach and the Peace Approach," and "What Could Peace between

Washington and Al-Qaeda/Iraq Look Like?" by Johan Galtung, Dr. h.c. mult, Professor of Peace Studies, Peace University.

Galtung (2004) calls the dominant approach the security approach, characterized by identifying and "othering" an evil party who presents a real or potential danger of violence; hence, strength to defeat or deter the evil party is needed to enhance security and safeguard "peace." The peace approach, on the other hand, is based on: a conflict to be resolved or transformed; a danger of violence to be settled; empathic-creative-nonviolent transformation of conflict; and peaceful settlement as the best approach to "security." He criticized the 9/11 Commission Report for: (a) writing and thinking "only inside a security discourse . . . and never inside a peace discourse . . . By constructing Other as merely evil there is no room for dialogue. Hence the singleminded, fatal focus on US strength," and, as a result, (b) the lack of focus on US acts of commission, "like about 70 interventions around the world since 1945 with 12–16 million killed, to be followed by recommendations about what not to do". If we are serious about "peace on earth," according to Galtung, we need to redouble our efforts to embrace the peace approach and cultivate enough equanimity to admit and atone for our own past mistakes. It is a disgrace rather than a virtue not to be able to do so. Galtung further states:

> "Building Peace Through Harmonious Diversity" is a marvellous title, combining three words of honour: peace, harmony, diversity. "Peace", in my view, is another word for equality, equity, equal rights/dignity, symmetry, reciprocity, diversity/symbiosis etc.; "harmony" is creative cooperation, beyond absence of violence; "diversity" celebrates our manifold, within peace and harmony. The Millennium Question is how to obtain all three when all over there is the opposite: direct, structural and cultural violence.

Galtung, who is a Norwegian sociologist and mathematician, is right on. To turn the culture of violence around, we need the ethics of respect and equality to resolve all conflicts wisely.

I was initially very impressed when I read "For a Vision of Common, Comprehensive, Cooperative and Sustainable Security" by Yang Jiechi (2015), Chinese State Councillor and former Foreign Minister:

> The Chinese Dream is a dream about peace, development and win-win cooperation . . . China follows the path of peaceful development, and upholds justice and pursues shared interests. China calls on all countries to foster a sense of shared destiny, forge a new type of international relations of win-win cooperation, and build a peaceful, harmonious and prosperous world. (p. 2))

Yang states, moreover, that:

> Countries need to foster a new vision of addressing security challenges through cooperation so as to promote peace and security through cooperation. We also need to seek peaceful settlement to disputes, conduct candid and in-depth dialogue and communication to increase strategic trust and reduce mutual suspicion, increase mutual understanding, accommodate each other's concerns, avoid conflict and confrontation, and seek benefits for all. (p.3)

A beautiful dream, I'd say! I wish China would act on such a dream. Sadly, though, this beautiful dream flies in the face of China's hardline policies such as those in relation to Tibet since China invaded Tibet in 1950—a topic being discussed at the 2018 Spring Session of the Edmonton Life Long Association (ELLA) Religious Extremism course at the University of Alberta. The Australian political scientist Ben Hillman's (2008) article, "Rethinking China's Tibet Policy," makes following references to China's failed hardline Tibet policy:

> Since the last major protests in March 1989, the policy has been carrot and stick—state investment for development

on the one hand, and zero tolerance of dissent on the other . . . Armed police reinforcements were sent to all ethnically Tibetan areas, including those free of protest. At the same time, the official media went on a publicity offensive, attempting to convince the world that Tibetan rioters were nothing but violent criminals. (p. 6)

This publicity blitz included more than the usual heated vitriol against the Dalai Lama, whom Beijing accused of orchestrating the mayhem in order to split China. Hillman continues to state that China's nationalist card, including demonizing the Dalai Lama, not only backfired on the international stage, but also has the effect of fostering ethnic hatred between Tibetans and Han Chinese. He therefore endorses a more open approach to policy on Tibet, as petitioned by some Chinese intellectuals, led by Beijing-based writer Wang Lixiong. The petition states:

In order to prevent similar incidents [the 1989 protest] from occurring in the future, the government must abide by the freedom of religious belief and the freedom of speech explicitly enshrined in the Chinese Constitution, thereby allowing the Tibetan people to fully express their grievances and hopes and permitting citizens of all nationalities to freely criticize and make suggestions regarding the government's nationality policies. (p. 7)

This is a hopeful sign. Should China further democratize and build a more cooperative society in which the rights of all people are respected and promoted, domestically and internationally, it would transform China's "peaceful rise" from a mere slogan to reality. "Peaceful rise" means cooperative resolution of any conflict to effect win-win solutions, rather than imposing one's solutions on reluctant others; then there would be peace at both the individual and the group level. I reflected different ways of conflict resolution in my poem:

On Conflict Resolution / The Lai / 2010

Conflicts shape our life.
How to avoid strife?
Stay calm.

Handle them wisely
Will make you holy:
How nice!

Handle them poorly
And you'll look silly:
That's life

4.4. Why Equality?

WE LIVE IN AN UNEQUAL WORLD. THAT'S OBVIOUS TO ME, AND YET THE myth that we are created equal, as stated in the US Declaration of Independence, is alive and well in America and possibly everywhere else. I wondered why the Republican Party has so vehemently opposed Obama Care, the Affordable Care Act, until I saw Kathy Seifert's (2013) explanation in the opening paragraph of her article, "We Are Not Created Equal":

> [T]he general sentiment was that we are all created equal and all have the same chances in life to succeed. Why is Obama Care necessary to even the playing field? Why should the rich have to pay more in taxes in order to subsidize health plans for the poor or low income?

Ah, I see! It's the myth of our being created equal that's behind the Conservative policy agenda! Would they still oppose taxing the rich more to help the poor if they were convinced of the inequality in our creation and that some really need extra help to care for their health?

In the final analysis, it all boils down to Iain King's concept of empathy and the helping principle. Misfortunes can strike anyone at any time, and we need others to help us pull through difficult times. What if we were born mentally or physically handicapped, and therefore had learning disabilities? What if our parents were abusive and made us feel we couldn't do anything right to please them? What if we lost our jobs—because our companies moved to China or Bangladesh, "racing to the bottom" in search for lower costs and higher profits—and we need retraining to find new jobs? What if we were the girls or women who worked in a garment factory in Bangladesh for $38/month, making clothes to be sold in Canada or the US, and whose factory collapsed because it didn't meet the building safety code, and we survived but lost an arm or leg—as reported in a CBC documentary, *Made in Bangladesh*? There is no question that we are born and raised unequally, and we need the help principle to make our world more equal. The question is *how*?

The conservative, neoliberal thinking has dominated public policy since the 1980s, after Margaret Thatcher and Ronald Reagan took power. These economists and policy-makers embrace market capitalism, equating the just distribution of income and wealth with a market-driven economic stimulation and distribution through the so-called "invisible hand." Even China's Deng Xiaoping, who ushered market economy into China in the 1970s, has been widely (mis?)quoted in the media as saying, "To get rich is glorious." As Martin White (2014) noted and also documented in *China Mike*, China was once a relatively egalitarian country with a Gini Index of less than 0.30. In 2011, however, China's Gini Index rose to 0.415 and ranked #53 in the world in terms of worse income inequality—as compared to the US's Gini Index of 0.400, which ranked #40. The accelerated income inequality in China is also indicated by the reported number of billionaires in China in March 2018, 819, surpassing the number, 571, of billionaires in the U.S. (Wright 2018). In the mid-2000s, 10% of China's wealthiest controlled 45% of the country's wealth, according to China's National Bureau of Statistics. Pew Research's Global Attitudes Project in

2012 found that 48% of Chinese in the survey said the gap between rich and poor was a very serious problem, up from 41% in 2008, and fully 87% considered it at least a moderately big problem. Even the world's super-rich now recognize the problem of income inequality. In a report entitled "Global Elites Finally Admit Income Inequality is a Problem," Michael Moran (2014), among others, quoted Oxfam's report, which found that the combined net worth of the world's eighty-five top super-rich people "equals the combined net worth of the poorest 50% of the planet—some 3.5 billion people." Many of these super-rich people attended the World Economic Forum (WEF), whose *Global Risk 2014* report contained a survey of 700 global corporate leaders who named "income disparity as the number one long-term threat to global stability."

In reaction to Oxfam's report, Kevin O'Leary, a.k.a. "Mr. Wonderful," was quoted as saying on his Canadian TV show, *The Lang & O'Leary Exchange*:

> It's fantastic. And this is a great thing because it inspires everybody, gets them motivation to look up to the 1% and say, "I want to become one of those people, I'm going to fight hard to get up to the top." This is fantastic news, and of course I applaud it. What can be wrong with this? (November 24, 2016)

Like many others like him, David Brooks also saw things differently. In his *New York Times* article on January 16, 2014, Brooks wrote: "Low income . . . is not the problem. To say it is the problem is to confuse cause and effect," because, according to him, it was the outcomes of the problems of single motherhood, low social mobility, high school dropout rates, the fraying of the social fabric, de-industrialization, etc. On that ground, he opposed raising the minimum wage since, in his view, only 11% of the workers affected by such an increase came from poor households, and most other workers were neither the primary bread earners nor from poor families. He reasoned, "The primary problem for the poor is not that they are getting paid too little for the hours they work. It is that they are not working full time or at all." Are the majority of Chinese and even the world's super-rich wrong to be concerned with income inequality? Is all minimum wage legislation unnecessary and even harmful as condemned by many conservatives?

O'Leary and Brooks, and others who think like them, are hopelessly wrong. It's obscene that so few people have so much while so many have so little, and it's ludicrous to urge and applaud those who dream and fight to be super-rich. I'd reply to O'Leary's question, "What can be wrong with this [dream]?" as follows: "Everything." It's not only outrageous but also obscene. In fact, that dream is, by and large, illusory and immoral. Why? I think the WEF report hit the nail on the head by confessing its unsustainability. Excessive wealth tends to promote extravagance and unhealthy/ wasteful lifestyles; it corrupts the political system through influence peddling, vote buying, etc., and hence is undemocratic—as shown by *Time Magazine*'s January 9, 2014, article on US politics: "Congress Is Now Mostly A Millionaires' Club"; it causes social discontent, envy, hostility, sense of unfairness, and social unrest (e.g., the occupy movements); it's often based on luck and market distortion, or on questionable means such as deceit and exploitation; it tends to promote anti-social thinking and behaviour, such as egoism, greed, cutthroat competition, etc., instead of empathy, cooperation, and mutual help; and it encourages, and is often based on, exploitation of human and natural resources, and on harming the environment and ecosystem.

All in all, it's socially irresponsible and environmentally unsustainable. That's exactly the message of China's deputy minister of the environment, Pan Yue. In his interview with *Der Spiegel* in 2005, he predicted that the Chinese economic miracle will end soon because of environmental unsustainability. He also warns us:

> If the gap between the poor and the rich widens, then regions within China and the society as a whole will become unstable. If our democracy and our legal system lag behind the overall economic development, various

groups in the population won't be able to protect their own interests. (Lorenz 2005)

On top of that, money does not necessarily bring them happiness, either. In an article, "Secret Fears of the Super-Rich," Graeme Wood (2011) quotes from *The Joys and Dilemmas of Wealth*, a Boston College study of those with assets in the tens of millions of dollars and above:

> The respondents turn out to be a generally dissatisfied lot, whose money has contributed to deep anxieties involving love, work, and family. Indeed, they are frequently dissatisfied even with their sizable fortunes. Most of them still do not consider themselves financially secure; for that, they say, they would require on average one-quarter more wealth than they currently possess.

Brooks too is incorrect to dismiss the issues of income inequality and to oppose raising the minimum wage to a living wage. First of all, those 11% of low-wage workers who work full-time are primary bread earners and need help, so it's natural to consider the direct measure of raising the minimum wage to the level of a living wage if the employer can afford it. Furthermore, it's a stretch of the imagination to think that the neoliberal market economy automatically distributes income and wealth fairly. The "invisible hand" is a descriptive, rather than prescriptive, theory. It's a "naturalistic fallacy," to use G.E. Moore's famous phrase, to justify unequal distribution of income and wealth on the basis of the neoliberal market economy. I've heard Kevin O'Leary on the CBC, characterizing taxation as "stealing money" from the likes of him, without acknowledging that the state plays a constitutive role by providing an infrastructure and services to enable the markets to function. It's possible, and indeed very likely, that the markets unfairly "subsidize" him by paying him too much—letting him appropriate all the surplus value rather than sharing it with the workers, thus "robbing" the poor by depressing their wages. Just distribution of wealth demands a living income for everyone, possibly by raising the minimum wage to a living wage, before endorsing some degree of income inequality.

We Get What We Deserve / Chant Royal / 2011

Imagine a world in which everyone
Has an opportunity to prosper and thrive
Life becomes beautiful and full of fun
Our dreams and potentials all come alive
All have goodwill towards each other
To make sure everyone progresses further
To live a life exciting and colourful
And our existence, joyful and meaningful
Everyone cares for everyone else
To make life lovely, caring, and truthful
And make sure we get what we deserve

I'm a dreamer, but also a realist
I know that our world is driven by greed
Which turns many of us into egoists
Ruthless competition becomes their only creed
And they thrive on conquest and excess
Desiring ever more bounties to possess
Concentration of wealth among the few
Isn't immorality they would eschew
Others then join the occupation movements
In hopes of bidding gross unfairness adieu
Knowing that we get what we deserve

I hear the gospel of capitalism
From CBC's Kevin O'Leary
Extolling the virtue of egoism
Which makes me inordinately leery
He denounces trade unions as evil
Although unions make us more civil
He applauds disparities in income
As a just and desirable outcome
And to worry about the crisis in Greece
For just 11 million people is dumb!
Remember, we only get what we deserve

I can't stand Kevin's bigotry and ranting
Knowing full well that he is revered by some
The show business loves dramatizing
The more the ideas clash, the more fun they become
That may be why the CBC made a choice
To give Kevin a prime-time role and voice
To air his neo-conservative view
For us to reflect and think anew
About civil unrest and raping of the earth
To come up with an alternative worldview
Because we only get what we deserve

The future holds no limit for egoism
Not even in its wildest dreams
Its rugged individualism
Abhors any regulatory schemes
It engenders waste and pollution
Which defies any sound solution
Even outer space is filled with junk
Rendering freedom unwittingly shrunk
Intoxicated with sweet delusion
The egoists act just like an unrepentant drunk
We always get what we deserve

For the next generations can we debunk
The myth of invisible hands, which have sunk
Our fortunes to a logical conclusion?
Neo-conservatism is all bunk
Of course we only get what we deserve

4.5. Capitalism, Democracy, and Socialism

IN 1989, FRANCIS FUKUYAMA PUBLISHED A PAPER, "THE END OF HISTORY?"
in the journal, *The National Interest*, stating that:

> What we may be witnessing is not just the end of the
> Cold War, or the passing of a particular period of post-
> war history, but the end of history as such: that is, the end
> point of mankind's ideological evolution and the univer-
> salization of Western liberal democracy as the final form
> of human government. (p. 1)

Isn't this statement, which has been amplified in his 1992 book, *The End
of History and the Last Man*, preposterous? Western liberal democracy, as

David Schweickart (2002) notes, is only a polyarchy, "a system in which a broad-based electorate select political leaders from competing candidates in elections that are reasonably honest." (p. 152) Capitalism is not compatible with democracy, which Schweickart defines as "a system in which a universal electorate is reasonably well informed, active, and unobstructed by a privileged minority class" (p. 153). Since the capitalist class in a capitalist society is a minority privileged class possessing enormous political power way beyond the average citizen, the struggle for democracy will continue at all stages of human development, under capitalism, socialism, or what have you, as long as the imbalance in political powers in any sphere of human activities continues. Western liberal democracy, therefore, is nowhere near "the final form of human development," which may not exist at all.

Capitalism, based on the myth of the invisible hand, is not sustainable in our finite world: it strives on cutthroat competition, creates a privileged minority class, indulges in ever-increasing consumption of goods and services, and exploits natural resources recklessly, thereby causes irreparable damage to the ecosystem that sustains human life. Garrett Hardin (1968) called our attention to what he called "the tragedy of the commons": "Therein is the tragedy . . . Ruin is the destination toward which all men rush, each pursuing his own interest in a society that believes in the freedom of the commons." Western liberal democracy must, therefore, continue to evolve to incorporate some form of socialism—to regulate and manage capital and the market more democratically and in a more sustainable way for the benefit of all. "The end of (human) history" will likely coincide with the extinction of *Homo sapiens*. Our search for utopias will doubtlessly continue, as proffered, for example, by Diane Elson's (2000) "Socializing Markets, Not Market Socialism":

> The way forward in the twenty-first century is not to dream of schemes for eliminating markets and money; but to envision ways of reclaiming and transforming markets and money, so that they become a means of facilitating mutually beneficial exchange, based on a

mutually beneficial division of labour, in an economy with an egalitarian distribution of economic power. This means embedding markets in egalitarian social relations, which in turn means exploring ways of transforming the property relations that underlie and shape the current configurations of market institutions. This will require building upon already-existing contradictions and dissonance in capitalist markets, and developing already-existing creative initiatives to socialize markets. (p. 68)

After experimenting with various forms of capitalism and socialism in the past, right combinations of the ideals of socialism and capitalism may emerge and shape our future, perhaps towards what Diane Elson called "a slower, kinder, gentler, more inclusive economy—one that really embodies, in this sense, the ideals of socialism". (p. 83)

A society, therefore, is like an individual: it's necessary to strike a right combination and balance between the yin energy of socialism and collectivism on the one hand, and the yang energy of capitalism and individualism on the other. While the latter drives creativity and wealth, the former ensures empathy, solidarity, and justice. Democracy is required to integrate the two harmoniously and peacefully in our interrelated world, indispensable for building a utopia:

Dystopia or Utopia / Free Verse / 2016

Do you see what I see?
A dystopia is now looming before us
I see sadistic winners and depressed losers
All frantically working their butts off
Rather than living their joyful lives

Naively, back in the 1970s, I mused about
The dawning of a leisure society, a utopia
Though that vision has since fallen off the radar
As reckless, hegemonic competition took hold
We may have now more liberty, but less equity

Inequity is a price we must pay for efficiency
Pronounced the American economist, Art Okun
No wonder, the world's richest sixty-two persons
Now hold the combined wealth equal to that of
A half (3.6 billion) of the world's poorest people

We want personal liberty and social equity
Can we have cake and eat it too?
Some of us have greedily eaten too much
Leaving too little to others and future generations
So, we must shift our course more toward equity goals

We could keep competing on a path to a dystopia
Or cooperate more on a path toward a utopia
Both liberty and equity are our prized goals
We need a just and equitable reward system for all
To have (some of the) cake and eat (some of) it too

5.
Beauty

BEAUTY, THE PRIMARY OBJECT OF LOVE ACCORDING TO PLATO'S *Symposium*, together with truth and goodness constitute Socrates' trinity. It's fitting, therefore, to delve deeper into this trinity's meanings and relationships.

Nobody can deny that beauty is what we love. We love that which we find beautiful and, as Confucius said, everything has its beauty, but not everyone sees it. In addition to beauty, we also love a whole lot of other things, such as chocolate, truth-telling, courage, tenderness, kindness, inspirational poems, funny stories, scientific theories, innovations, etc. I was somewhat surprised and taken aback, therefore, to read Professor Michelle Meagher's (2000) paper, "Jenny Saville and a Feminist Aesthetics of Disgust" in her Body Politics course at the University of Alberta. How can disgust be an object of aesthetics?

Aesthetics is called "Study/Knowledge of Beauty" in Chinese, so it's a contradiction in terms to talk about aesthetics of disgust. It seems, though, that the concept of aesthetics has evolved in the West over time so that it is often referred to as the study of both beauty and anything that is so outlandish as to shock our senses. I think this extension is like "drawing a snake and adding feet," to quote a Chinese proverb, totally unnecessary and unworthy. Jenny Saville's paintings of herself and others provoke the feeling of disgust, although many artists and art critics find these paintings great and powerful and declare that beauty is not an essential characteristic of art. I disagree. Beauty has to be an essential characteristic of art. If not beautiful, it is not art, pure and simple. Some people admire Jenny Saville's paintings to the extent that they find them beautiful—not necessarily in terms of physical bodies but in terms of the artistries of these presentations. Aesthetic experience is multidimensional. Any work of art has to be beautiful in some way, although it may also evoke other thoughts and feelings, such as a sense of disgust, in other ways. If they are the objects of pure disgust, I doubt that anyone would love them as works of art.

The most insightful aspect of beauty is perhaps in its new, dazzling revelation of reality and truth. Because of our love of beauty, we are drawn to it and eager to know more about it, leading to discoveries of a new kind of reality previously unknown to us. This is true in daily life when we love someone or something such as mathematics and science, when we ardently conduct investigations to go beyond what's already known to us, and end up with new insights about reality, which we find beautiful. Reality may appear to be messy, chaotic, and confusing, but truth often makes things appear much simpler and unified, comprehensible and harmonious. Such revelations are a source of beauty, which helps us understand and act according to the way of nature and actualize our authentic self.

Beauty, moreover, is an intrinsic good and a source of great pleasure. It inspires and enriches our lives. A life without beauty is dreary and unappealing. Beauty melts our hearts, soothes our minds, calms our senses, and uplifts our spirits. It makes us tender, loving, and kind to ourselves and to others. It renders us more empathetic and caring. Beauty, therefore, is goodness. On the other hand, goodness is beauty. Whatever act or behaviour that brings out goodness in us is beautiful. Goodness embodies courage, strength, honour, respect, nobility, admiration, empathy, kindness, grace, and above all, beauty. Shelley is right to proclaim that beauty is goodness and goodness is beauty. To talk about corrupting and immoral beauty is to confuse the issue. For example, in the film *Cloud 9*, Inge and Karl's love is beautiful, but Werner's reaction—jealousy—is not. It is their reactions, on the part of Inge and Werner, that precipitate Werner's tragic death. Most issues are complex, having both beautiful and ugly sides.

Beauty is mysterious, although I often know instantly when I see it. It puzzles me to no end to define what it is, what makes something attractive and wonderful. I have read amazing books such as *Survival of the Prettiest* by Nancy Etcoff and *The Beauty Myth* by Naomi Wolf, but I am no closer to understanding the nature of beauty. So I wrote the following poem:

The Riddle of Beauty / A Skeltonic Verse / 2011

Beauty is the riddle of eternity
Nobody knows it with certainty
It's our intellectual duty
To solve this riddle of beauty
At which we love to guess
Endeavour to express
Desperate to possess
But with little success
And with much distress

Beauty's the object of our love
It's a well-thought-of
Concept of true love
The best definition of
Beauty is (what we) love
Since beauty engenders love

And love's beautiful
Truth brings light, makes things graceful
Beauty is inspirational
Reveals a new kind of reality
Let's embrace its authenticity
And rejoice Keats's polarity—
"Beauty is truth, truth beauty"

Let's also defend the validity
Of "beauty's goodness, goodness beauty"
Beauty is love, and always uplifting
The world without beauty is boring
Utterly lifeless and even revolting
Goodness makes people more loving
More beautiful and inspiring
Tolstoy's wrong in his contention
That beauty's goodness is a delusion

5.1. Philosophy of Art

THE CONCEPT OF BEAUTY IS AN ENIGMA. I EXPERIENCE IT EVERY DAY IN nature, in architecture, in people, works of art, etc., but I am at a loss to characterize it. What renders something beautiful? Why do I deem someone more beautiful and like him or her better than someone else? Why do I like some works of art but not others?

I was very fortunate in the fall of 2011 to audit a course, Philosophy of Art, taught by Professor Jennifer Welchman. In the class, we discussed whether Marla Olmstead and Hong are "artists." Marla, an artist's four-year-old daughter, dabbles with paint on canvases and has sold over $300,000 of her paintings (see Figure 3). Hong, a nine-year old elephant in Thailand, does amazing representational paintings of an elephant holding a flower (see Figure 4).

Figure 3. A painting by the four-year-old Marla Olmstead. Her paintings were exhibited at the Brunelli Art Gallery in Binghamton in November 2004, and several of her works were sold for as much as $15,000.

Figure 4. Hong's painting, as "guided" by her "mahout", the trainer, who has trained
this elephant to do painting for two years. Elephant art has been promoted in
Thailand as a safe and creative source of income to care for domesticated elephants
and their trainers, as sponsored by the Asian elephant Art & Conservation Project.

Interestingly, the students in the class tend to regard Marla as an artist
because her patrons love her paintings, whereas Hong is not regarded as
an artist because her artwork is attributed more to the trainer than to her,
and the students questioned whether she is capable of producing other
artworks. I think such verdicts are questionable, based on a double standard, i.e., the patrons' reactions are used to judge Marla's but not Hong's
works. In fact, Hong seems to show the mastery of skills that Marla may
not have possessed. It's ironic, moreover, that the sale of Marla's paintings plummeted after the airing of a CBS *60 Minutes* documentary about
Marla having been coached by her father in producing her artworks.
Hong's skills too have been questioned, as a closer study later shows that
the trunk movements of all elephant "artists" are closely guided by their
caretakers, who tug and nudge the elephants' ears or other body parts to

control them (Morris, 2009). Therefore, Hong may also be disqualified as an artist by herself despite her amazing skills in muscle control—because she's responding to her caretaker's suggestions rather than expressing her own artistic ideas—although together with her caretaker, they may qualify as artists.

By the way, elephant tourism in Thailand and elsewhere is very controversial. As Claire Marshall (2017) reported, according to a study by World Animal Protection across Asia, it fuels incentives to capture elephants from the wild to keep for human entertainment. Of the 3,000 elephants inspected between 2014 and 2016, only 200 were found to be living in acceptable captive conditions—especially when there were no direct interactions with people such as riding, washing, circus tricks, etc. This may also apply to elephant art tourism. However, elephant art is justified on the Asian Elephant Art & Conservation Project website as follows:

> Asian Elephants are endangered and we believe that wherever possible they should be allowed to exist naturally in their native habitats. Unfortunately however, there are many elephants remaining in captivity with little protection and no habitat left to return to. Through this project we aim to educate the public about the elephants' plight, educate caretakers in humane care practices, and raise funds to provide support and care to both captive and wild populations.

Back on the issue of "What is (good) art?" I guess I am a Kantian who believes the mastery of skills to be necessary for someone to be called an artist. As Kant said: "A beauty of nature is a beautiful thing; beauty of art is a beautiful representation of a thing." I think all works of art are, or should be, representative—representing the artist's sense of beauty in something, concrete or abstract, material or immaterial. Without a beautiful representation involving the skills of an artist, there is no work of art. That's why when I look at any work of art, I always seek, first of all, its sensory and aesthetic impact (Is it beautiful?), but also its meaning—what are the thoughts and intentions underlying the work? (What is it about? What's its meaning?). And finally, I seek to know what the artist has accomplished in expressing, projecting, and conveying (Is it skilfully / superbly / well done?).

The above examples highlight the confusion concerning the meaning of "art." This prompted Mark Roberts (2011) to call for "Let's Abolish 'Art.'" This is his way "to show the fly the way out of the fly-bottle," which is the aim of philosophy according to Ludwig Wittgenstein, and also of morality, as urged by Elizabeth Anscombe. Roberts' advice, of course, is a non-starter. Morality is not just the product of Western, Christian culture, and moral disagreements are grounds for clarifying the concept, not for abandoning it altogether. Similarly, the task ahead is to elucidate the meaning of "art" and related concepts, which prompted me to audit Philosophy of Art.

Included in our course readings is an article by John Dewey (1934) entitled "Art as Experience." It is not an easy article to read, so I consulted Joseph Grange's (2001) exposition, "Dao, Technology, and American Naturalism." It's a beautiful elucidation of Dewey's naturalistic philosophy—of wholeness and respecting the way of nature (*wu-wei*) that unifies aesthetics (beauty), ethics (goodness), and realism (truth). We love life because it is dazzling and beautiful, thus enticing us to seek life's greater meaning and wholeness. Ethics (goodness) is a means to achieve that "end-in-view," which in turn requires authenticity and deep understanding (truth) of the way of nature. To do, for Dewey, is to grow in meaning, resulting from the perpetual emergence of novelty in time. We act naturally by integrating all these elements in a holistic and insightful way, which is the Taoist concept of *wu-wei*, to act "naturally" according to the way of nature. This interpretation, therefore, seems to tie together the concepts of love, beauty, truth, and goodness, which I have been exploring because they constitute what I surmise to be the most important things in life.

The above considerations inspired me to write the following poem:

My Kid Could Paint That—What's a Work of Art? / Skeltonic Verse / 2011

Art is what the eyes behold
In a true story we're told
Raised in an artistic household
Marla Olmstead, a four-year old
Has many of her paintings sold.
By splashing the paints around
Her kaleidoscopic pictures abound
Seeing them, many are spellbound
Until parental coaching formed her background

Cameras caught the "what" and "how"
In a CBS *60 Minutes* show.
Now that people know
That she is no van Gogh
Her paintings take a blow
Their sales plunge low

Are her paintings works of art?
If they were from the start
Their value wouldn't fall apart
If her works were wonderful
They should still be beautiful
And also remain meaningful

If my kid could paint that
Do you know what?
Many abstract arts also fall flat!

5.2. Beauty, Meaning, and Skill in Art

IN 2016, I AUDITED A COURSE, "CHINA ART NOW," TAUGHT BY PROFESSOR LISA Claypool. Much of the so-called "art" practised by contemporary avant-garde Chinese artists, as presented and discussed in that course, in my opinion, is juvenile and despicable. It is beyond me that so many people regard them as "works of art," engaged in their production and distribution, praising them and exhibiting them in reputable art galleries, and teaching them to art students, historians and professionals. To me, though, they do not meet my criteria of meaning, beauty, and skill to qualify them as works of art.

Xiao Lu's so-called "art performance" is instructive and illuminating. In 1989, she participated in the first avant-garde art exhibition in Beijing with her work, *Dialogue,* and two hours into the exhibition she fired two gunshots with a pellet gun at her work, causing the exhibition to be suspended for several days (see Figure 5). The reactions varied from high praise to condemnation, although few understood what her act was about. Four months later, with the occurrence of the Tiananmen Square massacre, her performance was dubbed "the first gunshots of Tiananmen."

After being detained by the Chinese authorities, Xiao Lu managed to make her way to Australia and lived and worked there for many years—before she went back to China again. Tang Song, her boyfriend, followed Xiao Lu to Australia, but they eventually split up. Then, in 2004, after their break-up, Xiao Lu confirmed with Gao Minglu, the curator of the avant-garde exhibition, that she was the sole author of the gunshot incident. Interestingly, this claim

> caused backlash in the Chinese art world, where people were not willing to remove authorship from Tang Song. Xiao Lu was accused of, among other things, lying and blowing off steam because of their break-up. (Oredsson, 2016)

Figure 5. Xiao Lu, *Dialogue*, February 1989. Just hours after the opening of China's first avant-garde exhibition, Xiao fired two shots into her work, causing military vehicles and riot police to come and seal off the museum, and arrested her. Although Xiao maintained her act was personal and not political, *Dialogue* would come to be embraced for its premonition of the fruitless dialogue between student leaders at the Tiananmen Square and Communist Party elders, which ended in the bloodshed in June 1989.

Only 25-years after the gunshot incident, in a 2014 interview with the *Sydney Morning Herald* (Wen 2014), Xiao confirmed that her "performance" was primarily personal and emotional rather than artistic and political. As Borgonjon (2017) reported, however, Xiao's (2010) memoir revealed that her 1989 Dialogue was a response to her being raped by her parents' close friend:

> A[s] she writes in Chapter 5 of her memoir, the sculpture expressed feelings of isolation, rage, and depression in the aftermath; the telephone spoke to her sense of being unable to communicate about the subject to family or

friends. When she called him in the last years of university to express her hurt and hatred, he hung up on her. That's how she conceived the sculptural component of *Dialogue*.

Reflecting on this piece of "art history," all I can say is "bullshit!" There is no beauty (nor grace) in Xiao's (and Tang Song's) performance, the meaning attributed to that performance is either non-existent or fabricated, and the skill involved in her/their act is unrelated or misrepresented, unappreciated or irrelevant to what Xiao intended. What kind of art is her performance? Nobody other than Xiao Lu knew its meaning and significance, so how on earth could anyone have truly comprehended and meaningfully appreciated it? The author of *How to Talk About Art History*, in the article "Artist Feature: Who is Xiao Lu?", shares my confusion when Xiao Lu's original artwork, *Dialogue*, in 1989 is described:

> It consisted of two telephone booths, one with a figure of a man and one with the figure of a woman, and a red telephone dangling between them. The artwork was considered a personal one by Xiao Lu, although we have no real idea of what its meaning could have been. It remains unclear how big a part the gunshots actually played in the meaning and conceptualisation of the work. (Admin 2016)

A fair amount of contemporary avant-garde art in the world today is of this nature: make something out of the ordinary, not revealing much about its intent, catch people off guard and keep them guessing, let them interpret and imagine any way they wish, and let that piece of work speak for itself. Postmodernism becomes a fad in the art world as in literature, culture, politics, and society everywhere. It's exhilarating as well as suffocating. We need a way out!

Here are a couple poems I wrote to express my feelings and aspirations:

Where Has Beauty Gone? / Memorial Stanza / 2016

I'm auditing China Art Now
Focusing on their avant-garde
Which are bad, I've lost my regard
For their sense of beauty anyhow

They say art needs not be beautiful
The concept is more valuable
Xiao Lu's act is justifiable
As rebellion isn't baneful

"Why is Modern Art so Bad?"
'Cause it's twisted and ugly
Pointless, arcane, and silly
Though bad taste becomes a fad

That's Robert Florczak's tirade
Which I'd also like to proclaim
Avant-garde art is to blame
For not showing it's not a charade

When the photograph was invented
Visual art turned more abstract
And obscurity became a fact
As artists overreacted

Artists, the onus is on you, artists
To show the purport of your work
Don't make me do the guesswork
So you can remain obscurantists

I'd like to know where you stand
So you won't leave me hanging
You owe me good explaining
As the nub's for me to understand

To Restore Beauty in Art is Common Sense / Spenserian Sonnet / 2012

Waking up from an incredibly bad dream
In which beauty no longer matters in art,
I want to undo this Dadaist blaspheme
And restore beauty in every artist's heart.

Duchamp's "readymades" are worlds apart
From the cherished aesthetic experience.
To claim these as art and not anti-art,
Like his urinal or "Fountain," makes no sense.

I still chuckle at the culture of pretence
That holds Dada's "readymades" in high esteem,
Amazed that many art "experts" have taken part
To turn Dadaism into the art world's mainstream.

But Dadaism can't be seen as works of art
Because its nihilism is a false start.
While Duchamp's works hold the public in suspense,
Picasso's *Guernica* shines as a work of art.

To treat any work as art is a sheer offence,
To restore beauty in art is common sense.

5.3. Beauty and Good Taste

BACK IN TAIWAN WHEN I WAS YOUNG, I REALLY LIKED LIN YUTANG'S BOOK, *The Art of Living* (in Chinese). It is only recently, however, that I read its English version, *The Importance of Living.* The book was first published in 1937, several months before I was born.

One thing that impressed me about this book is its emphasis on good taste in knowledge. The world is full of people with encyclopaedic knowledge about various aspects of the world, but with bad taste. Their photographic memories help them outperform and outmanoeuvre others, so they get their way and run the show in daily affairs, including scholarly pursuits, politics, finance, media, sports, and entertainment. They are also the ones, of course, who have driven our world into the present worrisome state because of their lack of good taste in knowledge. As Lin states, "Erudition is a mere matter of cramming of facts or information, while taste or discernment is a matter of artistic judgment" (p. 362). This is another way of saying that truth, goodness, and beauty are inseparable, and that only good taste in knowledge leads to wisdom. I just can't figure out why many people are oblivious to cultivating good taste and gladly savour what I consider to be bad tastes, such as unintelligible or disgusting art, rudeness and violence in sports and in daily living, deceit in politics and human relations, the cult of personality, and supernatural beings, etc. Perhaps my sense of bad taste all around us turns me against the so-called great historical and contemporary figures in all walks of life. It's so true that one of my prime criteria for judging an individual is the beauty or grace of his or her taste.

Notably, Lin Yutang wants us to apply the concept of good taste to all spheres of life, and places "art as recreation" (amateurism) above "art as creation" (professionalism). He says:

> As it is more important that all college students should play tennis or football with indifferent skill than that a college should produce a few champion athletes or football players for the national contests, so it is also more

important that all children and all grown-ups should be able to create something of their own as their pastime than that the nation should produce a Rodin. I would rather have all school children taught to model clay and all bank presidents and economic experts able to make their own Christmas cards, however ridiculous the attempt may be, than to have only a few artists who work at art as a profession. (1937, p. 366)

That's the inspiration I learned from my daughter, Solene, who used to give me birthday cards and handmade moccasins and cushions she made by herself, and engage in all sorts of artwork such as painting, music, and pottery. Now that I have taken up poetry, drawing, and painting, art and beauty have become more integrated into my everyday life, and Lin's philosophy resonates at this stage of my life more than ever. Solene also plants her own vegetables, and buy local, organic produce—so I also started to go to farmers' markets and organic stores for fresh fruits and vegetables. I used to go mindlessly, ages ago, to fast food stores like McDonald's, KFC, and Tim Horton's, and to big box stores like Wal-Mart, but I rarely go to these stores any more as a matter of good taste, which must have outweighed bad economics in my mind!

By the way, many people in the West do not realize that the naming convention in Chinese differs from that in the West (i.e., the family name comes before the given name). Thus, "Lin" is the family name for Lin Yutang. Siobhan Lyons (2014), for one, mistakenly thinks "Yutang" to be the family name in her article "On Happiness," when she quotes Lin as stating that sadness and thinking were related. She then jumps to the conclusion that "happiness is quite useless to the philosopher, and to the practice of philosophy." That's unfortunate, since "discontent is human," according to Lin, and "happiness" inspires the philosopher to hope, think, write, and do something about it.

Of course, Lyons is not the only one who commits this error. One of the textbooks for Culture and Identity in Taiwan, a course I audited, was Qiu Miaojin's *Notes of the Crocodile*. The book was available at the university bookstore, where all textbooks were arranged in the alphabetical order by the author. As I couldn't find the book under Q, I went to the M section, and sure enough, I found the book there on the shelf, as the folks at the bookstore thought "Miaojin" was her last name! Funny, isn't it? It also shows that truth, goodness, and beauty are intimately related: how can we behave gracefully and properly if we can't differentiate truth from falsehood, and good from bad? One criterion for being graceful is to respect everyone, as exemplified in the philosophy of amateurism:

In Defence of Amateurism / The Sestina / 2012

We pay lip service to health and happiness for all
By idolizing the extraordinary feats of the few
In sports, entertainment, and all walks of life
If we wish everyone a life that's fulfilling and good
We must accept every person's inherent worth
And help bring out the best talents in everyone

Life, without doubt, is valuable to everyone
So public policy must aim for a better life for all
To promote and enhance their sense of self-worth
Unlike elitist philosophies, which benefit only a few
Investing in amateurism boosts the common good
Through grassroots participation to foster our life

Let us engage in art and sport all our life
Even though excellence may not be reachable for all
Clumsy or mediocre, it would still make us feel good
Even though we can't master any sport or art at all
Notwithstanding the dazzling works of the few
Our creativity and enjoyment evince their worth

I sometimes wonder how much my life is worth
And wish for an answer to what do I want in life
While I admire the greatness of the gifted few
I value more the drive for excellence in everyone
A fulfilling life is to be shared and attained by all
Elitism that benefits only a few is a lesser good

I've been taught that human nature is basically good
Though I now question that very statement's worth
The nobility of some humans does not apply to all
As some are outright mean and selfish all their life
They guard their good fortunes against everyone
Uninterested in the well-being beyond the very few

By worshipping the best of the best, the top few
They treat elitism as an incarnation of good
Not only for themselves but also for everyone
Competition to them has an inherent worth
It becomes their central philosophy of life
The intoxicating doctrine of the winner-takes-all

Amateurism fostering creativity for all is good
Elitism benefiting only the few has little worth
An artistic and creative life is a right of everyone

5.4. Survival of the Prettiest

BEAUTY IS OF CRITICAL IMPORTANCE IN OUR LIVES. THE PROJECT OF
shaping our own mind and body as well as our living environment, according to our ideal images of beauty, to present and project ourselves to others
is a lifelong process. It is the work of art that we have to continually
engage in, like it or not, and consciously or unconsciously, all our lives.

Since there is a lot of truth in Nancy Etcoff's (2000) book *Survival of the Prettiest*, it is to our advantage if we pay proper attention to the art and science of cultivating and presenting ourselves to others. Since beauty is multidimensional, we should enhance all aspects of beauty, both internal and external. Outer beauty—a person's appearance of physical attractiveness—tends to impress us first before we pay attention to inner beauty. However, it is at least as important to cultivate our inner beauty—our character and personality such as being kind, considerate, empathetic, helpful, trustworthy, righteous, truthful, intelligent, knowledgeable, classy, graceful, etc. A common mistake is that we pay inordinate attention to some aspects of beauty at the expense of others, such as mannerism or hygiene, which become sources of irritation and annoyance. Some defects can easily be overlooked, while others cannot.

Now, there are terrible beauty and cultural practices all over the world because they are cruel and unhealthy, and not always beneficial—such as foot binding in old China, female clitoridectomy (genital mutilation) and male circumcision, breast implants, and other aesthetic surgical procedures performed for aesthetic rather than for reconstructive purposes. This is because these surgeries often have major or minor adverse effects and, according to Chinese medicine, would impede the smooth flow of vital energy and blood. It is not a good idea to mutilate one's body unless there is no better non-surgical alternative. Male circumcision is arguably among the most controversial of all these practices, and even then, the Canadian Paediatric Society does not recommend the routine circumcision of every newborn male. (Sorokan et al, 2015)

The first thing I learned in the early 1980s when I worked on quality assurance in food service at Misericordia Hospital in Edmonton was that diet and exercise are the one-two punch for promoting one's health. It is through regulating the input and the output of liquid, calories and nutrients that we maintain a healthy body. In many ways we are what we eat—as shown in Naomi Moriyama and William Doyle's 2005 book, *Japanese Women Don't Get Old or Fat*—and we keep our body in a good functioning order through mental and physical gymnastics and exercise. Medical and surgical interventions are necessary at times to correct serious health problems, but it is foolish to resort to them unnecessarily. Many dietary and cosmetic products, however, are toxic and harmful to our bodies, so it is of critical importance to know which products are health-promoting and good for us, and which are not. For example, my friend Jenny, a toxicologist, forbids her daughters to dye their hair because some of the ingredients in hair dyes are carcinogenic and can cause serious allergic reactions or hair loss in some people. The FDA, in fact, does not allow using hair dyes on eyelashes and eyebrows lest they hurt the eyes or even cause blindness.

Beauty, of course, is culturally conditioned, and is closely meshed with our personal and cultural identity. One of the most contentious issues relates to what we wear or not to wear. I remember when I was a student at the University of Toronto, the campus newspaper published a photo of a topless female student, which caused an uproar. The paper defended it, stating that it published the photo with the consent of the student, who was fighting for an equal right for females as with males to bare their bodies on hot summer days. In 1991, a woman named Gwen Jacob walked topless in Guelph, Ontario, and was charged with committing an indecent act. She appealed, and the courts vindicated her, ruling it legal for women to go topless in Ontario. However, it is not any easier for women to go shirtless today in Ontario even though it is legal to do so there.

At the other extreme is a woman's right, and obligation, to cover their whole body, including the face and hair. In 2017, the Canadian province of Quebec passed a ban on face covering, barring public workers from wearing the niqab or burqa, and obliging citizens to unveil when riding public transit or receiving government services. A Canadian judge, however, suspended this ban. Although 68% of Canadians want a similar ban in their province, Prime Minister Justin Trudeau has stated that it is not the government's business to tell a woman what or what not to wear. Muslim women justify their practice out of religious obligation or as an expression of their Muslim identity, according to a Canadian Council of Muslim Women (CCMW) report. Although I believe, with Trudeau, that women should have the choice in what they wear, I have the nagging feeling that face and hair covering is misogynous, as men are not expected to do the same, and women are subject to all sorts of verbal and physical abuse for not following such dress codes. Even my friend, Jenny, who wore leggings to work in Edmonton, was asked by a Muslim pharmacist not to wear them as they were too revealing. I told Jenny that he, the pharmacist, has a problem. Why is he here if he feels uncomfortable for seeing women in leggings, as most women in Canada wear them in winter?

So I wrote the following poems about beauty and fashion:

We Just Want to Be a Bit More Beautiful / Free Verse / 2010

Our bodies are the only place we live
So it's best to accept them and be happy
Luckily, we are free to reshape them
Turning them into works of art
It's the survival of the prettiest, we know
That's the law dictating our behaviours

So we join Weight Watchers and the like
But find out fewer than 5% actually succeed
Sadly, half of us are physically inactive
And heavier we'are, less active we become
A vicious cycle we find hard to break

We get depressed when looking in the mirror
We can't love ourselves the way we are
Diet and exercise do not do the trick
Cosmetic surgeons may be our only saviours
Carving our bodies just like sculptors do
Glamorous women (and men) love scalpels
As do many people in all walks of life

Isn't this "aesthetic health" what we need
Turning our bodies into works of art
Through the help of health professionals?

"The most dangerous idea in the world"
Decries Fukuyama re: "transhumanism"
For exploiting technology recklessly
To surpass biological limits
It can bankrupt our health care system too

Wait, it's our bodies that we are talking about
We are the artists, not the ones with scalpels
We must take charge and recreate ourselves
By empowering ourselves
To become comfortable in our own skin
Garnering enough willpower
We could embark on the role of an artist
Remodel and beautify our bodies

Beauty's precious, but it's not everything
We just want to be a bit more beautiful

Niqab, Male Chauvinism, and Colonialism / Carpe Diem / 2015

There is no better moment than now to act
On what you believe to be the right thing to do
Only by acting now can you shape the future
Or the future will unfold oblivious of your yen

So, the Tories seize niqabs as an election ploy
To prohibit its use at citizenship ceremonies
Fancying themselves as knights in shining armour
And Muslim women and men as victims and villains
They invoke the age-old image of "Orientalism" to
Rescue women under the spell of male chauvinism

That's their ruse in stealing a hotly contested election
After the court ruled twice against their unjust law
As wearing niqabs poses no clear threat to the public
No draconian measure for a legal ban can be justified
If there's any case for prohibiting any kind of clothing
It's not for niqabs, but for men's suits, jackets, and ties

Bangladesh banned Western business suits in 2009
As a measure for that country's energy conservation
To reduce air conditioning use in hot summer months
Pointless in design and uncomfortable for the wearers
The suits are relics of that country's colonial past
As they do not reflect their own culture and heritage

Is it fair to blame Muslim women for wearing niqabs
but not non-Western men for donning Western suits?
In the Philippines, Barong shirts are their formal dress
So why do men all over the world dress up like English men?
The answer is clear: globalization is Western hegemony
Wake up, men, chuck away your suits, and design your own!

6.

Racism, Culture, and Identity

WHO AM I, AND WHO AM I BECOMING? I ALWAYS KNOW WHO I AM. I MAY not be as smart as lots of other people, including my siblings, who were top students in their classes, but I have pretty good self-knowledge. My elder brother is a medical doctor with a PhD, my elder sister won a prestigious Lee scholarship after her bachelor's degree to study psychology at Ohio State University and completed her PhD in four years, and my younger sister came first, the very top mark, in one of the three categories in the nationwide entrance examination of all universities in Taiwan. Among our family friends, my younger sister and I used to play tennis during my high school years with Yuan-Tseh Lee, who went on to become a Nobel Prize laureate in chemistry in 1986. By contrast, I had to struggle hard and muddled through for a great many years as a professional student to finally earn my PhD. In the process, however, I learned my strengths and limitations: I know I'm a slow learner, but with perseverance and hard work I can and did do reasonably well throughout my life. I'm not quick and witty, but I can do good and decent work if given time to figure it out. That gives me a fair amount of confidence and some successes despite many failures.

All in all, I'm very much blessed. In the summer of 2011, my tennis partner, Jack, a physics professor engaged in biomedical research, forwarded me an inspirational video, Lighteninginajar.pps, in which it was stated that out of 100 people in the world, only one (1) would own a computer, and only one (1) would have a university degree. It further states that "If you have a full fridge, clothes on your back, a roof over your head and a place to sleep, you are wealthier than 75% of the world's population." It also said, "If you currently have money in the bank . . . you are one of eight of the privileged few amongst the 100 people in the world." Although I can no longer locate this video, one of the "Posters For Good" contains similar messages. (Tumblr 2010) Based on these and other insights, I'm unquestionably among the most privileged ones in the world. How can I not feel being immensely blessed?

There are, however, many people who are less fortunate, oppressed, exploited, voiceless, and being ignored. The black feminist movement that popularized identity politics in the US was a prime example. Feeling powerless and voiceless within the second-wave feminist movement (late 1950–1980s) dominated by white middle-class women, black feminists such as the Combahee River Collective painted a picture of sexism more pertinent to black women in the 1970s by foregrounding the intersection of racism, sexism, and class oppression in the fight for gender equality. They complained of white middle-class feminism universalizing claims about gender at the expense of paying too little attention to differences and variations among women. This black cultural identity gave them the confidence and passion needed to carry out more appropriate social analysis, critiques, and action plans to advance their causes. However, this concept of identity politics to advance the self-interest of one's own group remains questionable because of its exclusionist tendency. By treating those outside of their groups as "others," they often fall prey to narrow self-interest and cultural relativism without rising above them to seek common grounds with others. As a result, it fragments the movement and weakens the solidarity among the people involved.

As mentioned earlier, the world is full of unhappy, discontent, angry, confused, and depressed people; among them are the most privileged, talented, wealthy, accomplished, high-achievers. They include some of the most gifted poets in English literature and also many East Asian-Canadian writers, whose profound sense of exclusion and "otherness" from the mainstream Canadian culture permeates their writings. This sense of alienation radiates in writing such as Joy Kogawa's *Obasan* (1981) and Sky

Lee's *Disappearing Moon Café* (1990), both of which tell the tragic stories of racial discrimination by the Canadian government against Canadian citizens of Japanese and Chinese descent. Larissa Lai's (2001) paper, "Corrupted Lineage: Narrative in the Gaps of History", leaves no room for doubt when she states:

> Canada has not been an easy country for its first genera-
> tions of immigrants, those who remain forever outside the
> norms and expectations of mainstream Canadian society
> . . . Many sacrifice the past for an idealized future that
> never comes.

Even Fred Wah, who grew up in Canada's racist 1950s and wrote about it in his book *Diamond Grill* (1996), tried to be as white as he could, which was easy for him because the only overt trace of his being a Chinese was his name. These and most other writers and characters they portray, as far as I can tell, appear totally uncomfortable in their own skin and ill at ease with their own identity.

This is where I come in. I think the prevalent notion of multicultural-ism is problematic because it tries to embrace all cultures often uncritically without attempting to resolve the competing and conflicting claims among them. It's evident, however, that all cultures have strengths and weaknesses. The task of multiculturalism, therefore, is to assess all cultural heritages critically, adopt and incorporate the good elements and weed out the bad, and mould them into a unified whole. Each of us is obliged to undertake this process on a daily and ongoing basis, to shape and reshape our unique identity and, at the same time, dialogue and contribute to society—to shape and reshape our common culture. I was extremely fortunate to have come to Canada in 1969, studied and worked here, and made it my home. In all honesty, I wouldn't say I have encountered racism in Canada at all. Of course, we can, and we should try to be at home anywhere in the world and be a citizen of the world. I think the British Prime Minister Theresa May was dead wrong when she uttered, in 2016: "If you believe yourself a citizen of the world, then you are a citizen of nowhere." Local is global in this globalized world. Without global ethics, we would be less inclined to empathize with others and seek win-win solutions. So I wrote this poem:

Four Seas as Home / Poulter's Measure / 2011

Home is where we are now, not where we dream to be
Nor in the past, though it can be in the future we foresee

When longing to go home, we no longer wish to roam
In search of the place of hope and love that we can call our home

Yet the world has changed, nothing is the same anymore
While our fond memories may linger, there's no place like before

Our long-time friends and quiet homes are no longer there
And concrete jungles have replaced green spaces everywhere

We may not be totally happy with where we are
But we can make life enhancement our ongoing affair

If we want to find a home, this is where and how
Believe in "four seas as home," so we are home right here and now

6.1. Racism, Self-Confidence, and Identity

IN MY CASE, MY IDENTITY HAS BEEN FORMED BY WHERE I GREW UP AND lived (mainly in Taiwan, the United States, and Canada), the languages I speak (Chinese, Japanese, and English), what I have studied and read (Chinese and Western literature, society, politics, and philosophy; mathematics and statistics; art, science, health care and medicine, etc.), the activities I have engaged in and enjoy (e.g., basketball, tennis, ping-pong, squash, racquetball, Frisbee, cycling, tai chi, yoga), etc. I have been in Canada longer than the median age of Canadians (41.2 years as of 2016), so I am more "Canadian" than most (native and non-native-born) Canadians. As I haven't encountered any overt racial discrimination since I came to Canada in 1969, I have hardly been self-conscious of my ethnic background, and I have been writing mainly as a Canadian (not hyphen-ated Taiwanese-Canadian). It is like what Virginia Woolf said in *A Room of One's Own*, that a good writer has to have an androgynous mind and forget one's own sex when one writes. Why get hung up on one's race or sex or age? I am comfortable with who I am and who I am becoming.

In a nutshell, I identify myself with the naturalistic philosophy of Taoism and John Dewey, which guides me to navigate through this world. That identity is enhanced and refined by elements of the great Western philosophies such as humanism, romanticism, feminism, rationalism, empiricism, pragmatism, environmentalism, liberalism, and socialism. I disavow the authoritarian and hierarchical aspects of Confucianism as well as the adoration of hyper-masculinity and militarism the world over. I believe all countries, especially Canada, and all great powers, such as the United States, China, and Russia, should denounce the use of force, work together to engage in total disarmament and do away with all armed forces and weaponry, and re-channel those wasteful resources to more construc-tive use, such as increased international cooperation for the eradication of poverty, for learning and education, and for environmental protection. The world can be a much better place if we have a shared, common goal of cooperatively building a better world together to ensure that everyone has a decent and rewarding life, rather than fighting and competing to get ahead of others but leaving some of us losers behind.

Unfortunately, racism still exists in Canada, as in everywhere else. This was reported in the *Edmonton Journal*, April 23, 2010:

> A mixed-race couple from Nova Scotia who awoke one February morning to find a burning cross on their lawn and saw their car go up in flames this past weekend, say they're leaving town for their children's safety. (p. A6)

Most racist acts, however, are not as drastic and hurtful, and oftentimes they could not affect you if you have enough self-confidence. I remember the story about my niece when she was in grade school many years ago in Windsor, Ontario, where my brother-in-law was a chemistry professor at the University of Windsor. One day, she ran home in tears, telling her mom and dad that a boy at school called her names like "chinky" and "chink." My sister and my brother-in-law coached their daughter: "Name-calling can't hurt you if you stand on your ground. The next time he calls you names, just tell him, Yeah, so what?" The boy had nothing more to say the next day when he again called her names, and eventually, they became good friends. I retold this story (which my sister says she couldn't remember!) to the class when I audited a course in women's studies on Masculinities. We discussed, in relation to Cristyn Davies' (2008) article "Becoming Sissy: A Response to David McInnes," the devastating effects of naming someone as faggot or poofter, and what should be done about it. We all agreed that the one who did the name-calling be punished or dissuaded from doing it again, and the school be more vigilant in enforcing an anti-bullying policy to prevent future incidences like that. So I narrated this story to show the importance of counselling the victim for greater self-confidence in dealing with potentially nasty encounters, and the class burst out laughing when I said they became good friends.

Say Goodbye to Our Mythical Homeland's Past / Shakespearean Sonnet / 2012

Let's rejoice life's everlasting worth
Every phase of life is a gift
Mukherjee says immigration is rebirth
A start of a mind-boggling, life-changing shift

The rebirth metaphor connotes violence
As depicted in her novel, *Jasmine*
Who "murders" her past to gain transcendence
In a self-inventing, coming-of-age fiction

Diaspora opens up new gateways
To transmogrify ourselves in new cultures
It can be done in compassionate ways
In the spirit of wondrous adventures

Say goodbye to our mythical homeland's past
And be proud if labelled an iconoclast

6.2. Xenophobia and Authenticity

RACISM, HOWEVER, IS NOT NECESSARILY ABOUT RACE. IT MAY BE JUST about the perception of a group of people has against another group, even of the same race, whom they perceive to differ from them. A good illustration of this point is the 2015 film, *Wansei Back Home*, based on the book with the same title written by Mika Tanaka. While the book documents the stories of twenty-two Wansei, the film, directed by the Taiwanese director Huang Ming-cheng, focuses on eight of them on their return trip from Japan to Taiwan.

The term Wansei refers to about a quarter of a million Japanese who were born in Taiwan between 1895 and 1945 when Taiwan was Japan's colony. They consider Taiwan their home, growing up, going to school, working, living, and learning the local culture and language there. At the end of World War II, more than 470,000 Japanese were repatriated; over half of them were the Wansei. They were allowed to take only personal belongings and limited amounts of money. In the film interviews, they narrate how difficult it was for them to assimilate into Japanese society, as they were branded foreigners and faced hardship and poverty after their repatriation. To many of them, Taiwan is their home, and they recall with nostalgia their life in Taiwan.

So, to some of the Wansei, their "eternal home" was where they were born and grew up. They were still emotionally attached to Taiwan after many decades living in Japan. One of the reasons, I surmise, is that they were not welcomed and were discriminated against as "foreigners" even though they are authentic Japanese. As a result, they have not fully embraced Japan as their homeland. Treating a group of people as "others" has many causes, including racism and other forms of xenophobia—people are distrustful and even fearful of those who are perceived to differ from themselves. Another reason for their nostalgia may be that childhood memories are precious to them as to all of us. We all seek our roots, and their roots are in Taiwan.

The movie was nominated for the Golden Horse Film Festival Best Documentary in 2015; and also won the Osaka Asian Film Festival Audience Award in 2016. In 2017, however, the author and producer, Mika Tanaka, confessed to the publisher of her book that she lied about her identity and credentials—she actually is a Taiwanese named Chen Shuan-ju, born and raised in Kaohsiung, and not a granddaughter of a Wansei; neither has she studied at art schools in Tokyo and New York as she claimed. Furthermore, some of the stories in the book, such as the one on the Kamikaze Special Forces, are also taken from the memoirs of other documents and not from her interviews with the Wansei. The stories in the film, though, are by and large true and authentic, based on the interviews of the Wansei who came home to visit Taiwan.

It is too bad that Chen had to fake her identity and credentials to convince others of her worth and to raise money for the project. Many of her supporters understandably feel betrayed despite the film's artistic merits and the box office success. It is a tragedy of our competitive world of commerce where money talks and corrupts us. That's why we need to create a more supporting environment to recognize and support the talents and dedication Chen has to pursue her ideas and project. Unlike Doctorow's 1977 postmodernist assertion that there is no distinction between fiction and nonfiction, and that there is only narrative, authenticity is important because it reveals the reality of what is true and what is not. I can be authentic in my writing because I have the luxury now not to be encumbered by money or fame, as stated in my poems below:

Why do we write?
Proust is right
It's the writer's birthright
To contrive and shed light
And to gain greater insight
On life's delight and plight
To transcend all that's trite
Opacity as well as sleight

Dawkins is sure
That it's culture
Rather than human nature
That has a lasting future
Contributing to literature
May therefore reassure
One's continuing signature

We write
Because we love to write
Because it makes us special to write
Because we are the only creatures to write

6.3. Orientalism, Colonialism, and Native Rights

MOST CULTURES ARE XENOPHOBIC (I.E., FEARFUL OR DISLIKE OF PEOPLE from different cultures, those with different features, customs, dresses, languages, etc.). That sentiment is also referenced by the term Orientalism, one of the most celebrated themes in cultural studies theorized and popularized by Edward Said (1978). It is a popular Western misrepresentation of the Orient—the Middle East in particular, but also South Asia and the

Far East—as "primitive, irrational, violent, despotic, fanatic, and essentially inferior to the West," and hence, "enlightenment" can only occur when such "traditional" values are replaced by "contemporary" and "progressive" ideas of the West. Particularly after September 11, 2001, Orientalism metamorphosed into neo-Orientalism, which again generates an "us versus them" mindset—especially with regard to exaggerated fear and suspicion against people of the Muslim faith. Because of the possible racial profiling against those from the Middle East, many medical students and my former colleagues from the Muslim countries at the University of Alberta no longer wished to attend academic conferences in the United States.

Racism, of course, is still well and alive against Aboriginals in many countries of the world. It has been the legacy of colonizers to treat the Aboriginal populations as the Other—not only different from themselves, but also "less than human." A black eye for Canada and the United States to the international community, and an indefensible one at that, is how the Aboriginal (First Nations) peoples have been treated in the New World. Despicable and heart-wrenching stories of mistreatment of Aboriginals have been narrated, for example, in Richard Wagamese's *Indian Horse* (2012) about the horrors of residential schools and racism in the hockey world in the 1950s and 1960s, and in Thomas King's (2012) *The Inconvenient Indian*—stories that are not only in the more distant past, but also in the present day. The key to understanding the interactions between Natives and non-Natives, according to King, is the question of land—primarily a commodity for non-Natives, but "the foundation of history, religion, sustenance, identity" for Natives; that is what whites wanted and took from the Lakota Indians in the Black Hills, the Cherokee in Georgia, the Cree in Quebec, etc. It's a sad chapter of Canadian history to learn about the residential schools, poverty, and high suicide rates on First Nations reserves, alcoholism and family violence, missing women, etc., from King and other writers such as Tanya Talaga (2017) in Canada. However, the land issue remains central, and King uses the Alberta tar sands to illustrate his point.

It is a case of how the land is to be used: by whom, for whose benefits, in what way, at what cost, and how the costs and benefits are to be distributed and shared, etc. According to King (2012),

> It is, without question, the dirtiest, most environmentally insane energy-extraction project in North America, probably in the world, but the companies that are developing landscapes and watersheds in Alberta continue merrily along, tearing up the earth because there are billions to be made out of such corporate devastation. The public has been noticeably quiet about the matter, and neither the politicians in Alberta nor the folks in Ottawa have been willing to step in and say, "Enough," because, in North American society, when it comes to money, there is no such thing as enough. (p. 219)

It should be noted, though, that the project has also benefited not only the corporations and the provincial government but also the First Nations groups. By participating in the development, the Fort McKay Group and Companies, for example, generated $130 million in revenues, and with joint ventures will bring in another $400 million, enabling them to contribute to a $50 million trust fund for the community. On the other hand, First Nations communities are also concerned about the environment, and they, including the Beaver Lake Cree Nation around 200 kilometres northwest of Edmonton, launched a legal case against the provincial and federal governments "to protect the viability and longevity of the land" (Clancy, 2017). King also alluded to other court cases to oppose "building thousands of miles of pipeline—the Keystone Pipeline, the Northern Gateway Pipeline, the Transmountain Pipeline—that will take Alberta crude from Fort McMurray to refineries and markets in the United States (Illinois, Oklahoma, and Texas) and in Canada (Kitimat and Vancouver)"—or rather in the Far East (King, 2014, p. 220).

Now, whether the First Nations can legally stop the construction of these pipelines crossing their territories is questionable, depending on the extent of sovereignty they could exercise. Although the Canadian Constitution protects existing Aboriginal and treaty rights, Canadian courts have stopped short of recognizing the sovereignty or right to self-government by Indigenous nations. I can't imagine that the situation will change, even though the sovereignty of the Crown over all the lands and people of Canada is founded on the legal fictions of *terra nullius* and the Doctrine of Discovery—that the European colonizers "discovered" the "empty land" of Turtle Island, i.e., Canada—and ignoring all the past treaties signed on a nation-to-nation basis. How can we reconcile the differences if we are unwilling to face the truth of the sovereignty fictions, and seek just solutions to this impasse?

The issues are extremely complex, as they touch upon a great many issues—not only the Native rights and sovereignty but also the Albertan economy, environmental concerns affecting British Columbia in particular, and Canada's commitment to the Paris Agreement on cutting greenhouse gas emissions, etc. What I would like to see is a cooperative effort—an expert working group with members from the federal, British Columbia, and Alberta governments, and also from the First Nations and oil companies—to draft a comprehensive long-range energy and environmental plan to address all these issues. It is especially sad to see the bickering between the two NDP (New Democratic Party) governments of Alberta and British Columbia for and against the building of pipelines, rather than working together to find a win-win solution. Such a comprehensive plan is also required if we are to seriously consider the merits and feasibility of leaving the oil sand oil underground, as proposed by *The Leap Manifesto* (theleap.org).

A possible solution, according to the Green Party leader Elizabeth May (*CBC News*, March 14, 2018), is to process the oil sand bitumen right here in Alberta. That idea was not taken seriously in the past because of the high costs compared to exporting and processing in China or the United States. Since transporting through pipelines is problematic, perhaps we should reconsider the option of bitumen processing in Alberta, which is becoming more economically viable. In fact, Canada's first refinery in thirty years, in Sturgeon County near Edmonton, produced its first diesel from bitumen in December 2017. Owned 50% each by North West Refining and Canadian Natural Resources Ltd., the company has made the case to the Alberta government to support the second phase of the refinery as it supported the first 50,000 bpd phase—through loan guarantees and by committing its bitumen barrels to the project through a royalty-in-kind program (Morgan, 2017). Despite criticism and relatively high costs, the expansion of refineries in Alberta to enable exporting oil through existing pipelines may constitute a compromise solution for the national energy policy that all parties could support.

Due to the high cost of building full-upgrading facilities in Alberta, a more promising alternative may be partial upgrading in order to reduce the thickness of oil sands bitumen so it can flow through pipelines more easily without adding about 30% of diluent. The government of Alberta supports this initiative, with $1 billion—$200 million in grants, and up to $800 million in other financial support in 2018—aiming to deliver two to five commercial-scale partial upgrading plants in the province over the next eight years. Of note, Fractal Systems has already run a successful 1,000 bpd demonstration plant near the town of Prevost in Alberta from August 2016 to August 2017, with over 225,000 barrels of bitumen partially upgraded. The company is ready for commercial deployment of its partial upgrading technology in the oil sands. As the title of an article in *Oil Sand Magazine* February 6, 2018, shows, there may be another solution to "Increasing pipeline capacity—without building new pipelines." (Anonymous 2018)

On August 30, 2018, the federal Court of Appeal—which quashed the earlier federal approval of the Northern Gateway pipeline because Stephen Harper's Conservative government had fallen well short of listening to and addressing the concerns of various First Nations—also required Justin Trudeau's Liberal government to redo the federal environmental evaluation:

> "Canada was obliged to do more than passively hear and
> receive the real concerns of the Indigenous applicants,"
> wrote Justice Eleanor Dawson in a unanimous ruling that

quashed the Trudeau government's approval of the Trans Mountain expansion project. (De Souza, 2018)

With this confirmation of the longstanding criticism from affected First Nations that the Trudeau government also failed in its legal duty under the Canadian Constitution to properly address their concerns, isn't it time for the Canadian government, and the provincial governments, to take consultation processes very seriously in order to resolve differences and accommodate the interests of all parties involved? If we cannot rationally and justly resolve the pipeline issue domestically in Canada, how can we expect to resolve complex international disputes amicably?

On Native rights, I've composed the following poems:

Embrace Differences / Haibun / 2015

Canada's Aboriginal policy, described as "cultural geno-cide" by the Truth and Reconciliation Commission of Canada in 2015, remains an international embarrassment. Using state power to marginalize First Nations' sover-eignty, cultures and languages, and legal and political rights through the process of assimilation, Canada has doggedly obstructed First Nations' inspiration for politico-cultural survival and flourishing. Concocting the image of the Aboriginals as "barbarians" unworthy of self-government, the colonizer acted themselves out as barbaric oppressors. As a Chinese proverb says, "Whoever tied the knot on the bell is the one to untie it"; it's up to the Canadian government to undo its colonial policy. Canada must critically re-examine its individualistic, neoliberal political philosophy, embrace differences, and help promote First Nations' collective rights to their politico-cultural survival and participation in our one and only world.

Here's the haiku:

In one and only world
We must embrace differences
To dream dreamy dreams

First Nations' Issues / Katuatas / 2015

Don't blame First Nations
Let us respect their land rights
Sovereignty, and ways of life

Policy of Non-Recognition / Sedoka / 2015

Non-recognition?
Our settler colonialism
Vilifies the colonized

Just resolution
Demands the colonizer
To change unjust policies

Realpolitik / Tanka / 2015

For hundreds of years
Settlers and immigrants came
They dictated their rights
To the lands of First Nations
Curtailing the latter's rights

Let's Decolonize / Waka / 2015

Be "word warriors"[1]
Or rather "word philosophers"
Let's decolonize
Our colonial polity
Make it just 'n' harmonious

6.4. Sovereignty, Self-Determination, and Recognition

SOVEREIGNTY IS USUALLY ATTAINED BY A GROUP OF PEOPLE, THROUGH the use of force to prevent being dominated by another group. Conversely, the group is no longer sovereign if it does not possess the power required to resist being dominated by another group. While the Natives who have been colonized no longer retain full sovereignty, there are nations and peoples with full sovereignty although unrecognized by the international community. I am amazed to find out that there is an organization called UNPO—Unrepresented Nations & Peoples Organization. The UNPO was founded in 1991 at the Peace Palace in the Hague with fifteen members, and it has grown to over forty members worldwide today, including Brittany, Somaliland, and Taiwan.

I am interested in Brittany because I have a friend, Marie-Laure, who came to the University of Alberta from there to do her doctoral degree in physiology. I got to know her well after she enrolled in my daughter's yoga class. She told me that Bretons have been facing the progressive loss of their own distinct culture and language since the territory lost independence at the end of the fifteenth century and became a part of France

---

1 Dale Turner, Associate Professor of government and Native American Studies at Dartmouth College, New Hamshire, U.S.A., used this expression to refer to a person who has complete mastery over words and their use in order to engage in advocacy of Aboriginal rights.

during the nineteenth century. The UNPO (2015, July 8) website states the creation of the Parliament of Brittany, which aims to recover a certain form of autonomy through Breton national elections, to preserve their linguistic and cultural features, and to encourage their study and usage. In November 2016, 33 parliamentarians were elected in Brittany to work on a Breton Constitution as a step towards increasing self-determination.

Somaliland is another interesting case on the issue of sovereignty and international recognition. The UNPO (2017, February 1) website includes the following description:

> The Republic of Somaliland is a sovereign, democratic State in the Horn of Africa . . . Somaliland achieved its full independence from the United Kingdom on 26 June 1960, becoming the 15th African Country to do so. It voluntarily entered a union with Somalia in July 1960. However, following a civil war and the collapse of Somalia, it withdrew from the union and reclaimed its independence on 18 May 1991.

For a variety of reasons, the international community—the African Union, in particular—fails to recognize the de facto independence of Somaliland. Also included in the UNPO website is the following statements:

> Whilst Somaliland remains a "state-in-waiting," it nevertheless continues to satisfy all the criteria for statehood in customary international law. It possesses a permanent population, a defined territory, a government and the capacity to enter into relations with other states. In 2016, over a million Somalilanders signed a petition supporting the country's recognition (*Somaliland Sun*, August 23, 2016; VOA news, 24 August 2016).

Taiwan's case, of course, is of great interest to me. Like Somaliland, it is a de facto independent country since the end of the Chinese civil war in 1949. The government of the Republic of China, after it retreated to Taiwan from Mainland China, continued to occupy the China seat at the United Nations until 1971, when the seat was replaced by the People's Republic of China. The UNPO (2018, July 19; https://unpo.org/members/7908) website states that:

> Taiwan is well known around the world for its successes first in economic development, and more recently in democratization. However, as a result of its lack of UN membership and recognition by most major states, coupled with the threat posed by China, it remains in a precarious state in the international arena, which prevents the Taiwanese people from being able to fully enjoy their newfound prosperity and human rights.
>
> UNPO believes that Taiwan should be allowed to fully participate in the United Nations, as well as all its specialized agencies. Denying Taiwan's international recognition is preventing Taiwanese people from their right to self-determination and thus constitutes a violation of international law.
>
> A non-violent and democratic solution to all disputes with People's Republic of China (PRC) must be both countries' priority; therefore UNPO condemns the permanence and increase of Chinese military presence in the Taiwan Strait as well as the Anti-Secession Law (2005), that purports to grant China the right to use force against any attempt of independence coming from Taiwan.
>
> UNPO commends Taiwan's government democratization efforts and its work in contributing to a flourishing democratization of the Asia-Pacific region. UNPO also welcomes the country's attempts to embrace its indigenous peoples and to build a more inclusive and open society.

As these cases illustrate, it is extremely challenging, if not impossible, to resolve the conflicting values between unity and separation, between solidarity and self-determination, and between emotion and reason. The fear of international recognition to encourage other secessionist movements prevents Somaliland from being recognized as a state, and the same reason may also have prompted China to enact the Anti-Secession Law in 2005. However, the right to self-determination is an issue affecting many countries, including Spain, Russia, Belgium, Iraq, etc., and even Canada. Since it is among the highest of the values widely upheld by the United Nations and international law, it is necessary to agree internationally on the conditions under which separation would be recognized, legitimized, and even promoted, through a transparent and fair referendum conducted democratically, as in Quebec, Canada, in 1980 and 1995. As much as possible, we must rely on cooperative and negotiated mechanisms to settle disputes, and avoid confrontational means such as the bloody Russo-Georgian war of 2008, or the bewildering state of Catalan independence from Spain in 2017–2018.

Some disputes cannot be resolved at the given time, in which case it is better to defer decisions for the time being, and keep clarifying and negotiating the terms of win-win solutions—rather than resorting to unilateral, punitive measures, competing, and ending up with a win-loss or no-win solution. Action begets reaction, and the cycle of violence could escalate so nobody wins, not even the victors.

Feminism is a prime example. Women have been struggling for equality for a long time, to resist domination by men. Divorce used to be a taboo in many cultures, and even today there are often news stories about homicide by jealous and possessive partners who couldn't or wouldn't bear to let go of their relationships. If you truly love someone, don't you hold that person's welfare highest in your mind? If you are so possessive, isn't it just self-love, rather than loving someone else? The same goes for anti-secession laws in countries like China, Spain, Belgium, Canada, etc. It is better to clarify just solutions—the terms under which secessions are justified and the relations that should prevail after the secessions. It is a failure of human intelligence and morality to resort to imprisonment, threat of violence, or war.

One of the differences between Eastern and Western cultures is the degree of autonomy and freedom that the parents accord their children. I was amazed to see how much my daughter, born and raised in Canada, lets her children do their own things, e.g., feeding themselves when they were still very young, therefore making a big mess, spilling food all over the place, rather than feeding them as Taiwanese parents would do for their children. As a result, her children are much more "spoiled" and yet more outgoing and adventurous, more inquisitive and innovative. In contrast, many parents in Taiwan are more "authoritarian," demanding of their children, dictating them to do this or that, such as studying medicine or law, discouraging them from working part-time, so as to concentrate more on studying, etc. Although Asian students score very high in international achievement tests, in mathematics, science, etc., it is widely acknowledged that they are not better off after university in terms of general knowledge about the world, motivation and preparedness for work, and creativity.

Apparently, a culture of self-determination is as important at the personal as at the national level to foster self-confidence and self-reliance, and also to promote and maintain family and group cohesiveness and goodwill. It is a challenge to find a good solution between authoritarianism and anarchism, and yet we must, since peace and prosperity within family and society depend on it. I was horrified, therefore, to read the Yale law professor Amy Chua's 2011 article, "Why Chinese Mothers Are Superior." She toots her own horn as a tiger mother—having a "triple package" of first, a group superiority complex (of being a Chinese), second, a sense of insecurity, and third, controlling impulse (resisting temptation). Chua is of course right to insist on the virtues of "self-control, discipline, resilience" in order to succeed in this competitive world, but what I object to is the vision of such a world: do we want to be complicit and perpetuate such a world? Shouldn't we change our way of life, be more cooperative, working together and excelling together, to create a kinder and gentler world, rather than fighting to get ahead of others and to climb to the top of the hierarchy? Wouldn't the world be in perpetual turmoil if everyone subscribed to her triple package and fought it out ruthlessly, at work, in politics, and militarily? Shouldn't we rely more on positive reinforcement to motivate our children to be the best they can be in search of excellence, so that they willingly work hard to excel in what they do—rather than resorting to punitive measures, which may result in unintended emotional scars in the children? Is that the kind of (Chinese) culture worth promoting? I wonder, so I wrote a poem:

Battle Hymn for Tiger Mothers? / Sijo / 2011

"Chinese mothers" are proud of producing
Math/music prodigies
Showered with admiration for their kids
They love what they do
Battle Hymn of the Tiger Mother
A song for child abuse?

6.5. The Politics of Recognition

Nonrecognition or misrecognition can inflict harm, can be a form of oppression, imprisoning someone in a false, distorted, and reduced mode of being. (Charles Taylor, 1994, p. 26)

AMONG THE SADDEST STORIES I HAVE READ IS EVELYN LAU'S *Runaway: Diary of a Street Kid* (1989). Evelyn, whose parents are Chinese, grows up in Vancouver. This autobiography is about her parents' non-recognition or misrecognition of Evelyn's needs, wants, and aspirations—e.g., discouraging and forbidding her from writing creatively, which becomes a cause of her having low self-esteem, becoming suicidal, running away from home at age fourteen to become a street kid, and experimenting with drugs and sex. She craves for her parents' love and recognition, the denial of which devastates her—and yet her parents are clueless as to what harm they have inflicted on Evelyn. As I read, I kept wondering: Why is Evelyn the only one who is required to go for psychiatric counselling, and not her parents, who caused Evelyn's problems in the first place? By not addressing the failure of parenting on the part of Evelyn's parents, the whole social and medical systems are "blaming the victim," identifying the problem solely with Evelyn, thereby dealing only with the symptoms and ignoring the root cause!

The issue of recognition, moreover, is closely related to that of identity and authenticity, as discussed in the Canadian philosopher Charles Taylor's (1994) seminal paper, "The Politics of Recognition." It is true that one's identity is primarily related to his or her unique nature, but the failure to recognize one's true nature, by oneself or by others, can have grave moral consequences—making life less meaningful or more tragic, for instance. Everyone is unique, and yet our true nature is not obvious to us. It is our lifelong task to "know thyself." In Taylor's words:

> Being true to myself means being true to my own originality, which is something only I can articulate and discover. In articulating it, I am also defining myself. I am realizing a potentiality that is properly my own. This is the background understanding to the modern ideal of authenticity, and to the goals of self-fulfillment and self-realization in which the ideal is usually couched. (1994, p. 31)

The non-recognition of Evelyn's originality—her true nature and potentials—by her parents prevents Evelyn from being authentic. She is lucky to have her writer's dream realized after two years of being a street kid, although many others are not as fortunate.

The issue of recognition, furthermore, is closely related to the opposing concepts of honour and dignity. As Taylor explains, "honour," in the sense he uses the term, is intrinsically linked to inequalities, so that for some to have honour, not everyone should have it—such as honouring someone with the Order of Canada (1994, p. 27). "Dignity," on the other hand, is universal and egalitarian, as when we talk about "the inherent dignity of human beings," which is "the only one compatible with a democratic society." In a democratic society, therefore, we should strive to accord "equal recognition" to the aspirations of all individuals and groups as much as possible, rather than withholding it in the name of honour. While the politics of equal dignity emphasizes equality (and universality), the politics of difference honours liberty (and authenticity), and the two come into conflict throughout history. Since both universality and specificity are of critical importance to all of us, the challenge is for us to find a proper balance, individually and collectively, based on critical thinking.

Multiculturalism is a case in point. As it is often debated today, it has a lot to do with the imposition of some cultures on others, with the presumed superiority that powers this imposition—in contradiction to the principle of the equal worth of all cultures. Now, it is obvious that all cultures have strengths and weaknesses, but do they have equal worth? Instead of bogging down on such debates, it would be more productive if we were to critically examine all the cultures in question, and propose ways to overcome deficiencies and enhancing promising features. As all societies are becoming increasingly multicultural and some minority cultures are being marginalized, it is of critical importance to respect the politics of difference as appropriate, and not to impose the dominant culture on others by the draconian policies of assimilation. Instead of blindly worshiping the dominant culture and being assimilated, all of us, even for those in the dominant culture, must critically assess all cultures and purge any deprecating self-images—just as Evelyn Lau has tried against her family's culture. If the dominant culture is problematic and intolerant of the practices of the minority cultures, the best way forward is to reform the dominant culture to make it more empathic and accommodating. At least we should resist it and try to live a life according to our own images—which is possible in a democratic society.

However, the collective rights of peoples, such as French culture in Quebec or Aboriginal rights of peoples in many countries, are irreconcilable with those of dominant cultures, so that more prudent, tolerant, and collaborative approaches are required to resolve, or at least set aside, policy differences. We must value diversity and specificity, as new ideas of improvement hinge on it; as well, life is boring and uninspiring if it is monotonous without variation. We all learn from different cultures regarding what to do and what not to do, to make our own cultures more inspiring and supportive of our vision of good life. We need to be critical, self-confident, and tolerant enough to accommodate alternative visions of good life. I think Taylor is right to insist not to dictate the concept of good for others, only to insist the procedural norm for universality between peoples and cultures. In fact, the imposition of the goals of good life is at the heart of colonialism and imperialism and is to be resolutely rejected in the future.

Unite, No Contest / The Knittelvers / 2016

To survive, we must fight or flight!
To thrive, we must join hands and unite

Work hard, getting rich's not a crime
Play hard, making good life more sublime

Compete, win, it's the only thing
Cooperate, we are not playthings

Be bold, so we'll have a head start
Be kind, and treat us as your sweethearts

Hang tough, life is for endless tests
Soft power, smart lives need no contest

Fight to the end until we're done
Unite, so our lives won't be undone

7.
Feminism

"ALL OPPRESSION CREATES A STATE OF WAR," DECLARES SIMONE DE Beauvoir in *The Second Sex* (1989, p. 717). That's exactly what happened in the gruesome tale of the butcher's wife by Li Ang (1986), an internationally acclaimed Taiwanese author. The story may have been inspired by an actual event in the 1930s in Shanghai, about a wife who dismembered her husband. In Li's story, the heroine, Lin Shi, was adopted by her uncle after the death of her father and the disappearance of her poverty-stricken mother, and was forced to marry a butcher who abused her physically and sexually. While she endured his brutality throughout the story, in the end, she, in a delirious state, used the butcher's knife and maimed him while he was asleep.

More recently, I read Khaled Housseini's *A Thousand Splendid Suns* (2007), an equally gruesome story of wife abuse. In the story, two women, Mariam and Laila, both married Rasheed, a shoemaker. Eventually, Mariam, the older wife, killed her brute husband, who was strangling his younger wife to death; as a result, Mariam received a death sentence from the Taliban justice system in Afghanistan. It is often assumed—in Taiwanese and Muslim cultures, as well—that when a woman kills her husband, it is because she has an affair with another man. It is clear, as shown by Li's and Housseini's stories, among others, that wife beating and sexual abuse can also lead to extreme measures by the abused, and feminism is instrumental in spreading this message. Family violence is no longer considered exclusively private, and should not be tolerated in any culture. Feminism demands gender equity the world over, that men and women treat each other with respect and without discrimination. There is no room ethically for unequal power relationships between men and women.

Feminism is universal. Any form of cultural relativism that excuses gender violence is a farce. Any kind of brutality has no place in any culture. The personal is political. Unfortunately, that is not the case, as attested in the events throughout human history, inside and outside our homes. Far too many people worship hyper-masculinity, as exemplified in aggression and violence against other human and living beings, exacerbated by more and more powerful weapons and other deadly technologies. It's ludicrous for any country to spend valuable resources on arms rather than using those resources to improve the general well-being of its people. We need more "soft power"—the ability to persuade and win the hearts and minds of others—rather than "hard power"—the ability to use force to coerce others—to create a more caring and compassionate world. We have too much excess, brute masculine/yang power and too little, gentle feminine/yin power in this world. We need to rectify this yin-yang imbalance through feminism, humanism, and other ethical teachings. Feminism is, and should be, promoted for that purpose. Beauty and beast! They are the images I often conjure up when I think about yin and yang, femininity and masculinity. Femininity is grace and beauty, and masculinity is something that is often ugly, brutal, and powerful. Power without grace makes me shudder with fear and disgust. We have too much of it, and we need to find ways to inject grace into everything we do if we are to prosper and have a happy life, individually and collectively.

Not all brands of feminism are equally appealing to me, however. Radical feminism, for instance, tends to be advocated by lesbians who do not want to do anything with men. This happened to Adrienne Rich in 1980, whose later life became increasingly militant. She was separated from her husband, Alfred Haskell Conrad, an economics professor at Harvard University after seventeen years of marriage. Conrad then shot himself to death, and Rich refused to see any of her former male friends. Her lesbianism led her to reject the ideal of androgyny, as advocated by

Virginia Woolf and others; Rich promoted a "woman-centred" vision. Many feminists followed her advice and androgyny became a dirty word.

This anti-naturalistic stance, of course, is utterly unfortunate because, as I presented in the Masculinities course in 2010, androgyny is in each and every one of us, regardless of sex—biologically, psychosocially, psycho-analytically, and also in the Chinese philosophy of Taoism and Chinese medicine. Radical feminists were rightly incensed by the devaluation of women and femininity within a patriarchal culture and, as a consequence, refrained from having anything to do with it, but humanism and Taoism, among others, do not endorse patriarchy. Indeed, I maintain that ideal androgyny in the form of the best combinations of femininity and masculinity (or yin and yang) should be the goal for all of us, both men and women. In this framework, there are good and bad feminine and masculine traits, and good feminine traits are as valuable as good masculine traits, if not more so. It is up to each one of us to keep developing, selecting, enhancing, and balancing desirable traits throughout our lives, based on what we inherit biologically and are required environmentally. For instance, we should be, at the same time, adventurous and prudent, courageous and graceful, truthful and compassionate, passionate and cool, physically and mentally resourceful, etc. We need to accept the way we are, yet keep learning and reinventing ourselves to make us more loving, truthful, ethical, and beautiful.

Jade, my poetry teacher, used to introduce me at poetry-reading gatherings as a "feminist." Well, I explained to the audience that I am not a feminist because in my mind a "male-feminist" is an oxymoron. I am a humanist who values the feminist ideal of gender equity. My "feminism," which is just an extension of my humanist thinking and my Taoist egalitarian philosophy, gives me a sound intellectual grounding. It is fitting, therefore, to include in this section two related poems that I wrote in 2009:

In Praise of Femininity / Confessional Poem / 2009

Shush, I confess, I love femininity
More so than over-prized masculinity

Femininity is like water, soothing
Indispensable, and all empowering

Who can be blamed for liking women better?
Women are more graceful, gentler, and softer
They are more compassionate and caring
And they tend to be less domineering

It's time to boost the feminine soft power
To counterbalance masculinity's lure
Love and cooperation are what we need
To rid the world of malice and greed

Are reason and enlightenment mirages?
Why continue to use force in this day and age?
Enough! Let's say *no* to violence
And to hyper-masculinity, its base

We need a cultural renaissance
To promote a gynocentric response
When the yin and the yang are in balance
The world will know harmony and peace

You Can Be Fully Androgynous Too! / Free Verse / 2009

Why aren't women and men communicating?
Why can't they communicate?
Because they don't know how,
Because they don't dare,
And because they don't want to.

Why, why, why? Don't we all live in the same world?
Don't we all want peace and harmony, not gender wars?
Why are gender wars or apathies still raging?
Why aren't there more cross-gender participations
In each other's studies and each other's movements?
Why is a male-feminist still an oxymoron?
Where are women in men's movements?
Why do the two genders still live in solitude to this day?

Have we forgotten the tale of androgyne?
The union of woman and man in the same body,
So powerful that Zeus had to cut and separate,
Making each half seeking a reunion with the other
In loving and harmonious complementation?
Transcend the Freudian myth of male aggression
And resist sliding into disharmonious hermaphroditism
You can do better!

We are all born androgynous, all endowed with
X chromosomes and female and male sex hormones,
Feminine and passive, and masculine and active psychosocial traits,
Feminine unconscious self and masculine conscious ego,
Negative elements of yin and positive elements of yang.
The right brain is feminine and yin, and the left is masculine and yang—
Be sure to activate the best of both feminine and masculine traits.
As Woolf said, a great mind like Shakespeare's is fully androgynous.
You can be fully androgynous, too!

7.1. Third-Wave Feminism?

FOR A LONG TIME, EVEN AFTER AUDITING COURSES IN FEMINIST PHILOSO-
phy and feminist theory, I was still baffled by the so-called third-wave

feminism. Recently, I made a point to read Claire Snyder's paper, "What is Third-Wave Feminism? A New Directions Essay" (2008), which confirmed my suspicion that the third "wave" is a kind of farce. Third-wavers tend to be individualists, anarchist, and postmodernists, and hence uninterested and incapable of presenting a unified vision of feminism. They even denounce the very category of "women" as "essentialist" and "universalizing," because it allegedly treats all women similarly without taking into account their diverse experiences outside of the dominant groups. Their desire to be all-inclusive, moreover, leads them to embrace a philosophy of non-judgement and individual choice. I maintain that such a stance, especially their version of "pro-sex feminism," inevitably leads to some embarrassing, anti-feminist consequences.

In the name of individual choice, third-wavers' "pro-sex feminism" is said to defend women who enjoy sexual objectification (pornography), who service male sexual needs for money (prostitution), and who eroticize relationships of inequality (sadomasochism). This amoral stance is clearly contrary to the feminist ideals of freedom, equality, justice, and self-actualization for all. Surely, eroticism could be advocated, as it can be beautiful and self-actualizing; and prostitution may be justified in dire circumstances as Emma Goldman almost did when she was penniless and wished to visit her anarchist lover in jail, or when no one is exploited and victimized. However, sexual objectification that is disrespectful of the subject involved is never justified, and sadomasochism—like mutilating self or others—is never healthy and can lead to serious mental and physical harm, or even death. My idea of pro-sex feminism is to promote beautiful, tender-loving eroticism to mutually gratify the sexual needs of the parties involved. According to Confucius, eating and sex are human nature, so the right thing to do is to satisfy the needs of each other lovingly, beautifully, truthfully, and ethically. Unequal relations based on violence and domination, which are often socially conditioned, have no place in "pro-sex feminism."

I learned a lot about third-wave feminism when I audited Dr. Michelle Meagher's course, Feminist Popular Culture. I realized that the "post-feminist" culture since the 1980s had been dominated by the philosophies of individualism and neoliberalism, which were often anti-feminist.

Even then, many self-professed feminists fell for such cultural products as romance fiction, soap operas, punk and rap music, *Twilight* fantasies, *America's Next Top Model*, "gangster feminism," etc. I came to understand the rise of Riot Grrrl bands in the 1990s as a backlash against masculine, misogynist rock culture—a feminist act of resistance and defiance—but feminism failed in its encounters with popular culture, which thrived on providing entertainment and pleasures to target audiences, feminists and antifeminists alike. Feminism—and indeed, our culture as a whole—failed because of its reluctance to embrace and promote the types of pleasures that are life-enhancing and also to vigorously critique and denounce those that are not. Serah Summers' (2010) article, "Twilight Is so Anti-Feminist that I Want to Cry: Twilight Fans Finding and Defining Feminism on the World Wide Web", for example, sheds valuable light on the issue. An internet forum was created for adolescent girls and women to voice their opinions and reflect on the various meanings of feminism. They talked about the protagonist, Bella, who was given limited gender roles and little opportunity to develop and assert herself. This portrayal was discussed in relation to the author Stephenie Meyer's Mormon religion and conservative values, including valorizing women's status as a stay-at-home mom. I understood that the pleasures derived from reading her work were related to the universal yearning for love, romance, and devotion, although the vampire aspect of the story turned me off completely, no matter how much more humane the image of vampires had evolved in recent times. Even now, it's still beyond me why so many people fancy such vampire fiction . . . it just makes my stomach turn. I have no use for such imagery.

The following two poems best summarize my views on sexual objectification and third-wave feminism:

Sexual Objectification and Beauty / Elegy / 2009

Sexual objectification
Is to treat you as an object
It's a despicable offence
Especially against women

A woman feels like being sliced to
A nice piece of ass or bosom
Rather than a whole and thinking person
A subject with feelings and needs

I may enjoy your cute body
In silence or with loud catcalls
But I'll treat you with respect
In hopes of earning affection

Some claim there are times when one can
Regard you as a mere object
Such as in a sexual embrace
While wholly intoxicated

I say that's a flimsy excuse
To impose my will on you
Ignoring you as a subject
And forgetting about your needs

So do not stop looking pretty
For fear of being objectified
To embrace and create beauty
Is an important gift of life

It's not your fault if you have been
Treated as a sexual object
It can happen to anyone
Whether you are pretty or not

Let's treasure all forms of beauty
In our body, mind, and spirit
Let's make the world more beautiful
A path to our liberation

Third-Wave Feminism is a Farce! / Terza Rima / 2011

Third-wave feminism is a farce
'Cause these are not true feminists
And their convictions are rather sparse

They are self-serving individualists
With a philosophy of non-judgement
To avoid being called dogmatists

Their downfall is in their commitment
To their version of pro-sex feminism
With a sense of righteous entitlement

Why on earth do they condone sexism
Such as sexual objectification
And even sadomasochism?

They become a source of contention
And "personal choice" is no defence
Against any debasing action

Violence against anyone is an offence
This third-wave feminism a farce
Consensual violence is a lame pretence

7.2. Family, Romance, and Work

IN THE MID-2000S, I ORGANIZED A PHILOSOPHY CIRCLE WITH SOME friends. We brainstormed topics of interest to us for discussion. Feminism was among those we picked and talked about. We read Anne Kingston's *The Meaning of Wife* and Warren Farrell's *The Myth of Male Power*. On top of these, we discussed Susan Kwilecki and Loretta Wilson's online pre-publication article, "Feminist Follies: Facing Facts At Fifty", (which was subsequently published in *Women in Higher Education*, and referenced here: Kwilecki and Wilson, 2003). We were extremely disappointed with Kwilecki and Wilson's article, because they blamed feminism for their disastrous romantic and family relationships, which they regarded as the natural consequences of their feminist quests for independence and excellence in career development. They wrote:

> Facing fifty, we find ourselves ostracized and disinherited by our natal families, approaching old age without the support of spouses or children, and unrecognized and wounded at work . . . we believe these circumstances are the natural, albeit unintended, consequences of feminist self-cultivation. (p. 26)

They, therefore, posed the question, "Are we, as feminists, better off than our mothers?" (p. 26) Their answer in the pre-publication article, but not in their 2003 paper, was:

> After decades of living and defending the feminist ideals of the 1970s, over and against the traditional gender model of our upbringing, we are forced to concede that our mothers may, indeed, have had better lives.

In the 2003 paper, they state:

> We can't help comparing ourselves unfavorably with our mothers and sisters whose traditional femininity won them enduring financial and emotional support from decent men. Who, we have to ask, is "empowered," that is, realizes her objectives in relationships with men? (p. 26)

Well, despite the absurdity of their logic and conclusion, we may empathize with their personal plight. What went wrong with their lives, and why?

I and my friend, Marie-Laure, who was working on her PhD in physiology at that time, thought the biggest flaw in their lives lay in their one-dimensional view of feminism, which was all about independence, self-determination, and career accomplishment. These were their preoccupations. Thus, they wrote: "The possibility of compromising our objectives for traditional female satisfactions never occurred to us." (p. 25) They, like many other second-wave feminists, didn't view life as a constant balancing of many and often conflicting and competing needs and wants, and didn't attribute enough importance to pleasures and fulfilments in other "mundane" things like leisure activities and personal/family relationships. We saw in Kwilecki and Wilson the caricature and stereotypical images of second-wavers as painted by some postfeminist third-wavers.

Closely related to the above is that their feminism valorizes independence at the expense of interdependence. This is a common mistake, especially in our Western cultures. When I did quality assurance in hospital rehabilitation medicine in the early 1980s, the same philosophy of independence predominated in clinical practice. So I tried to emphasize the importance of the concept of interdependence, since people with disabilities often needed help from others and, at the same time, they were perfectly capable of helping others. Interdependence enriches the lives of those involved, making us realize and value the need to rely on each other, help each other, rather than always "going it alone," based on rugged individualism. This greater awareness of our interdependent world—requiring more cooperative and reciprocal arrangements with others—is missing in their version of feminism, thus contributing to their inability or unwillingness to work out more satisfactory love and family relationships.

Marie-Laure and I maintain, moreover, that their version of feminism lacks conviction and therefore is not internalized. They constantly craved external approvals, especially from their mothers. They were devastated when such approvals were not forthcoming, as when they got doctoral degrees and tenured positions, and also when they got their papers published in prestigious journals. Why couldn't they be simply proud of themselves and celebrate their achievements? Why were they so upset when they perceived their mothers to exercise favouritism, giving extravagant gifts to their siblings but not to them, since they were far from being in dire financial straits? Why were they still convinced of the stereotypical images of women, when they wrote:

> But feminism has not significantly changed the game of romance. Still, to attract men, women must brush their hair, not brush up their resumes; eyeliner pencils, not wits, must be sharpened. How many men seek feminist partners? (p. 26)

Am I a nerdy oddball who likes intelligent women with natural looks and dislikes cosmetic makeup, which tend to diminish, rather than enhance, women's beauty? I don't think so. A cursory browsing of the internet shows a sizable number, perhaps a quarter, of men prefer natural-looking women, although I didn't find any credible study quantifying the proportion of such men. There is also Kate Springer's (2012) "The 'Naked Face Project': Two Months, Sans Beauty Products". For two months, two ladies from Charlotte, NC, Molly Barker, aged fifty-one, and Caitlin Boyle, twenty-seven, "decided to give up makeup, shaving, jewelry, heels, straightening irons—you name it—and go *au naturel*." They said they were actually inspired by questions from young girls whom they work with: "'If you tell me I'm beautiful just the way I am, why do you color your hair or wear makeup?'" Springer also reported:

> Realizing their hypocrisy, Barker and Boyle decided it was time to practice what they preached. After booting everything from antiwrinkle creams to deodorant from their daily routines, the pair have made some refreshing observations. "There's a natural flush to my cheeks," Barker told *USA Today*. "There's no need for blush there." The project has perks unrelated to looks. Less time primping means saving time and money. According to WFMY News 2,

Boyle says she is no longer running late constantly and both women have saved about $300 over the course of the commitment.

They found out that naked faces were more common than they thought, noting: "At least 30 other women are trying the experiment." They also have a better answer for those little girls looking up to them: "What I would tell little girls is that I don't like feeling like I have to do certain things, and I'm the same person whether I follow these routines or not," Boyle says. "Real sexiness and real confidence come from within." As well, the no-make-up trend is said to be gaining popularity, especially among women who are comfortable with themselves and their appearance—"that they desire to be seen more authentically—to be accepted for how they actually look, without camouflage or enhancements." (Well 2017)

Kwilecki and Wilson's hunch about the importance of family, however, is very true. Friends often come and go, but family ties tend to last. It's crucially important, therefore, to nurture loving family relations, because "family makes us who we are." It saddened me, therefore, to learn that their families were so dysfunctional, and didn't value their achievements. I'm blessed to have had a very supportive family. It all started when my elder sister earned a big, fat scholarship to study in the US, so she used that money to finance my elder brother's airfare to study in the US—and later also paid my younger sister's airfare to study in Canada. My brother, in turn, supported me, $30/month for a number of years, out of his meagre medical residency income, until I got my scholarships to support my graduate studies in North America. It's the family support that made me who I am. Our family has always placed the utmost importance to education, so we provided funds for university education to our children, and I'm still amazed to hear the stories of tens of thousands of dollars of student loans owed by many if not most Canadian university graduates. Isn't it a parental responsibility nowadays to provide funding for one's children's education, at least to the university level if possible, to give them a head start to face the challenges of life?

There is no question, though, that our world can be an unforgiving place. Like what Kwilecki and Wilson had experienced, women in their late twenties and throughout their thirties, in particular, are facing especially challenging choices in relation to work, romance, and family. Nobody can have it all, at least not all at once, and it's heartbreaking at times to witness what some of my young lady friends and family members have had to go through to cope and make difficult choices. At least in my lifetime, within my limited experience in Far Eastern and North American cultures, I have seen tremendous cultural changes in gender relations. Women were not as powerless as they used to be in my parents' generation. My mother was not allowed to pursue higher education like her male siblings did, in contrast to my younger sister who felt a slight sense of unease with her two master's degrees as compared to my elder sister's doctoral degree. My mother went through an arranged marriage, while my younger sister and I picked our own partners . . . although my elder sister and elder brother had semi-arranged marriages. Did my mother have a better life than my sisters? It's hard to say, but I doubt it. Once, I read my father's diary in which he described how hurt he was when my mother tried to help in planning their upcoming trip. He felt she distrusted him, and had no confidence in his ability to do the planning. Indeed, it was men's role in that era to provide for and protect women, who were not to make decisions without the consent of their male guardians. Would any woman be happy in such unequal power relations?

Everyone has to hone skills in the art of living, navigating through the labyrinth of numerous opportunities and barriers. True feminism is to fight for a better world, with better opportunities and less restrictive barriers for women, in partnership with men (and other women), to find ways and shape their futures according to their dreams. It would be silly to fantasize "that our mothers may, indeed, have had better lives." No life is easy, but who would voluntarily want to go back to the "good old days" when women had many fewer choices and rights than men, and must depend on the approval of their male heads of household? The best course of action for women is to make their feminist dreams come true in all spheres of their lives—in relation to work, romance, family, etc. The reality may be bleak, as depicted by Kwilecki and Wilson, but unless people and institutions change, there is no hope for a better future.

Happiness is indeed elusive to many people in this seemingly idiotic world. Can we still be happy? I wrote the following poem to address this question:

Can We be Happy in this Seemingly Idiotic World? / Persona Poem / 2010

Can we be happy in this seemingly idiotic world
Where bad things happen mercilessly to good people?
Long ago, the Taoist philosopher Chuang Tzu told a story
Of Tzu Shu who fatally opposed his king's unjust policy
Witness the fate of the whistle-blowers in recent times
They can't be happy without trying to right the wrongs
Then tragically ruin their careers and their lives in the end

In the eyes of Sigmund Freud, happiness is a paradox
In a world full of betrayals, injustices, and miseries
Toe the line, follow the rules, adapt, and be good . . .
We're driven into self-doubt, depression, and anxiety
From a heightened sense of nervousness, guilt, and sin.
Stop looking inward and blame ourselves, says B. Russell
For the culpability, guilt, and sin of our imperfection

The Buddhist philosopher Daisaku Ikeda fully concurs
It's futile to strive for perfection, nobody is, or can be
Just accept the way we are and strive to do our best
Keep challenging our weaknesses and only compare
Who we are today against who we were yesterday
Without comparing ourselves against others
Simply celebrate our efforts and have no regrets

Bertrand Russell also advises us: we can't be happy
By kidding ourselves, with over-inflated egos, or
With the love of power, which is unlikely to last
We can be happy, though, if we look outward more
Restore our childlike curiosities and constantly
Explore the world with a wide range of interests
Interact, make connections, share and care for others

Beware! Even then, happiness can still be elusive
As revealed in *Mother Teresa: Come Be My Light*
Her inner emptiness and lasting crisis in her faith
Were masked by her public smiles and demeanour
As the Buddhist philosopher ever so wisely urges us
We need a strong inner self to be genuinely happy
True happiness is to be found only within ourselves

So, it's not easy to trust those who say they are happy
Since we aren't sure if they are wearing a mask or not
Research shows the conservatives to be overtly happier
Than the liberals, but this may just be plain hogwash
Putting up happy fronts to please themselves and others
Like women in Betty Friedan's *Feminine Mystique*
We don't know until we're truly in touch with ourselves

The secret of happiness lies in the timeless trio of virtues:
The lifelong quest for truth, goodness, and beauty.
We won't be in touch with ourselves without truth
We won't be in harmony with others without goodness
And we won't rise above mere existence without beauty
It's at the intersection of truth, goodness, and beauty that
We find love, meaning, serenity, harmony, and happiness

Can we be happy in this seemingly idiotic world?
Yes we can, I say, by replenishing our zest for life
Strengthening our inner self, live fully and lovingly
For the present, with a deep sense of joy and wonder.
Because life is fleeting, imperfect, and wondrously uncertain
It's miraculously free, unpredictable, and unknowable.
Let's celebrate life's mysteries and wonders, and be happy

7.3. *Hannah Arendt* and the Banality of Evil

FEMINISM, AND INDEED PHILOSOPHY AS A WHOLE, IS AT A CROSSROAD. Life is challenging for all of us, but doubly so for women in a patriarchal world. Therefore, it is crucially important for all thinkers, women as well as men, to engage in a pursuit of a greater understanding of the world, to make the world a better place for all of us.

It was timely that I read Yasemin Sari's (2014) review of the film *Hannah Arendt* with the description, "about a courageous thinker and her views on responsibility and the nature of evil"—directed by Margarethe von Trotta. The nature of evil was of great interest to me since I started at that time to compose a paper advocating a shift toward the cultural paradigm that values cooperation more than competition. After decades of neoliberal political agendas, since the early 1980s, the world has become increasingly unequal in income, wealth, and power. This uneven distribution of cost and benefit has caused unending conflict and misery all over the world. A possible solution, I figured, was to deemphasize and stop glorifying the virtue of competition, since competition would create winners and losers, and only cooperation would entice people to work towards win-win solutions. Is competition really good and necessary as we are led to believe, or is it evil and should it not be valorized?

Hannah Arendt focuses on the controversy surrounding Arendt's report on the 1961 trial of Adolf Eichmann in *The New Yorker*, and she published it in 1963 as a book, *Eichmann in Jerusalem*. Arendt—a German Jew who studied philosophy under eminent philosophers Martin Heidegger and Karl Jasper, witnessed the rise of the Nazis and the collaboration of her trusted Jewish friends, including Heidegger, with the Nazis, escaped to the United States in 1941, and authored major philosophical classics such as *The Origins of Totalitarianism* in 1951 and *The Human Condition* in 1958—was eminently qualified to report on the trial of Eichmann, a mid-ranking Nazi official who sent millions of Jews to gas chambers. One of the most contentious claims that Arendt advanced, also as a subtitle of her book, was her characterization of Eichmann's crime as "the banality of evil." As Sari (2014) stated in the review of the film:

> Adolf Eichmann, however, did not think; hence, he did not judge. In turn, through his actions, he demonstrated what Arendt infamously labelled "the banality of evil." Here she put forth neither a general rule nor a philosophical thesis concerning the nature of evil, but rather, an explanation of a particular phenomenon in order to show how this instance of evil was possible. Von Trotta forcefully presents Arendt's judgement as she is conversing with her old Zionist friend Blumenfeld, and says: "Eichmann is no Mephistopheles." (p.43)

This characterization of Eichmann as a normal yet unthinking individual who just followed the orders and not a devilish monster (Mephistopheles), as he is widely presumed to be, has been hotly disputed. However, I think Arendt hit the nail on the head in characterizing many of the tragic events in the world—especially in relation to the evil of competition, which is ubiquitous and committed by ordinary people in everyday life. Most people want to get ahead of other people, often at the expense of others, in this competitive world, rather than taking time to think ethically and find win-win solutions cooperatively. Evil, according to Arendt, is a result of thoughtlessness, which I agree, although others do not, like Richard Brody's (2013) review of the film entitled "'Hannah Arendt' and the glorification of thinking." So I wrote in a paper with Professor Joy Fraser (Chang & Fraser, 2017):

> It is often due to pressures of competition that we fail to think rationally, and to resolve conflicts cooperatively. Ethics, after all, is about rational decision-making, to think and find worthy, common causes/objectives plus the best course(s) of action to achieve such objectives. (p.11)

No, we can't overestimate the importance of thinking, since ethics is all about thinking and rational decision-making. The concept of the banality of evil provides us with new insight and helps us understand why people often misbehave and act horribly to themselves and to others. To be a good feminist, you have to be a good thinker too.

Nobody is perfect, and the same goes for Arendt. Her characterization of Eichmann as thoughtless functionary together with her indictment of the Jewish Councils for cooperating with the Nazis has been disputed and shown to be not totally true (Ezra, 2007). These likely shortcomings notwithstanding, I'm grateful for her concept of "the banality of evil," which is very insightful of human nature and what all of us must do to think ethically on a daily basis if we are to make this world a better place.

Dreaming Beyond Our Violent World / Confessional Poem / 2012

I must confess my despair about our future
When faced with our incessantly violent culture

School bullying, goon tactics in hockey, wife beating,
honour killing, love affairs with guns here at home

We have to reengineer our psychology and mindsets
So we could rid ourselves of our violent past

I just can't believe my eyes when I read in *Maclean's*
A story about Chris Brown, the convicted wife-beater

His winning and twice live performances at the
Grammy awards were too much for some to bear

Miranda Lambert, the country music singer
Sent a tweet, expressing her disbelief and outrage

Then came an onslaught of tweets from Brown's female fans
Saying they'd "relish the opportunity to be beaten by him"

More shocking is the news about his wife, Rihanna
Who has forgiven him and collaborated with him

They worked on a sexually explicit song, saying
He'd like to "give it to [Rihanna] in the worse way"

I shudder in anguish about our culture of amnesia
Turning a deaf ear to feminism's *no means no*

Then I am heartened when the same issue of *Maclean's*
Features Jody Williams, the Nobel Peace Prize laureate

Courageously she shouted "Happy Women's Day" on March 8th
In the Honduran capital, "the most murderous city in the world"

She was risking herself to protest murders and femicide
And drug wars occurring daily all over Central America

I rack my brain trying to figure out how we could
Rid ourselves of our violent mentality and behaviours

Make love, not war, I say; it's time to make war history
Cherish international solidarity; banish genocides

Watching the Arab Spring and the Occupy Movement
I dream of peace on Earth, and a flourishing life for all

7.4. Martha Nussbaum, the Professor of Parody and Nationalism

ANOTHER FEMINIST THINKER I ADMIRE GREATLY IS MARTHA NUSSBAUM (born 1947). While auditing a women's studies course reading Judith Butler's hugely influential *Gender Trouble* (1989), I came across Nussbaum's devastating critique of Butler, "The Professor of Parody" (1999). In this paper, which may be viewed as a second-wave feminist's critique of third-wave feminism, Nussbaum has articulated many of my concerns about how feminism, and indeed our culture as a whole, has evolved and is heading.

On the new feminism, Nussbaum states, "It is the virtually complete turning from the material side of life, toward a type of verbal and symbolic politics that makes only the flimsiest of connections with the real situation of real women." (p. 38) This trend, Nussbaum also noted, owes much to European postmodernist thinkers like Michel Foucault:

> We are prisoners of an all-enveloping structure of power, and that real-life reform movements usually end up serving power in new and insidious ways. Such feminists therefore find comfort in the idea that the subversive use of words is still available to feminist intellectuals. (p. 38)

Due to Butler's influence among young scholars, Nussbaum laments about new feminism's "quietism and retreat" from social engagement:

> The great tragedy in the new feminist theory in America is the loss of a sense of public commitment. In this sense, Butler's self-involved feminism is extremely American, and it is not surprising that it has caught on here, where successful middle-class people prefer to focus on cultivating the self rather than thinking in a way that helps the material condition of others. (p.44)

Nussbaum also critiques Butler's writing style, which is often obscure, full of unexplained jargon, imprecise, open-ended without clear assertions, difficult to decipher and understand the intended message, etc. This verdict has been corroborated by Butler's winning the first prize in 1998 in the annual Bad Writing Contest sponsored by the journal, *Philosophy and Literature*. Recalling my struggle to understand *Gender Trouble*, I chuckled at Nussbaum's following passage:

> One afternoon, fatigued by Butler on a long plane trip, I turned to a draft of a student's dissertation on Hume's views of personal identity. I quickly felt my spirits reviving. Doesn't she write clearly, I thought with pleasure, and a tiny bit of pride. And Hume, what a fine, what a gracious spirit: how kindly he respects the reader's intelligence, even at the cost of exposing his own uncertainty. (p. 40)

Nussbaum also takes issue with Butler's assertion that not only gender but also sex is a social construction. Butler famously speaks about gender performativity—i.e., a repetitive performance of acts associated with the male and the female—and frequently quotes Simone de Beauvoir's famous dictum: "One is not born, but rather becomes, a woman." However, Nussbaum wants Butler to answer those who believe that human beings have at least some pre-cultural desires (such as for food, comfort, cognitive mastery, survival, etc.), and that this personality structure is crucial for our development as moral and political agents. This anti-naturalistic stance relates to Butler's rejection of universal, normative notions such as human dignity on the grounds that they are "inherently dictatorial." Butler's "dangerous quietism," according to Nussbaum, is due to her lack of a normative theory of social justice and human dignity. The best alternative for Butler, therefore, is to mock, which is personal and private rather than un-ironic, organized public actions for social change.

In all fairness, my assessment is that Butler (born 1956), as a lesbian in her early thirties under the influence of third-wave feminism when she wrote *Gender Trouble*, provided a penetrating and creative analysis of issues surrounding sex, gender, and power relations. Her ideas may not have been truly original, and the scope may have been too narrow because of her distrust of universal ethics, as Nussbaum has pointed out, but her synthesis of the teachings from many poststructuralist thinkers, especially from Foucault's *Discipline and Punish*, to form her idea of "regulatory discourses"—which provides "frameworks of intelligibility" or "disciplinary regimes" for deciding what are socially permitted—strikes a chord among many third-wave feminists, influencing political, particularly queer, discourses and activism all over the world even to this day.

Butler, moreover, became much more politically active in the subsequent years, broadening her theory of gender performativity to deal with contemporary biopolitics, addressing issues of precarious lives, social justice, racism, nationalism, among others. In her book, *Parting Ways: Jewishness and the Critique of Zionism*, for example, Butler (2012) criticized Zionism and its practice of state violence, nationalism, and state-sponsored racism, etc. Following Edward Said, moreover, she advocates a one-state solution since, in Hannah Arendt's words, "we cannot choose with whom we cohabit the world." In proposing a one-state cohabitation model for the Israeli-Palestinian conflict, Butler has no illusions. As she reiterated in her interview by Roy Filar:

> ...living with one another can be unhappy, wretched, ambivalent, even full of antagonism, but all of that can play out in the political sphere without recourse to expulsion or genocide. And that is our obligation. (Filar, 2013)

In defending her one-state solution against those who dismiss it as idealistic and will never happen, Butler (2012) quotes Mahmoud Darwish's poem, "a possible life is one that wills the impossible," (p. 222) Butler says that in politics, sometimes what is thought would never happen actually starts to happen. So I love it when she says that one of philosophy's jobs is to elevate principles that seem impossible. It would be an impoverished world, as Butler says, if no one wants to tackle the tasks that seem impossible.

When the German city of Frankfurt awarded the prestigious Theodor W. Adorno Prize to Butler in 2012, members of the Jewish community, academics, and commentators denounced the decision, in view of her criticisms against the policies of the state of Israel, plus her open support for the boycott and sanction against Israel. Like Hannah Arendt, she was condemned for being anti-Semitic and self-hating—as a Jew herself. Coincidentally, this kind of blind nationalism is exactly what Adorno argued against, and what Arendt called "unthinkingness" that characterizes "the banality of evil"—since such critics would not, or could not, differentiate between just and unjust condemnations. I agree with these superlative feminist thinkers like Arendt, Nussbaum, and Butler that nationalism is not sacred, while critical thinking is. And I applaud the members of the Adorno jury for defending the decision and awarded Butler for her outstanding contribution to humanity. As Nussbaum (1994) stated in her opening section:

> I believe, with Tagore, . . . that this emphasis on patriotic pride is both morally dangerous and, ultimately, subversive of some of the worthy goals patriotism sets out to serve—for example, the goal of national unity in devotion to worthy moral ideals of justice and equality. These goals, I shall argue, would be better served by an ideal that is in any case more adequate to our situation in the contemporary world, namely the very old ideal of the cosmopolitan, the person whose primary allegiance is to the community of human beings in the entire world.

I wish those who defend patriotism and nationalism as a highest value would read Nussbaum's article containing the above quote and reflect on it. Shouldn't our ultimate allegiance be "to the community of human beings in the entire world" rather than to a particular country or nation?

Nussbaum's harsh criticism of Judith Butler has naturally invited rejoinders from other third-wave feminists. Endorsing Carol Gilligan's view that women have "a different voice," Defalco states that ethics of care is distinctly "anti-universal in its approach," seeking to expose the problematically "reductive tendencies of 'grand theory'" and develop a philosophy that, in contrast, "emphasize[s] the ethical irreducibility of specific situations" (2016, p. 13). Smaro Kamboureli also echoes such anti-universalism, and characterizing Nussbaum's concept of communal attunement as "remarkably totalized," and the fulfilment of this promise as "concomitant with eradicating difference" (2007, p. 952).

I think this kind of gendered response based on anti-universalism is self-defeating. If ethics of care is, in fact, "anti-universal," then we need to change it to make it universal for everyone, regardless of gender, so as to make our society more caring. If we care about others, then we are likely to cooperate and seek win-win solutions when we are faced with interpersonal and intergroup conflicts. If we don't care about others, then we would likely compete based on self-interests, which would result in win-lose or lose-lose tragic solutions. Hence, ethics of care has to be a universal imperative and cooperation a universal virtue. I also don't think there is substantiating evidence of "totalizing" in Nussbaum's universalism. In defending some versions of essentialism, e.g., for sentiments such as compassion and respect, Nussbaum (1992) states:

> We see that such compassionate identification need not ignore concrete local differences; in fact, at its best, it demands a searching analysis of differences in order that the general good be appropriately realized in the new concrete case. But the learning about and from the other is motivated as it is in Aristotle's own studies of other cultures: by the conviction that the other is one of us. (p. 241)

So Kamboureli may have committed "the failure to read": the charge she levelled against her opponent. To me, it is obvious that the universal and the particular—and the theory and the practice—are complementary, and that they need each other to gain meaning and legitimacy. It's at one's peril to denounce the one or the other.

It is shocking to me that anyone would be totally against universalism and essentialism. I too value writings that are "shocking" and thought-provoking, as long as they are reasonable and evidence-based. So I wrote this poem:

Inspire Others / Acrostic / 2011

I try to write poems that are shocking
Not just something sweet and fleeting
So the reader would do serious thinking
Poems, I say, should be mind-provoking
Inspiring others to do soul searching
Reminding them that life is challenging
Expecting nothing less than enchanting

Other times I just do storytelling
To narrate my experience and feelings
Have I got something that's captivating?
Especially revealing and penetrating?
Recording those that are life-affirming?
Sure, that's what I dream of becoming

8.
Graceful Ageing

When memories exceed dreams, the end is near. (Thomas Friedman, 2005, p. 553)

EVERYBODY IS GOOD AT SOMETHING AND NOT AS GOOD AT OTHER THINGS. What I can truly take pride in and often receive compliments from others is graceful ageing. Despite signs and symptoms of ageing—such as baldness and grey hair, wrinkled and spotted skin, frequent and difficult urination, diminished sex drive, heart problems that required angioplasty and stenting, receding gums, etc.—I still can do most of the thing as I could fifty years ago when I was in my twenties. At age eighty, I still cycle everywhere and play tennis as well as ever before, I climbed China's fabulous Yellow Mountain at age seventy-five, and I'm still inspired to learn new things every day by going to classes and book clubs, reading, watching films, drawing, painting, creative writing, etc. It was Anais Nin (1969) who said this: "Writers do not live one life, they live two. There is the living and then there is the writing. There is the second tasting, the delayed reaction." (p. 73) The living is a prerequisite to the writing. To be a profound writer, one has to live profoundly. That's what I now realize and try to emulate, by exploring new avenues, new possibilities, new experiences, and new dreams.

When my young lady friend, Marie-Laure, was asked by her young male friend why she liked to hang out with me, she simply said I was "young at heart." When a friend of mine too asked about my secrets, I proffered my advice half-jokingly, "Like Peter Pan, never to grow up!" Indeed,

I feel I have not changed much since I was young. I'm still same old me, a wild-eyed dreamer-idealist. Funny, isn't it, that I have remained a socialist throughout my life, and I've always voted for the New Democratic Party since I was able to cast my first vote in Canada.

I have a friend, Nina, in her late sixties, who came to Canada from Russia more than fifteen years ago. She was an engineer back in Russia, but when Mikhail Gorbachev started Perestroika—which resulted in the collapse of the former Soviet Union and its economy—she lost her job and all her pension. To make a living, she used her dressmaking skills to start a successful business. She opened her own shop in Toronto after she immigrated to Canada, and became a vocal opponent of socialism. She teased me, calling me a dreamer who's totally out of touch with reality. I said to her that our future would be bleak if we kept continuing our current practice of cutthroat competition under neoliberal capitalism, and she agreed with me. I said, therefore, that we had to change more toward socialism and cooperation while designing better work incentives. She maintained, however, that people worked hard only under free-enterprise capitalism; hence, socialism would not work. In this way, the debate raged on between idealism-socialism and realism-capitalism, and I gained new insight as to why and how so many people have lost their idealism and become more conservative as they embraced the reality of power politics and cutthroat competition.

Fawzi Ibrahim is probably right when he declares that humanity faces a stark choice in his book, *Capitalism Versus Planet Earth*: "save the planet and ditch capitalism or save capitalism and ditch the planet." The key question, of course, is *what* to replace capitalism with. Well, in the past many versions of socialism failed, in Russia, China, Cuba, Eastern Europe, etc. What's lacking in these experiments is "economic democracy" as outlined in David Schweickart's *After Capitalism* (2011). In fact, he proposes a form of market socialism, which includes workplace self-management (including the election of supervisors), social control of capital investment by a form of public banking, and fair trade between countries. My prescription of cooperatives as a better and more democratic form of business models (Chang & Fraser, 2017) is in line with Schweickart's ideas of economic democracy.

Nina is understandably distrustful of any form of socialism, but, from my perspective, that's no excuse for giving up on socialism. We should learn from all social theories and experiments—including the practice of social democracy in Scandinavian countries. Nina works hard during the weekdays, and plays hard during the weekends—going hiking in the summer, Nordic skiing in the winter, to art galleries, operas, etc. all year round. She does not know the meaning of not working. On the other hand, I'm "retired" but "work" as hard as ever to do the things I want to do. My life is as good or perhaps better in many ways now after retirement than ever. However, retirement can be hell if we don't know what to do with it. This is most vividly depicted in a 2002 film, *About Schmidt*. After Warren Schmidt's retirement from his position as an actuary at an insurance company in Omaha, Nebraska, his life literally falls apart. His wife dies suddenly, and he is devastated to find out about her love affair with one of his close friends. He tries, but is increasingly alienated from everyone, including his friends, his only daughter and her fiancé. Nobody seems to appreciate him any more. He becomes nobody. He questions what he has accomplished in life, and can only see the total futility of his life. It's one of the most depressing films I've ever seen—despite its commercial success and critical acclaims. It makes me wonder about old age and the implications of retirement. So I wrote a poem reflecting on the meaning of retirement:

Retirement Is What You Make It Out to Be / Shakespearean Sonnet / 2009

I had a gift of life called retirement
No more alarm clock and fussy bosses
No more work pressure and peer resentment
Free to pursue youthful dreams without stresses

Beware! Retirement can be hell for some
Look what happened in the film *About Schmidt*
He becomes nobody and feeling lonesome
Desperate for love to lift his spirit

For me, it's a golden time to go back
To the classrooms to survey the frontiers
Of knowledge, write and get feedback
And share inspiration with my peers

Heaven or hell, agree or disagree
Retirement is what you make it out to be

8.1. A Sense of Purpose, Social Connections, and Physical Activity

WHAT HAPPENS TO MANY SENIORS IS OFTEN THE LOSS OF SOCIAL CONNECtions. As Eric Tangalos, a professor of medicine at the Mayo Clinic who specializes in Alzheimer's disease research and ageing issues, noted: "I would argue that as each of us gets older, we shrink our environment to get better control of it." (Moeller 2012) Retirement may inadvertently "shrink our environment"; it brings about social isolation in seniors as their social networks are altered, their friends and family move or pass away, and their mental and physical limitations increase. It's a challenge, therefore, to keep up with social connections, renewing and enhancing them. That's why it's of critical importance to pay increasing attention to the social aspect of the senior's life, since its shrinkage is a major cause of their mental and physical demise.

Physical activity is another key to graceful ageing. Nina told me about a CBC radio program on June 24, 2013, called *The Longevity Puzzle* by Susan Pinker (2013):

In a cluster of quiet mountain villages in Sardinia, Italy, something unusual is happening. A remarkable number of people are living into their hundreds. And in this global hotspot for longevity, there are nearly as many male as female centenarians. Psychologist and author Susan Pinker takes us to Sardinia as she searches for the answers.

Some of the factors Pinker (2014) identified are: a sense of purpose, physical activity (occupation as a shepherd), and genetics. I think we need to pay special attention to physical activity, in addition to the sense of purpose, since that is a modifiable factor which we can easily do something about. When I play tennis or engage in more strenuous cycling, I tend to sleep well and get up fewer times in the night. As the Sardinia example shows, there may not be a biological basis as to why men can't live as long as women, who now tend to outlive men by five to eight years in most countries in the world. Indeed, it isn't outrageous for us to aspire to be a centenarian. Our "natural lifespan" was already projected at 100 years in *The Yellow Emperor's Classic of Internal Medicine* over 2,000 years ago, and at 120 years according to Taoist Chinese medicine. A premature death is at less than half of 120 years, or before 60 years of age; and key milestones are at the ages of 72 (60%), 84 (70%), 96 (80%), and 108 (90%) years.

An important element of graceful ageing is "grace," which has physical, mental, and social aspects. First, a graceful body is one that is appealing and attractive in some important ways. As revealed by the Canadian Health Measures Survey, 2009 to 2011, it's a sad reality that in Canada about two-thirds of men and about half of women are either overweight or obese, and these phenomena become more pronounced as people age. Thus, the proportion of normal-weight Canadians aged 18–39, 40–59, and 60–79 decreased from 45% to 24% and 21% among men, and from 55% to 40% and 30% among women, respectively. This means that a vast majority of seniors aged 60–79—i.e., four in five of older men and over two-thirds of older women—are not in ("normal") shape, according to the Canadian Body Mass Index (BMI) classification. I often wonder why it's harder to find graceful-looking older people in the crowd, and these statistics, instead of lying, tell us why. I'm, of course, aware that beauty and grace come in many shapes and forms, but as a health researcher I also know that normality in terms of BMI is also related to optimal health and longevity. So it's not totally outrageous to view grace from a BMI perspective.

A person's grace also has a lot to do with his or her composure, comportment, and movement, which, in turn, represent and reveal his or her personality, character, and mental state. It's an integral component of our concept of a person's beauty, which is reflected in the way a person speaks, gestures, sits, stands, walks, runs, jumps, falls, stumbles, smiles, laughs, cries, frowns, curses, shouts, acts, writes, sings, behaves, expresses, lives, etc. Graceful ageing is to live gracefully in old age, with equanimity, calmness, serenity, joy, zest, vitality, taste, class, and above all, with a right balance—neither excessive and extravagant, nor deficient and wanting. This just-rightness of the makeup of a person is what graceful ageing is about. Somehow, my attitude toward ageing impressed one of my young classmates, Monika, in one of the courses I audited, after she interviewed me for her assignment in an ageing course she was taking in human ecology. I told her my story of lifelong learning after retirement, taking or auditing courses in art, philosophy, and literature, and engaging in physical and social activities like cycling, playing tennis, going to theatres, walking, etc. Then I sent her a poem, a pastiche of Dylan Thomas's villanelle, "Do not go gentle into that good night," which urges his dad to fight against old age, cancer, and death. I told her that Thomas' poem lacks grace towards ageing, so I wrote a more uplifting version to express my attitude towards ageing:

Go Gently Forward into That Good Night / Pastiche / 2010

Go gently forward into that good night
Old age brings wisdom and light at end of day
Cheers, cheers for life's miraculous delight

Wise men, through their lives, know life is right
Because their minds are enlightened they
Go gently forward into that good night

Good men, living for the present, know how bright
Their deeds have illuminated Nature's way
Cheers, cheers for life's miraculous delight

Wild men who soared 'n' topped a creative height
Find happily that they did have their way
To go gently forward into that good night

Brave men, who face death squarely without fright
Know when to fight and let go and be gay
Cheers, cheers for life's miraculous delight

And you, my friend, enjoy life with all your might
Count your blessings and shed joyful tears, I say
Go gently forward into that good night
Cheers, cheers for life's miraculous delight

She really liked my poem and my attitude towards ageing, telling me through an email after the interview that "I was just beaming all afternoon and shared some of the highlights of our day with my friends and family who found you to be as fascinating and inspiring as I do!" It made my day.

8.2. Celebrating Life and Death

WITH A BIT OF LUCK AND HARD WORK, BARRING UNEXPECTED SERIOUS illness or injury, we may attain healthy ageing to old age as I have now entered the eighth decade of my life. It's a cause for celebration, so my son and daughter suggested that we do something special for my birthday.

We originally toyed with the idea of celebrating my birthday in warm Mexico since my birthday is in December. We changed our plan to San Diego in California because of the threat of the Zika virus in Mexico in late 2017 and early 2018. We rented a spacious, five-bedroom house with a swimming pool and a hot tub in early February 2018 to accommodate my daughter's and my son's families, and me and my good friend, Jenny. There were eleven of us. My daughter, son-in-law, and their three kids drove all the way from Vancouver Island to California, stopping by at Lego City on their way there. The rest of us flew from Calgary and Edmonton over to San Diego. We had a swell of time there, walking on the beach, surfing, watching sea lions, swimming, dipping in the hot tub, playing tennis, exchanging stories, etc. Some of us also took an excursion into Mexico to sample what's like over there. Everyone had a memorable time.

We celebrate life, so why don't we celebrate death as well? Some deaths are indeed unfortunate and untimely, such as promising young writers, artists, or scientists who died of a plane crash, car accident, or mass killing, incurable cancer, etc. Such are heartbreaking losses and occasions of immeasurable sadness. But when someone has lived fully to old age, it is appropriate to choose a time to gather family and friends to celebrate life and bid farewell to the loved ones. Why should we be preoccupied with, and terrified of "the Nothing," to use Martin Heidegger's euphemism for the idea of death? Why should we insist on prolonging life to the very bitter end, resorting to every drastic measure at one's disposal, without taking into account the quality and meaning of life to the person? The key to a good death is to live well. By living well, we can face death with equanimity as a natural event, one more time to rejoice life and bid a last farewell to the loved ones.

There are many who are terrified and fascinated by death, among them was Ludwig Wittgenstein, who frequently contemplated suicide. As Peter Adamson stated in "Wittgenstein & the War" (2018), Wittgenstein wrote in one of his notebooks that "only death gives life its meaning," so he enlisted and volunteered for the most dangerous duty during WWI. And yet, he chastised himself for the fear he felt, that to fear death comes from a "false view of life." (p. 41) As I stated earlier, life has its inherent meaning even though we become aware of it often at the time of death. We fear death because we are dissatisfied and want more from our lives. This, I maintain, has nothing to do with a "false view of life."

As discussed earlier in relation to love, Antonia, in the Dutch film *Antonia's Line*, holds the life-affirming female principle, rejoicing in death as a natural event when the time comes and sharing it with her loved ones at her bedside. Similarly, I have quoted "the most important letter" ever written by the Queen of Romance Novels, Chiung Yao (2017), in Taiwan. It was a letter addressed to her son and daughter-in-law in which she rejected life-prolonging measures and requested a simple send-off after her death; she had already lived to seventy-nine years of age, "by heaven's grace," so she would "face death with a smile." She also wrote, "I have approached this letter with a positive mindset to live like a spark burning to the last moment and die like snowflakes floating to earth, becoming dust."

I have hardly ever read any of her novels, but her attitude towards life and death strikes a chord with me. As an atheist, I don't expect any after-life or reincarnation. When my body ceases functioning, my spirit will be gone, and "I" will no longer exist. My body will disintegrate, although not totally disappear. The zillions of molecules that constitute my body at the time of my death will still be there, and, in time, possibly scatter all over the world. After reading a beautiful poem, "Do Not Stand at My Grave and Weep" by Mary Elizabeth Frye, a Baltimore housewife "who lacked a formal education," I was inspired to compose the following poem:

Come and Celebrate My Life With Me / Elegy / 2016

Come and celebrate my life with me
Before I bid you my final farewell
Let's revel in our zillion achievements
In work, leisure, and the art of living
To gauge which way and how far we've
Travelled, and how far we have yet to go

Life's full of sadness and joyfulness
I may not have been the smartest
But surely I'm among the luckiest
To achieve wellness and happiness
Thanks to you who enriched my life
Which I'll let go with equanimity

So let's all celebrate our dreams of
Making our lives worthy and beautiful
Only the fool would give in to sadness
When we can make merry and be gay
I'm ready to dissipate with grace, as
I've lived and loved, and also been loved

Honour my "last" wishes with deference
On the when and the how of my adieu
It's a cosmic law that we came
From the earth and return to it
So, cremate me and scatter my ashes
Somewhere in the vast Pacific Ocean

Then, I'll be the current in the sea
The wind over the Canadian Rockies
And the Taiwan Central Mountain Range
I'll be the spectacular clouds and rain
Over Vancouver Island and beyond
In zillions of molecules, I'll be there

8.3. Sex, Online Dating, Pornography, and Old Age

SEX IS IMPORTANT FOR PEOPLE AT ALL AGES ALL OVER THE WORLD, AS shown by "A Global Survey of Sexual Behaviours" by Kevan Wylie et al.

(2009). The percentage of respondents who "agreed or strongly agreed" with the statement that "sex is beneficial for your general health and well being" ranged from 91% in Brazil to 28% in Thailand. The frequency of having sex weekly tended to be lower for seniors aged over 65 (40%) as compared with those aged 20–49 (65–70%); and just 44% of all participants and 41% of seniors aged 65+ were "fully satisfied" with their sexual life. A study by Stacy Lindau et al. (2007) of 3,005 US adults 57–85 years of age also found that sexual activity declines with age: 73%, 53%, and 26% for the those aged 57–64, 65–74, and 75–85 years, respectively. About half of those who are sexually active reported at least one bothersome sexual problem: low desire (43%), difficulty with vaginal lubrication (39%), and inability to climax (34%) among women and erectile difficulties (37%) among men.

Thus, it would seem that many seniors are still active sexually and are enjoying it despite some sexual problems, although over half of them are not sexually active. Public perceptions, however, are often negative, as Belinda Kessel pointed out in "Sexuality in the Older Person" (2001): "Sexuality simply does not exist," "Sexuality is funny," and "Sexuality is disgusting." (p. 121) It is not easy for seniors to have a healthy sexual life, as depicted in the movie, *All Together*, a French movie about five 70-something seniors who decide to live together. In order to have sex in that movie, Claude spends his time photographing young, nude prostitutes at local cathouses, and he pays for the service rendered. Jeanne, who is afflicted with terminal cancer while her husband begins losing his memory, can only talk frankly about her romantic life with a young German student, hired as a dog-walker, who is doing research for his thesis on these five septuagenarians. How tragic! So many barriers for seniors to find sexually compatible, loving partners! Besides, sex is such an awkward topic that even after forty years, infidelity remains an explosive, emotional issue among these friends in that movie.

It is doubly difficult for many elderly women than for men to find compatible sexual partners, since women tend to outlive men, and men often find younger sexual partners. As sexual needs for older men and women are not that different than those of their younger counterparts, it's important that more socially acceptable opportunities be created and provided to seniors. This is particularly the case for seniors living in institutional settings such as nursing homes, where there is little privacy to be had. Therefore, opportunities for finding a suitable sexual partner are extremely limited for the elderly, especially if they are also disabled, overweight, ugly, and socially isolated.

Since beauty is in the eyes of the beholder, all you need is to find one person who appreciates you and you reciprocate. Internet dating has become increasingly popular these days, and according to Anderson (2016), "Statistics suggest that about 1 in 5 relationships begin online nowadays. It's estimated that by 2040, 70% of us will have met our significant other online." I was curious a few years ago, thinking as a writer I need to know what internet dating was about, so I signed up with *match.com*, a leading online dating site. I met online a number of ladies both locally and faraway, and several of them in person. Seeing their profile descriptions and pictures online was one thing, meeting them in person was another, as I found out that the two often did not jibe and did not generate the same kinds of chemistry in person as anticipated. Indeed, the chemistry between two people is such a mysterious yet critical phenomenon that it makes or breaks relationships. This reminds me of one of my tenants, Diane—my little house near the university has a basement suite as a rental unit—whose dad in Toronto mail-ordered a bride from Taiwan. Can you imagine that in this day and age? Anyway, according to Diane, her dad took a dislike of the bride with just one look, but didn't have the heart to send her back. That first impression sealed the fate of that family: her dad's neglect of her mom by being a workaholic, her mom's resentment towards her dad transferring towards her. In addition to abusing her, her mom eventually became psychotic, thus resulting in a very dysfunctional family.

Online dating works, sometimes, however. I spotted my Russian friend, Nina, on the internet and contacted her some years ago. She looked so elegant in her posted picture, and no wonder . . . she was a fashion designer in Toronto . . . and she was an outdoor enthusiast. We hit on each other well and became pen pals. When she was going to join a research team to do fieldwork in the wilderness of Northwest Territories via Edmonton, I invited her to stay at my house. She accepted my invitation without hesitation, and I let her stay in my sunroom, which she appreciated greatly, as she was able to see the trees and sky through the glass ceiling when lying on the bed. I took her to Elk Island National Park to hike and see the bison, to the University of Alberta's Devonian Garden to participate in a Japanese tea ceremony, and we biked to the Provincial Museum to see the natural history exhibition. We had a great time together.

Nina kept saying that St. Petersburg is the most beautiful city in the world, and we talked about travelling to Russia together, to also visit Moscow, and then taking trans-Siberia railway all the way to China. If we were to do that, though, it would take more than a month! I asked her what she'd like to see in China, and she said the most scenic places. I told her that Kweilin is known to be the most scenic place in the world from my high school geography course, and the Yellow Mountain is the best known of all the sacred mountains in China. When I showed her the pictures of these two places after she returned to Toronto from the Northwest Territories, she was so taken in by the beauty of these places that she set her mind for the China trip. Since I hadn't been to these places either, I concurred. At my suggestion, Nina also convinced her two daughters and the younger one's boyfriend to join us. So I found a reputable travel agent, negotiated a travel package for the five of us—including an itinerary for climbing the Yellow Mountain with a guide, accommodations there and at Kweilin, the train tickets to Kweilin and a travel guide at Kweilin. I also pre-booked hostels in Shanghai, Suchow, and Hangchow so we could visit famed Chinese gardens and West Lake. We had a great time together in China.

After the China trip, Nina and I continued on to Taiwan while the young ones went back home. I kept telling Nina that we were leaving China for Taiwan, but Nina insisted that we were still in China. I guess I didn't convince Nina that we had left China when we boarded the plane heading toward Taiwan, where I had booked a bed-and-breakfast place near the gorgeous Taroko National Park, and also at Jiaoxi, to enable us to go to Japanese Bathhouse for a dip in soothing hot springs. While in Taipei, we visited the National Palace Museum in Shilin, which has a collection of nearly 700,000 pieces of ancient Chinese imperial artefacts and artworks. We had a fantastic time in Taiwan, and Nina thought Taiwan's Taroko was more spectacular than the Yellow Mountain. Maybe it was because Taroko was where the impressive gorge was located along a cross-island highway that took us to the Hehuan Mountain Pass. Our itinerary there included a bicycle trip from the pass down along the highway back to the lodge. It was an exhilarating ride, and I had an accident falling from the bike because I was following Nina down a hill. Seeing that we had to go uphill again, I accelerated trying to pass her from the left when I spied a car coming from the opposite side. So I veered to the right, but Nina did the same. In order to avoid crashing into her, I braked hard and fell, landing on my left hand on the pavement. Luckily, a car stopped for us, and a lady helped me bandage my left hand. Farther down we stopped at a fruit stand, and the lady owner also helped me to put some herbal ointment on my wound to prevent infection. Eventually, my bike brake gave way because of the steepness of the road, so I phone the lodge owner from the roadside telephone to come and pick us up. Nina, though, did not take the ride and rode all the way back to the lodge. It was a highlight of our trip despite the mishap, and I was grateful to the two ladies as my hand healed in a couple weeks without any infection.

Nina told me after the trip that her daughters asked her why she had trusted me—having met me through the internet. She told them that she could tell I was trustworthy and not faking to take advantage of her. It's interesting that our friendship has been platonic all along—even when we slept on the same bed during the trip in Taiwan, it never occurred to me to treat her as a sex object, and I suspect she responded likewise. Sex is important, but we don't treat everyone as a sex object. Sexual attractions are special . . . isn't that something?

Well, if you are single and do not have a sex partner, a fuck buddy, you could look through adult classifieds, pick a spa, and find a partner there. Or you could go to a red-light district and pick someone on the street. But there are risks involved, as buying sex may be illegal, and having sex with a prostitute or a stranger may result in you contacting a sexually transmitted disease. It may be safer, less embarrassing, and less expensive—even free—to watch pornography for sexual gratification. I was amazed, when I was studying acupuncture at MacEwan University, that the campus newspaper published an article on pornography and listed an internet site featuring free sex videos. Again, out of curiosity, I clicked on the site and sure enough, all sorts of sex videos were there: women of all ethnicities and different hair colours, teens, mature women, European, Asian, black, etc. I wonder, though, why these women, and men, are willing to perform sex acts for video recordings; money must have been paid handsomely—but since viewings are free, how do the producers make money? Do they sell the videos to someone else? I have no idea. Well, unlike the good old days, sex scenes can be seen everywhere nowadays in the movies since many movie actresses no longer have any inhibition to appear nude and perform sex on screen. The internet has changed everything, and we can watch sex scenes in the comfort of our homes for free or pay nominal fees. Self-gratification isn't as satisfying as good partner sex, but it still is something most of us can have—regardless of how unattractive we are or how we feel about ourselves, because of age, looks, disability, etc. True, most of the videos may be unappealing, since they may be violent, vulgar, or ugly, not your type, and so on, but we can choose the ones we like. In addition to sexual gratification, we may get sex education out of watching, learning what to do and what not to do, so that we'd have more beautiful and more satisfying experience when we have a sexual encounter with a partner we love. Actually, Saad (2010) makes a surprising claim based on scientific evidence-based authoritative studies, which is: "pornography is good for you."

Of course, not all forms of pornography can be endorsed, such as those involving paedophiles, sexual exploitation or objectification disregarding the feelings of others, violence against the partner, inflicting bodily or emotional harm, etc. However, we may have to re-examine our attitudes toward sexuality and sexually explicit material as well as opportunities for human interaction, especially in relation to the elderly and other disad-vantaged individuals, in order to promote sexual and social health for all. Moreover, we need to be increasingly vigilant about the internet scam-ming . . . so I wrote the following poem:

To an Anonymous Internet Scammer / Free Verse / 2015

I have a good, healthy, and creative life, but
I'd have a better life in a much nicer world
I long for a world where duplicity is history
A just society where we treat each other civilly

I can't reshape the world all by myself
But I can alter how I relate and react to it
I can't change the way you do your business
But I'll deal with people like you more wisely

We'd have better lives by trusting each other
So why didn't we treat each other more nicely?
Why did you kowtow to the almighty dollar
Scamming me on the Internet with sweet lies?

Do you realize what you've actuary done
Fantasizing that the world of deceit is fun?
By scamming for your personal financial gain
You've helped create a broken, guileful world

You know, the truth is, we are all interrelated
So, no one can be truly happy if others aren't
If you don't try to make other people happy
It will likely come back and haunt you later

You see, the world is in a horrendous mess
'Cause people like you only care about yourself
It's the same stories of selfishness everywhere
At the personal, national, and international levels

So, treat others as you'd like to be treated
To make the world a better place for all
I have a good life no matter what you do
But I'd have a better life if I could count on you

I'd like to thank you, though, for your trickery
Through which I experienced a real-life crime story
As a writer, I could narrate your clever scheme
And who knows, it could become a best seller!

9.

Culture and Environmental Sustainability

> If human vices such as greed and envy are systematically
> cultivated, the inevitable result is nothing less than a col-
> lapse of intelligence. (Schumacher, 1999/1973, p. 18)

I CAN'T AGREE MORE WITH SCHUMACHER'S (1999/1973) STATEMENT:
"Excessive wealth, like power, tends to corrupt...They corrupt themselves
by practicing greed, and they corrupt the rest of society by provoking envy."
(p. 236) I can understand, and even forgive, Deng Xiaoping, who may or
may not have uttered the famous line, "To get rich is glorious"—since
China needed to reform and promote an entrepreneurial culture in the
late 1970s and early 1980s. However, it's "a collapse of intelligence"—to
use Schumacher's phrase—and it's highly immoral to perpetuate that
mentality in the twenty-first century, as O'Leary and others like him are
still preaching.

Why? Because we have a colossal problem: the world is getting to be full
and too small for us. The earth can no longer accommodate the continued,
explosive expansion of human populations, activities, and interests without
negatively affecting all living creatures. In Alberta, Canada, where I live,
there have been high-stakes conflicts over oil sands pipelines: Keystone
XL to the US Gulf Coast, and Northern Gateway to the Pacific Coast.
The $15.1 billion takeover of Calgary-based Nexen Inc. by China's state-
owned company, CNOOC, has also raised the eyebrows about Canada's
energy and foreign takeover policies. China has an insatiable appetite
for oil to sustain her industrial development, and is investing globally in

oil-producing countries around the world. As China's deputy minister of environment, Pan Yue, noted in his *Der Spiegel* interview (Lorenz, 2005), China's miraculous economic growth isn't sustainable because of massive environmental degradation:

> Acid rain is falling on one-third of the Chinese territory, half of the water in our seven largest rivers is completely useless, while one-fourth of our citizens does not have access to clean drinking water. One-third of the urban population is breathing polluted air, and less than 20 percent of the trash in cities is treated and processed in an environmentally sustainable manner. Finally, five of the ten most polluted cities worldwide are in China.

Pan was concerned, because:

> We are using too many raw materials to sustain this growth. To produce goods worth $10,000, for example, we need seven times more resources than Japan, nearly six times more than the United States and, perhaps most embarrassing, nearly three times more than India. Things can't, nor should they be allowed to go on like that. (Lorenz, 2005)

Obviously, all of us must do things differently to reduce resource inputs and use: by working smarter, improving efficiency and quality, cutting waste, foregoing the needless use of materials and procedures, living simply and more frugally, etc. Thomas Friedman, the author of *The World Is Flat* (2005), was asked by a young Chinese woman, "Why should China have to restrain its energy consumption and worry about the environment, when America and Europe got to consume all the energy they wanted when they were developing?" (p. 500) Friedman didn't have a good answer to this question, but the answer is obvious—times have changed, and we are in this all together. The United States and Canada, in particular, should be shamed into accepting their moral responsibilities for drastically reducing their energy consumption, in addition to helping China and other countries develop renewable energy sources and technologies to improve/reduce energy use. We should all cooperate, rather than compete, to solve our common problems, to make the only world a better place to live. Competition will make the matter worse, not better.

What we need, therefore, is to critically re-examine and reshape our cultures to render them kinder, gentler, more empathic and collaborative, more democratic, and more sustainable. Every year at Christmas time, a huge neon sign, "PEACE ON EARTH," graced the top of the entrance to the University of Alberta Hospital. We should make peaceful resolution of conflict a 24/7/365 affair in all corners of the world, and forbid the use of force except as a last resort—justifiable only for self-defence. To make this work, democracy is a must—to allow for protests against perceived injustices through peaceful means. I used to admire China for promoting internationalism. Even today, large placards are affixed to the Tiananmen gate in Beijing, which read, in Chinese, "Long live the solidarity of the people of the world." Interestingly, "Long live the solidarity of the people" remains a slogan for the European Left to fight against neoliberal austerity measures and to defend "solidarity, justice, and equality." We definitely need to promote a culture of solidarity, empathy, collaboration, and mutual help as the dominant philosophy of globalization.

We are indeed very short-sighted, not thinking beyond our own immediate interests. But how about other people and the next generations of people who need to share Earth's precious resources? To those who are oblivious of the rights of other people, including those who come after us, I wrote the following poems:

On Intergenerational Morality / Analyzed Rhyme / 2012

Why does ethics between generations
Pose extreme difficulty to philosophers?
Isn't it evident that we have obligations
To our future generations and ancestors?
Moral relativism is the culprit
Seeing justice as "local" in place and time
And not between generations in its paradigm

The trans-generational community
Is a necessary ethical framework
For intergenerational morality
Let's fight relativistic irrationality
To resolve conceptual difficulty
Which involves a historical perspective
Of all generations as an imperative

On the Kyoto Protocol and Intergenerational Justice / Satirical Verse / 2012

Climate change? Bah humbug! Just a racket
To bring confusion to our scientific mindset
Global temperatures have changed cyclically
But stayed flat for over a decade, magically

Human activity isn't the one causing
Arctic ice sheets to be decreasing
Hotter climates may lead to more illnesses
But we'll triumph and cope with any distresses

The Kyoto protocol must be a joke
So the Tories have to denounce and revoke
The treaty signed by the Liberal government
Risking international embarrassment

Now that the Liberals are gone and no more
The Tory majority ignores the uproar
Choosing economy over ecology
Sticking righteously to their ideology

The oil from the tar sands may be "dirty"
But it's a ticket to our prosperity
We have the right to do what we please
Though future generations may feel unease

They are yet to be born and have no rights
They can't gain voices by initiating fights
Rawls' just saving principle won't save them
Cost-benefit discounts won't solve the problem

Don't our children's grandchildren need our love?
Don't the Tories want their rights well thought of
In their ethical theory and practice
As intergenerational justice?

9.1. Cooperation, Competition, and Globalization

I HAD A CAR ACCIDENT ON THE CHRISTMAS EVE IN 2009, ON MY WAY TO
my daughter's house in a small town of Rimbey an hour-and-a-half drive
from Edmonton. The car hit black ice on the shoulder of the south-bound
highway, went into the median strip between the south- and the north-
bound highways, and overturned in the snow-packed strip, and the car

was totalled. Luckily, my daughter's sister-in-law (who was sitting in the passenger seat) and I escaped unhurt, not even a scratch. As the Chinese saying goes, "After surviving the worst, great fortunes will follow." I resolved to be carless since, and it was a blessing. I walk or bike every-where—to go grocery shopping, to my classes, or just to go for a walk or a bike ride. And, of course, I also get rides from my friends, and use the public transportation from time to time. On rare occasions, I hire a taxi/Uber; and I have kept my driver's licence so I can rent a car when a friend or relative comes for a visit. My life is simpler and yet, on balance, healthier and more satisfying than before. I can live a simple life because I can do a vast majority of my day-to-day activities close to where I live. Nearly everything is right there: a university, a hospital, a community centre with tennis courts, a public library, several supermarkets and health food stores, restaurants, movie theatres, all sorts of little shops, and even a farmers' market. I have neither a need nor a desire to visit fast food stores or coffee shops such as Tim Horton's, Subway, McDonald, Starbucks, etc., and, of course, I rarely shop at big box stores like Wal-Mart and Best Buy, which aren't within walking/biking distance anyway. By default, necessity and choice, I've been practising "Buy local, think global," and I think I have a much healthier and better-quality life than before my car accident.

One of the biggest challenges facing us all is to minimize our eco-logical footprints, to aim for a more sustainable future. We need to keep reminding ourselves: "It's the quality, not quantity, stupid!" and "Less is more." A life without a car is free from worries about purchasing, operat-ing, and maintenance and insurance expenses for a car, so I've more money in my pockets now to do things I want to do: exploring, experiencing, learning, and writing. This way of living and thinking, I know, is going against the philosophy of neoliberal market consumerism, which is based on greed, competition, and "more is more." When I travelled to Japan, Taiwan and China, or to France, I always wondered why Starbucks, KFC, and McDonald's were there. As a tourist, it's nice to be able to sip a cup of coffee once in a while and use their clean washrooms, but I really, really wonder why they are there, since the locals have better, more interesting, and more nutritious foods and beverages. As I read about "4 Countries

That Wal-Mart Has Failed To Impress" in *Business Insider*, October 11, 2013, it puzzled me to no end as to why Wal-Mart even wanted to expand its operation into India, Russia, Germany, and South Korea. What drives this business ideology of insatiable expansion and quest for more and more profit? Haven't they driven out enough competitors at home and abroad and made enough fortunes already? When is enough, enough?

I audited a course on international development in 2013 offered by Professor Jennifer Hsu, and learned a great deal about the winners and losers of globalization. China and other East Asian countries benefited the most, as indicated by a reduction in the share of extremely poor people in the world from 57% in 1980 to about 23% by 2005. Globalization, on the other hand, didn't benefit Latin America and Africa as much. Nevertheless, for many people all over the world, "there is simply no alternative but to jump on the globalization express train . . . Capitalism has triumphed worldwide . . . Developing countries have to conform, and if they do not they will be left out" (Beaudet, 2009, p. 108). Some of my friends in Taiwan too didn't want to move their factories or businesses to China, but they did. They felt they didn't have any choice if they were to remain competitive. This "hollowing out and offshoring" of Taiwan's economy worries Taiwan's youth and small business owners, and it was a motivation behind the 2014 student Sunflower Movement in opposition to the service trade pact with China. According to Shelley Rigger of Davidson College, the author of *Why Taiwan Matters: Small Island, Global Powerhouse*, however, it's Taiwan's globalization, stupid!

> [I]t's really not China that's driving Taiwan's economic malaise—it's globalization and twenty-first-century capitalism. So I'm not sure that refusing to integrate further with the PRC economy will solve their problems, but I admire them for standing up and saying, "Stop!" (Wasserstrom, 2014)

Taiwan's problem, therefore, is no different than those faced by the Americans and the Canadians, and people in many countries around the globe for decades. For the Taiwanese, however, the elephant is right in their midst and next to them. To many of us, the globalization express train is clearly on a disastrous track and out of control, fuelled by the neoliberal ideology of greed and market competition, benefiting some at the expense of others. It does not benefit everyone. We really, really need a better vision of globalization, to focus on international (and domestic) collaboration on maintaining peace, eliminating poverty, protecting environment, and sharing energy and other resources, so as to provide a decent living for all. That was the intent of my open-access paper (Chang & Fraser, 2017) to plead for a cultural shift from competition to cooperation. We need to create a sense of community for the entire world, a world citizenship, to work toward the goal of health and well-being for all. We should cooperate always and say *no* to competition, lest we create more losers and leave them behind. Such a cultural shift would entail working towards a cooperative society at personal, community, and policy levels, including education, health, worker and consumer cooperatives, etc., to advance democracy at the workplace and everywhere else. Evidently, we have the task cut out for us.

One of such cooperative tasks may be interstellar travel, as suggested by the Cambridge University physicist Stephen Hawking. He called on the world to dedicate 0.25% of all its financial resources towards setting up settlements, first on the moon, then on Mars, and beyond. Hawking was not totally optimistic about the future of humankind, and he was quoted as saying "that primitive life is relatively common, but that intelligent life is very rare . . . Some would say it has yet to occur on Earth." (Barak, 2008) Well, I couldn't agree more with Hawking's "undisguised dry humour." Seriously, though, our priority should be to make our planet a better place for all of us before thinking of colonizing the moon or Mars, lest we risk perpetuating human conflict in future space colonies. An intriguing question, in my view, therefore, is whether we are intelligent enough to cooperate and work together for hundreds and thousands of years to ensure long-term human survival and prosperity. Therein lies the rub! Some people adore competition, saying we can have "healthy competition." Really? I say it's an oxymoron:

No Such Thing as "Healthy Competition" / Free Verse / 2016

Competition is our cultural obsession
Creating some winners and plenty of losers
The rich and powerful, and the poor and powerless
To us, winning's everything, it's the only thing

Why do we compete if someone has to lose?
We know losing is bad for you and me
It creates inferior-superior states of mind,
Rewarding the winners but not the losers

Research clearly shows that competition is bad
It drives a wedge among us, makes us jealous
Focuses less on doing well than on winning
So, why do we compete when we don't have to?

"Healthy competition" is an oxymoron
There is nothing healthy about competition
It's immoral to feel good for beating someone
Turning us into sadists, knowingly or not

Competition does boost our morale at times
Make us work harder to avoid being failures
It's just a negative prop like electric shock
So we could dodge being taunted and called chicken

But winning and doing well are not the same thing
We can easily do well without competing
We can and should live life cooperatively
In work and leisure, politics and economics

I play tennis year-round for its athleticism
Just rally the balls with my partners, no games played
It's good for our health, and we are having fun
We've improved our skills over time, and we're happy

We should live our world more cooperatively
So we don't keep turning most of us into losers
Knowing the devil we must avoid is the first step
The next is to find ways to live our lives better

9.2. The Truth About Sustainability

TRUTH, LIKE THE EMPEROR'S NEW CLOTHES IN THAT FAMED HANS Anderson's fable, can be so transparent that it escapes people's notice. That happens to competition in our daily life and especially in the business world, since monopoly often reigns without it—as John Stuart Mill pointed out more than a hundred years ago—and goods often become unaffordable and inaccessible. Therefore, we take competition for granted. It has always been seen as a virtue, and we can't imagine a world without it.

Times have changed, however, and so has our relationship with the world. The Earth used to be so vast, its resources so inexhaustible, relative to human activities that we were free to do and take whatever we want without affecting the integrity of its ecosystem. With the rapid technological advancement and the human population growth, that era of uninhibited freedom to do whatever we want is rapidly coming to an end. We have come to the painful realization that the Earth's resources are limited, and we have to cooperate and share such resources as air, land, water, plants, fish stock, etc. in order to prevent our societies from collapsing.

This situation is closely related to what the American ecologist and philosopher Garrett Hardin in 1968 called "the tragedy of the Commons"— that if ranchers graze their animals in a common land, unregulated over-grazing to maximize self-interest would lead to the depletion of that resource to the benefit of no one. Jared Diamond (2005), in a fascinating book *Collapse: How Societies Choose to Fail or Succeed*, documents why once-mighty cultures such as those of the Maya cities in Central America, Angkor Wat in Indo-China, and Easter Island in the Pacific Ocean disappeared. Due to deforestation, soil erosion, water management problems, overhunting, overfishing, human population growth, toxic chemical pollutions, etc., there had been food shortages, starvation, violence, and wars, etc. in these societies, leading to their collapse. It is time, therefore, to re-examine and repudiate our ethics and especially economic theories based on maximizing self-interest which sanctions competition, so as to head off the collapse of our globalized society.

I feel like the little boy who yelled, "But the Emperor has no clothes!" The culture of competition is not what people make it out to be. It is neither virtuous nor necessary. In fact, it's crystal clear to me that it is immoral, and it will lead us down the garden path of destruction. The use of competition as a means of conflict resolution is to sanction the ethics of "the might is right": to reward those with more intelligence, more strength, more power, more wealth, more greed, etc. It's a sure way to create winners and losers, and to maintain an unequal society in terms of social status, wealth and power—in addition to the overuse of resources since "more is better." It is totally against the philosophy and goal of sustainability. To be sustainable, we have to work together to live within our Earth's means, and sooner the better.

As I mentioned in relation to Native rights in Section 6.2, my home province of Alberta is facing monumental, strategic planning decisions by the new NDP government—which came to power in 2015 after forty years of the Tory rule. Alberta used to rely on the export of agricultural products such as wheat and beef until a major oil field was discovered at Leduc near Edmonton in 1947. When the oil prices soared during the 1967 Oil Embargo, the 1973 oil crisis, and the 1979 energy crisis, Alberta's economy boomed, and Alberta became a land of opportunity. Following the slogan of that time, "Go West, young man," I packed all my belongings into my beat-up Volkswagen van in 1975 after completing my doctoral degree at the University of Toronto, drove all the way across the vast

Canadian prairies, and settled down in Edmonton, the capital city of the province of Alberta, where I've stayed ever since. Like Alberta's economy, my fortune rose and fell with oil prices—I was laid off twice from my positions in hospital care: once during the oil glut in the mid-1980s when the entire research department at the hospital I was working was closed down, and again in the mid-1990s when the Conservative government cut public health care spending by 21%.

I was extremely fortunate to find good employment soon after my layoffs, but I kept thinking we could have managed economy much better, like Norway with a trillion-dollar heritage trust fund. Why didn't Alberta do the same when times were good, rather than squandering the fortune away to a puny $17.5 billion as of December 31, 2017? Looking at a bigger picture and thinking globally, why can't we manage the economy more sustainably worldwide, so we can share the fruits of our productions to provide a decent living to everyone in the world while protecting Earth's ecosystems? Isn't that the goal we should set locally, nationally, and globally?

Living in a cold climate, my utility bill—including water, gas, electricity, garbage collection—for a small, 1-bedroom house is $4,500 for the year 2017, or over $12 a day. Thus, energy is a big deal here, perhaps more so than in warmer places in the world. We are, however, blessed with the world's largest oil reserve outside of Saudi Arabia; thus, we have been enjoying a higher standard of living than the rest of Canada—and even higher than the United States—in recent decades. Now that we are at a crossroad of balancing economic development with the environment, not only here in Alberta but also in Canada, North America, and globally, we really need to garner all the necessary wisdom to navigate the treacherous waters of domestic and international politics to negotiate, design, and implement a sound energy policy—to meet the energy, environmental, and income expectations of so many domestic and international players—for the present and future generations. Instead of fighting out politically and legally, it is better if all the players engage in a more collaborative and conciliatory approach and work out mutually satisfactory solutions to this complex undertaking.

I still recall, at the 2016 NDP national convention, the Leap Manifesto was presented, urging, among other things, the adoption of proposals for Canada to shift away from fossil fuels so that Canada gets 100% of its electricity from renewable resources within twenty years, and no fossil fuels by 2050; and no new infrastructure projects, including pipelines, to be built to increase extraction of non-renewable resources. The manifesto didn't go over very well at the convention, as Alberta NDP Premier Rachel Notley, who supported pipelines, blasted it. I can't imagine why the sponsors of the manifesto didn't consult and work together with the Alberta government to come up with more satisfying proposals that would include a strategic plan, plus concrete and workable steps, to bring about a transition to renewable resources that would also be acceptable to the Alberta government. At present, about 87% of the electricity in Alberta is produced from fossil fuels—47% from coal, and 40% from natural gas. Without a plan, the Leap proposals, although well intended, are just naïve, utopian, unenforceable goals. In fact, the authors of *The Leap Manifesto* may have come to different conclusions and recommendations, had they done an in-depth analysis of Canada's demand and supply of energy to 2050—as done by David Hugh (2018) in his report, *Canada's Energy Outlook*, which documents how difficult and challenging for Canada, including Alberta, it will be to make a transition to renewables and aspires to reduce emissions 30% by 2030 and 80% by 2050 from 2005 levels. No wonder Alberta's Environment Minister Shannon Phillips called *The Leap Manifesto* "ungenerous" and "short-sighted." Can we transcend the "stone-age mentality," work better together, and agree on a good public policy?

Our Future / Free Verse / 2011

Our stone-age mentality, which is myopic
Temperamental, irrational, and egoistic
Together with threats of natural calamities
Will lead to the downfall of humanities

Our failure to live in harmony with nature
Has imperilled the next generations' future
Enamoured and driven by insatiable greed
We blindly follow the more-is-better creed

Our relentless quest for absolute dominance
Engenders widespread anger and resistance
The hell with winning the heart and mind
We will be worshipped even if we are unkind

That logic will lead to an impending doom
And not to an overall prosperity and boom
The wind of change is blowing everywhere
Everyone wants to be treated fair and square

But then, we need a cultural makeover
To resist the stone-age mentality taking over
We must denounce the use of force
To settle any dispute as a matter of course

9.3. Ecological Footprints and Economics

ONE OF THE BEST MEASURES OF ECOLOGICAL SUSTAINABILITY IS THE ECO-
logical footprint, the concept created by Canadian ecologist William Rees
and his Swiss urban planner-student Mathis Wackernagel. The ecological
footprint is "a land-based surrogate measure of the population's demands
on natural capital," and is defined as "the total area of productive land and
water required continuously to produce all the resources consumed and to
assimilate all the wastes produced, by a defined population, wherever on
Earth that land is located" (Rees & Wackernagel, 1996, pp. 228–229).

According to their calculations, there are only about 1.5 hectares (ha)
of such land available for each person in the world, whereas the ecological

footprint of residents of richer countries has steadily increased to, for example, 4–5 ha per capita for North Americans. This is "three times their fair share of the Earth's bounty," which they acknowledged to be an under-estimate. In their view, therefore, our current level of consumption is clearly unsustainable:

> By extrapolation, if everyone on Earth lived like the average North American, the total land requirement would exceed 26 billion hectares. However there are fewer than 9 billion hectares of such land on Earth. This means that we would need three such planets to support just the present human family. (Rees & Wackernagel, 1996, p. 238)

Not only our current and future levels of economic activities are unsustainable, Rees (2010) further argued that growth-inducing globalization and trade "actually contribute to unsustainability," because "conventional economic logic is based on false assumptions and monetary measures of efficiency that are wholly divorced from biophysical reality" (pp. 1-2). Moreover,

> The economic benefits of trade-induced growth go primarily to the already wealthy who don't need them while the collateral social costs weigh most heavily on the poor. Meanwhile, trade effectively extends the ecological footprints of importing nations halfway around the globe. (Rees, 2010, pp. 1–2)

Thus, importing nations extend their ecological footprints to other nations beyond their own national borders, contributing to the ecological degradation and future export capacity and sustainability of exporting nations. The continuous expansion of global trade is seen as creating "an inherently unstable 'entanglement of nations' that accelerates the entropic dissipation of the ecosphere" (Rees, 2010, p. 2)

Thus, from the point of view of ecological footprints, all of us—rich or poor—need to re-examine our worldview and our way of life. For the rich, we may be living way beyond our means, and we need to drastically reduce our personal ecological footprints by using less of Earth's resources. For the poor, who aspire to obtain a better-quality life, it is also necessary to achieve it in such a way as to minimize wasteful resource use. Instead of blindly advocating globalization, which tends to further increase our ecological footprints, we must promote "buy local" more, as appropriate, to encourage local production and consumption.

It is possible to reverse the trend of ever-increasing ecological footprints with a global consensus and concerted efforts to implement a technology-driven transition to low-carbon energy. As Christiana Figueres et al. (2017) states:

> In the past three years, global emissions of carbon dioxide from the burning of fossil fuels have levelled after rising for decades. This is a sign that policies and investments in climate mitigation are starting to pay off. The United States, China and other nations are replacing coal with natural gas and boosting renewable energy sources. There is almost unanimous international agreement that the risks of abandoning the planet to climate change are too great to ignore. (p. 593)

It was this trend that made the 2015 Paris climate agreement possible, and yet, as Figueres et al. also noted: "The political winds are blustery. President Donald Trump has announced that the United States will withdraw from the Paris agreement when it is legally able to do so, in November 2020" (p. 593)

Now, there are those, like President Trump, who dismiss the need for collective actions to combat global warming, which has already happened 1.0 °C above the preindustrial temperature, aiming to limit the rise below 2.0 °C by reducing human CO_2 emissions. However, as Will Steffen et al. (2018) warn us in the Proceedings of the National Academy of Sciences in the United States, even if the Paris Accord target of a 1.5–2.0 °C rise in temperature is met, the Earth's system may still cross a planetary threshold due to a cascade of feedbacks, pushing it irreversibly onto a "Hothouse Earth" pathway and leading to "a much higher global temperature than any interglacial in the past 1.2 million years and to sea levels significantly higher than at any time in the Holocene." A safer personal and public policy, I maintain, is to do as much as we can to minimize carbon emissions and reduce ecological footprints. While I try to do my best to do just that, we need to redouble our efforts—and good public policies to help design and enforce such practices.

For developing such public policies, we need a new paradigm of ecological economics—what Herman Daly (2005) called "economics in a full world"—one of the topics featured in Professor Laurie Adkin's fall, 2018 course, "Ecology and Politics", at the University of Alberta. According to Daly,

> When the economy's expansion encroaches too much on its surrounding ecosystem, we will begin to sacrifice natural capital (such as fish, minerals and fossil fuels) that is worth more than the man-made capital (such as roads, factories and appliances) added by the growth. We will then have what I call uneconomic growth, producing "bads" faster than goods—making us poorer, not richer... Once we pass the optimal scale, growth becomes stupid in the short run and impossible to maintain in the long run. (p. 100)

Since, in his opinion, we may already have entered the uneconomic growth phase, he further pleads: "Humankind must make the transition to a sustainable economy— one that takes heed of the inherent biophysical limits of the global ecosystem," otherwise "we may be cursed not just with uneconomic growth but with an ecological catastrophe that would sharply lower living standards. (p. 100) Clearly, we urgently need to move away from our current growth paradigm, towards a new economic paradigm that also aims at safeguarding the integrity of our ecological system. This is because, in Capra & Jakobsen's (2017, p. 836) words: "In ecological economics, the economy, interpreted as an integral part of society and nature, is filled with meaning. Every economic activity should be a servant of life."—so that it aims at maximizing wellbeing of entire ecosystems, including human and non-human beings, since "the well-being of the ecology of our planet is tied to the quality of human life." (p. 837)

Daly, of course, recognizes that avoiding uneconomic growth is not easy, since "some people benefit from uneconomic growth…In addition, our national accounts do not register the costs of growth for all to see." (p. 100) One way to effect changes at the organizational level is to promote what Marjorie Kelly (2012, p. 11) called "generative ownership"—designed to put organizational control in the hands of people who have a natural interest in the health of their communities and local ecosystems—in contrast to the dominant ownership models, which Kelly calls "extractive". Such organizations include worker-owned and consumer cooperatives, customer-owned banks, wind farms operated by "wind guilds, and so on—e.g., the Evergreen Cooperative Laundry, Ohio Cooperative Solar, and Green City Growers in Cleveland, Ohio. (Kelly, 2012, pp. 1-2) As Kelly puts it,

> Ownership is the gravitational field that holds our economy in its orbit, locking us all into behaviors that lead to financial excess and ecological overshoot. (p. 8)

The key to promote sustainability, therefore, is to tackle the ownership issue to ensure its community orientation and ecological friendliness—e.g., by incorporating the concept of eco-housing, villages and communities that strive to live sustainably, restore the land, and often experimenting with new forms of communal governance and decision making. (Capra & Jakobsen's (2017, p. 839)

At the personal level, too, it is not always easy to change our lifestyles to minimize our ecological footprints, for example, as the promotion of designated bicycle lanes in our city of Edmonton has generated mixed reactions from car drivers. Having been corrupted by the convenience of automobile, fast food, etc., we need a wakeup call to act smarter!

Biking to the Farmer's Market / Memorial Stanza / 2009

Off to the farmer's market I biked
Energized by strong pedaling
Touched by a cool autumn feeling
I smiled and whistled as I liked

But, alas, bikes and cars don't mix
Rude, mindless drivers make me cry
To busy Whyte Ave I bid goodbye
A neighbourhood street is my fix

It is great to shop there weekly
Buy local and get fresh produce
Healthy mind-body I induce
Good for me and my family

9.4. Violence, Domination, and Sustainability

IT SHOULD BE NOTED THAT ECOLOGICAL FOOTPRINTS ONLY PARTIALLY estimate the ecological impact because such calculations neither take into account the natural disasters such as windstorms and floods, nor human violence such as bombing and chemical warfare, which harm the sustainability of human ecology. According to the Institute for Economics and Peace (2016), the impact of human conflict and violence in 2015 on the global economy alone is enormous: $13.6 trillion in purchasing power parity (PPP) terms, 13.3% of world GDP, or $1,876 per person per annum. Military expenditure constitutes 45% ($6.16 trillion) of that total, followed by the internal security expenditure (26%, $3.53 trillion) involving police, judicial, and prison systems spending, among others; and homicide accounts for another 13% ($1.79 trillion). The remaining 16% includes private security spending ($672.8 billion), sexual and violent assault ($544.6 billion), etc. Violence due to civil war affects Syria the most, costing that country 54.1% of GDP in 2015.

Such expenditures on human conflict and violence are totally unnecessary if all conflicts are resolved cooperatively and peacefully rather than competitively and violently. Armed conflicts also have devastating consequences socially, economically, and environmentally, and in fact, are major obstacles to sustainable development. The financial resources devoted to conflict and violence may be viewed as "stolen" from the current and future generations and also from sustainable development. As Botta and Abbasi (2015) emphasized further, it is necessary to promote peaceful conflict resolution as an alternative to violent confrontation, including going beyond one's own social and cultural group and seek "familiarity" with others without "othering" Others (i.e., treating and discriminating against others negatively as different from ourselves). Since causes of violence and war are often due to past grievances, which have often been relegated to the deep recesses of the subconscious mind or the collective memory, it is of critical importance to deal with any past grievances and seek just and collaborative resolutions.

With competition, moreover, many losers would be devastated, becoming anxious and/or depressed. According to the World Health Organization (2016), the number of people suffering from depression and/or anxiety increased by nearly 50% between 1990 and 2013, from 416 million to 615 million; nearly 10% of the world's population is affected, and mental disorders accounted for 30% of the global non-fatal disease burden. The cost of depression and/or anxiety to the global economy is an estimated $1 trillion USD per year.

Depression, moreover, is highly correlated with problem drinking (Sher, 2004; Geisner et al., 2012), as well as with drunk driving (Zhang and Sloan, 2015). Globally, in 2012, 3.3 million deaths resulted from harmful use of alcohol, representing 5.9% (male 7.6%, female 4.0%) of all deaths; and such alcohol-related deaths happened relatively early in life (e.g.,

25% of all deaths in the 20–39 age group) (World Health Organization, 2015a). In fact, road traffic injuries are the top cause of death among those aged 15–29 years, as alcohol is implicated in over 50% of such accidents. Thus, a reduction in road traffic deaths and injuries by 50% by 2020 has been among the Sustainable Development Goals of the World Health Organization (2015b).

Bullying, mental harassment, or physical violence, is a pattern of "unwanted aggressive behaviour" associated with the motivation and practice of domination involving "a real or perceived imbalance of power" (United Nations Educational, Scientific and Cultural Organization 2017). Bullying is particularly devastating for school-age children, and yet according to that report, an estimated 246 million children and adolescents experience school violence and bullying in some form every year, ranging from 10–65% in various countries. Cyberbullying is a growing problem, affecting 5–21% and girls appear to be more likely to experience it than boys. Indeed, global estimates indicate that one in three (35%) of women have experienced physical or sexual violence from their intimate partner or non-partners in their lifetime (World Health Organization, 2017).

Violence, therefore, is a way of life for most of us, affecting us personally or our loved ones. Such a culture is unsustainable, as we are likely to destroy ourselves even without catastrophic natural disasters. The way forward, however, is not to dwell on past-oriented thinking, but to focus on the future, seeking cooperation and peace among us, and for future generations. Unfortunately, as Milojevic (1999) stated in the context of former Yugoslavia, there is a widespread belief that there are just wars, that violence is justified to achieve "just" resolutions, that ends justify means, that the destruction of environment does not matter, that human well-being can be sacrificed for higher goals such as to defend national interests, and that it is necessary to glorify violence and build up military power. As a result, competition and power politics often take precedence over cooperation and negotiation, rendering true reconciliation impossible. As ecological sustainability increasingly depends on human choice, activity, and impact, however, we can no longer take ecological sustainability for granted and assume that Mother Earth will sustain and nourish us forever regardless of what we do. In order not to abuse and safeguard ecological integrity, we need a more sustainable global culture based on the partnership, rather than the domination models, to deal with all others, human and non-human (Eisler, 2007). We must reflect and elevate our "human nature" for a better future.

Human Nature / Senryu / 2015

Human nature is
To place all blame on others
Never on oneself

10.

Living Authentically and Magnanimously

IN TOLSTOY'S NOVEL, *The Death of Ivan Ilych*, THE PROTAGONIST IVAN Ilych assimilates the values and behaviour of those with high social standing. He single-mindedly pursues his career until he hurts himself and gets seriously sick. Only at his deathbed does he realize that only his son and his country-boy nurse, Gerasim, genuinely care about him, while all others, including his wife and his physician, despise him. All his achievements throughout his life—his official life, his family, and social relations—seem artificial to him. In the end, he feels sorry for his son and his wife, and yet he experiences a sense of extreme joy; and in the middle of a sigh, Ivan stretches out and dies.

The world is full of people like Ivan Ilych, pursuing "the American dream" all their lives. And yet they feel sad and empty at their deathbeds; despite the fact that some find peace of mind like Ivan Ilych (though only at the end of his life), others are not as lucky. Why the pervasiveness of such remorse? I'd say, first of all, that people like Ivan Ilych do not know the *truth* about themselves—not until it is too late. Ilych doesn't realize that there are more things in life than his lifelong pursuit of high social standings. Self-realization, or "knowing thyself," is a lifelong project. Like Betty Friedan's "the feminine mystique," it is often the "problem that has no name" and is unconscious in most people's mind. Most of us are so caught up in the busy day-to-day rat race to make a living and keep improving our lot that we have no time to pause and reflect on the philosophical question of authenticity. To an extent, Albert Camus (1913–1960) is right to state that, to be authentic, one must be aware of the absurdity of a world without objective morality and purpose and strive to create one's own meaning of life through rebellion against the absurdity. The inability to launch such a rebellion condemns us to inauthenticity.

The above notion of authenticity is widely used in humanistic and existential philosophy—e.g., by Heidegger—to refer to ideal or optimal ways of living. In that sense, it is related to virtue ethics. Being authentic means to live up to one's ideals—to be and to become the best, or as good as, one can be. As Guignon (2008) explained in the article "Authenticity,"

> Being human, we are "coming from somewhere" in the sense that each of us has a set of motivations that give us an orientation and a frame of reference. And we are "going somewhere" in the sense that we are always engaged in projects and commitments concerning what we hope to accomplish in our lives. (p. 283)

Each of us, therefore, is a project, "to live in the tension between 'thrownness' (coming from somewhere) and 'projection' (going somewhere)." An inauthentic person is one who drifts with the crowd while avoiding any responsibility for his or her own actions. An authentic person is one who "owns up to" the temporal structures of thrownness and projection into what Heidegger calls "being-a-whole" and truly realizes what each of us is in potentiality.

Not all human potentials and ideals are virtuous, however. In addition to being *truthful* about oneself and to the world, one must also commit to *goodness*—cultivating the *good* and repudiating the *bad*. We must not only rebel against inauthentic and immoral world, but we must also rebel for a *good cause*. Sometimes white lies are justified, like the father in the 1997 Italian film *Life is Beautiful*, who employs his imagination and shields his son from the horrors of internment in a Nazi concentration camp. On the other hand, while many of us know what we should rebel against, few know what we should rebel for. The 1955 James Dean film *Rebel Without a Cause* had a huge impact on the youth of the time the world over, which strengthened our convictions, as exemplified in a 1960s Red Guard slogan of the early Chinese Cultural Revolution, that "to rebel is justified" . . . against oppressive authorities and social norms, but we weren't sure about what we should rebel for, and the film was silent about it. The subsequent world events, such as the Arab Spring in the 2010s, demonstrated clearly the continued widespread perplexities about what goals to aim for—in politics as well as in everyday life.

Authenticity could also be a ticket to success. The director of the hugely successful 2008 Taiwanese film, *Cape No. 7*, Wei Te-Sheng, for example, reflects on years of fruitless search—for what he would like to do in his life in a 2008 interview—before embarking on film-making, his true love, as his career goals. Having set his goals, he is finally inspired to put all his energy into the necessary tasks—e.g., doggedly writing screenplays in his spare times and learning the art of making films. To raise money, he even put his house as a collateral with the grudging consent of his wife. Finding his authentic self gives him the self-confidence he needs to carry on his conviction, often against the advice of others.

Most people are like Wei Te-Sheng, clueless in what they like and what they are good for, often until they are in their middle ages or beyond. As Wei states, our education systems should be more flexible and caring to help all students succeed and find their authentic self. This is exactly the philosophy as practised in Finland's education system:

> An essential element of the Finnish comprehensive school is systematic attention to those students who have special educational needs. Special education is an important part of education and care in Finland. It refers to designed educational and psychological services within the education sector for those with special needs. The basic idea is that with early recognition of learning difficulties and social and behavioural problems, appropriate professional support can be provided to individuals as early as possible. (Sahlberg, 2012, p. 24)

So when a child temporarily has a learning difficulty, the teacher immediately designs and carries out a remedial plan, either in the classroom or after school, any additional cost being funded by the Finnish government. I think there should be a similar individualized, quality, egalitarian system in every country to provide assistance and counselling to all students for self and social exploration, improvement, and experimentation.

To work towards a caring society in which nobody is left behind, we must live *magnanimously*, cooperating with and respecting each other; we must not take advantage of one another, we must not try and get ahead at the expense of one another, etc. Such goals are obviously necessary—at least to me. Otherwise, there would be ceaseless conflicts between individuals, groups, nations, etc. If some were left behind, there would be resentment, and eventually, they would react and strike back, and there would be no peace, no goodwill. We would constantly be on guard for the cycles of cheating, fraud, theft, violence, threat, or abuse (physical, mental, verbal), etc. If we do not want to continue living in a society like that, we must change. We must repudiate the culture of competition and opt for a culture of cooperation instead. I used to not lock the door when I went out for a quick errand, but once, when my daughter came for a visit, and we went out for breakfast at a nearby health food store. Someone walked right into my house during that time, ransacked my desk drawer, and took about $1,000 worth of foreign currency from my prior out-of-country travels, plus my daughter's camera. Since then, I started to lock the door, of course, but I hated it, as it has made my life more uptight and less carefree. How can I live magnanimously if I have too many worries and no peace of mind?

My idea of goodness, moreover, is closely related to that of *health*. It is an intrinsic good, as we all desire it and strive for it as an individual or a society. Contrary to Jean-Paul Sartre's claim that "existence precedes essence," all biological beings are endowed as their essence the potentials to strive for survival and healthy growth. Although our individual freedom is absolute and unbounded according to Sartre, we are constrained internally and externally in reality to actualize individual potentials. To the extent possible, though, our goals should be to cooperatively develop healthy body and mind for all individuals, and extend it socially, culturally, and ecologically. Remember the World Health Organization's characterization of health as "a state of complete physical, mental and social well-being?" It connotes the concepts of perfection and *beauty*: perfectly beautiful body, mind, human relations, etc. Our goals should definitely include the maintenance, enhancement, and creation of a world that is beautiful and breathtaking. We should all engage in "healthy living" in our daily lives of work and leisure, keep learning, be creative in the production of art, science, literature, food, crafts, etc., and share the fruits of our labour fairly and equitably in the communities in which we live. Where there's a will, there's a way to excel, individually and collectively!

Slimming Down Like the Japanese? / The Rubaiyat / 2012

Our fantasy is to look slim and handsome
With diet and exercise we shall overcome
Japanese Women Don't Get Old or Fat[2]
We could surely hope for the same outcome

But we are too self-centred and indulging
Spoiling ourselves with sweets and beer drinking
Flipping the remote, watching TV or video games
We delude ourselves, calling it good living

When our bodies become bloated and oversized
We get anxious and our thinking, paralyzed
Half of us are overweight or obese, thus
Our dream for a right weight is fetishized

---

2 The title of a book by Naomi Moriyama.

Though one in four Japanese are overweight
They are obliged to slim down and relate
What they eat and drink with how they look
They pay heed or their health premiums inflate[3]

We won't do the same to curb our waistline
Because we'd rather see our health decline
Than give up our precious "freedom of choice"
To live a life without a timeline and deadline

But if anti-smoking campaigns are the guide
Anti-fat campaigns will surely make strides
It's a matter of time to see the groundswell
That drives against this fat epidemic worldwide

10.1. Culture and Identity in Taiwan

FROM JANUARY TO APRIL 2018, PROFESSOR CLARA IWASAKI OFFERED A course, "Culture and Identity in Taiwan," in the Department of East Asian Studies at the University of Alberta. Through the course, I deepened my understanding of the issues surrounding Taiwan's—and my own—culture and identity.

The culture of Taiwan evolves with the unfolding of the unique histories of various peoples of Taiwan—the Austronesian aboriginals, the Dutch and the Spanish, the (early and post-WWII) Chinese, the Japanese, and the South Eastern Asian immigrants, etc. The first novel for the course is Wu Zhuoliu's *The Doctor's Mother* (1944). It is a story during the late Japanese colonial rule about a Taiwanese doctor who is mainly

---

3 Jose Manuel Blanco. (December 17, 2011). *CNN Fatbusters:*
Japanese told to slim down. Retrieved from http://www.youtube.com/
watch?v=gqBShaDE5QA.

interested in making money and eager to "become more Japanese than the Japanese"—talking and dressing and showing off as a Japanese, adopting a Japanese surname, etc.—for advancing his social status. He wants his mother to Japanize too, yet the doctor's mother scolds him for abandoning his Taiwanese language and culture. It is a satire against the doctor and other intellectuals of the time like him who supported Japanization of the Taiwanese to be a proud Japanese.

I became curious, since my father resisted an intense pressure to adopt a Japanese name. In fact, he was a prime target as a graduate of the prestigious Waseda University in Tokyo and was teaching English at his hometown high school, a profession for which only the Japanese could normally qualify. I found out that only in the 1940s, in order to support the war effort, the Japanese imposed the conversion to a Japanese name, and yet only 7% of the Taiwanese Japanized their names by the end of WWII (Kinoshita, 2016; Kim, 2016).

I am also fascinated by a 2013 survey conducted by the Interchange Association, Japan, Japan's de facto embassy in Taiwan, which found that 65% of the Taiwanese feel either "close" or "really close" to Japan, which stands in stark contrast to the Chinese, over 90% of whom have either an "unfavourable" or "relatively unfavourable" opinion of Japan:

> Japan is overwhelmingly the most popular country among Taiwanese. When asked what their favourite country was in the same survey, 43 percent said Japan, while only single digits said Singapore, the US or China. The support for Japan is even stronger among Taiwanese aged 20–29, with 54 percent of respondents in that age group listing Japan as their favourite foreign country. By contrast, only 2 percent of respondents between ages of 20 and 29 said China was their favourite foreign country. (Thim & Matsuka, 2014)

In fact, the manga artist and author Hari Kyoko (2013) coined a new word "Hari", in the Hoklo dialect, to signify a deep love of Japan, and the "Hari tribe" those who are a fan of Japan.

A more recent survey conducted by the Taiwanese Public Opinion Foundation in 2017 showed Singapore, Japan, and Canada as the top three favourite countries, while Philippines and China are among the least popular countries. Japan remained the most popular among young Taiwanese, especially among the respondents aged 20–24 and 25–34.

Such cultural preference is a huge mystery to lots of people, especially to the Chinese and the South Koreans. The brutality of the Japanese army during WWII, including the Nanking Massacre and the treatment of comfort women, is unforgivable, and yet Japan fails to come to terms with its ugly past. As Jennifer Lind (2009) of Dartmouth College writes:

> Tokyo's official apologies for its past aggression and atrocities are dismissed as too little, too late. Worse, they often trigger denials and calls of revisionism in Japan, which anger and alarm the country's former victims.

It is a mistake, however, to attribute the Taiwanese fondness of Japanese culture to the Taiwanese's colonial mentality. As mentioned earlier, my father was so upset with the Japanese colonial rule that even though he was most fluent in Japanese, he refused to be a writer in that language and instead opted to write in English . . . although unsuccessfully. He had great personal friendships with many of his former Japanese students and friends, who always threw huge, warm welcome parties for him whenever he visited Japan. The most important reasons for Hari, I surmise, were the mistakes committed by the Chinese Nationalists and the Communists. The former relates to the 228 Incident and the massacre, the White Terror, and the four decades of martial law. The latter concerns China's hostility towards Taiwan since 1949—including the One-China policy, the use of force against Taiwan, and the various measures to exclude Taiwan from participating in international organizations. While the Taiwanese welcomed being a part of China after the defeat of Japan, the subsequent internal and external "friendly fire" from both the KMT and the CCP turned them off, switching public opinion increasingly against China. The diplomatic isolation of Taiwan imposed by the Chinese government further prompted the Taiwanese to seek support from neighbouring countries, especially Japan.

The lessons are clear: good relations are built on good will. If you are mean and do not respect others, don't expect others to act differently. Good Cross-Strait China–Taiwan relations are also built on good will. The cooperative approach that I have been advocating requires both sides abandon the antagonistic rhetoric, policy, and action of the past, and be more respectful of each other's rights and aspirations, work together, and seek win-win rather than win-lose solutions that characterize the combatant, win-at-any-cost strategies of the past. The apparent first step, of course, is to renounce the use of force. Then China would be less of a threat to Taiwan's security, and less likely to be regarded as its enemy. Another way of developing good will is for China to support Taiwan's re-entry into the world organizations, and cooperate in promoting measures and initiatives that would benefit both sides of the Taiwan Strait. This is not difficult to do, as the former Soviet Union had three seats at the United Nations. Patriotism can be a positive force of uniting one's own people or country, but it can turn into a negative force such as racism, chauvinism, imperialism, and colonialism. We cannot uncritically and emotionally commit to the doctrine of "My country, right or wrong!" That didn't go over well at the Nuremberg trials for following the Nazi ideology and the atrocious orders of one's superiors! We need to transcend nationalism if we are to genuinely aspire to be citizens of the world and promote world peace.

The last reading for the course is the novel *Green Island* by the American author Shawna Yang Ryan (2013). The novel traces the story of Dr. Tsai's family from the time of the 228 Incident through the White Terror and martial law era to the present. This part of history affected millions of Taiwanese in different ways. My philosophy professor, Yin Hai-kuang, a former editor of the Nationalist Party, the KMT's, *The Central Daily Newspaper*, was persecuted and placed under house arrest for being critical of the KMT rule and policy in Taiwan. He defended liberalism and translated Friedrich Hayek's influential work, *The Road to Serfdom*. When Hayek came to Taiwan, he was not allowed to meet with Professor Yin, whose work was banned, and he was prevented from giving lectures to students. Only in 1990, after the end of martial law, that a 20-volume edition of Professor Yin's complete works appeared (see Figure 6).

Figure 6. Yin Hai-kuang (1919-1969). Born in China's Hubei province, he came to Taiwan in 1949 and taught philosophy at the National Taiwan University. As an editor of the *Free China Journal*, he promoted freedom and democracy and became an outspoken critic of Chiang Kai-Check's authoritarian leadership.

His student, my classmate Chen Gu-ying, was blacklisted for speaking out against the KMT government, and the authorities would not allow him to teach philosophy at the National Taiwan University. Eventually, he was allowed to go to the United States, and from there he went to teach at Beijing University until 1997, ten years after the end of Taiwan's martial law, when his professorship at the National Taiwan University was restored. In my case, I decided to leave Taiwan, and while in the United States, a KMT informer reported me to the Taiwanese authority for being critical of the KMT government (which was true) and making donations to anti-KMT organizations (which was false). So I wrote to my father, denying my involvement in such activities to pacify the authorities in Taiwan. I am convinced that, had I stayed in Taiwan, my life would likely have mirrored what happened to my teacher and my classmate. The KMT government did not tolerate anyone who dared to disagree with them, as Professors Yin and Chen were mainlanders who came to Taiwan at the end of the Chinese civil war, and I was born and raised in Taiwan. While the victims were of any ethnicity, the oppressors were mainlanders—a cause for a deep political chasm between the mainlanders and the native-born Taiwanese. Nobody dared, or wanted, to talk about it, especially the mainlanders, for fear and embarrassment before the end of martial law . . . and even for many decades that followed. The silence has been deafening—until the opposition DPP came to power for the first time in 2000, and especially in 2016, with a majority in the Legislature Yuan.

Of course, the fate of hundreds and thousands of people who were imprisoned on Green Island—like Dr. Tsai (in Ryan's novel), who spent a tortured life there for eleven years, and some, like him, returned as broken men—is immeasurably worse off. As a result of arbitrary arrests, imprisonment, and the execution of tens of thousands of people during the White Terror and martial law era under Chiang Kat-shek and his son Chiang Ching-kuo, the new DPP government is faced with a challenging task of transitional justice, through a Truth and Reconciliation Committee, including the removal, renaming, or addressing of authoritarian symbols (e.g., Chiang's statues, and the streets and schools named after him). President Tsai Yin-wen (2016) stated in her inaugural address:

The goal of transitional justice is to pursue true social reconciliation, so that all Taiwanese can take to heart the mistakes of that era. We will begin by investigating and sorting through the facts. Within the next three years, we plan to complete Taiwan's own investigative report on transitional justice. Follow-up work on transitional justice will then be carried out in accordance with the truth unveiled by the report. We will discover the truth, heal wounds, and clarify responsibilities. From here on out, history will no longer divide Taiwan. Instead, it will propel Taiwan forward.

Her pursuit of transitional justice, as Ian Rowen and Jamie Rowen (2017) contend,

signal a departure from the ROC's authoritarian past and to draw a distinction from China's authoritarian present, while demonstrating adherence to international norms of human rights, democracy and self-determination.

It is an ambitious and risky measure, however, since it will have a significant impact on politics inside and outside of Taiwan, highlighting and accentuating the differences between the DPP and the KMT on the one hand, and between the DPP and the CCP on the other. While the DPP policy is to promote Taiwan's own culture and identity by reversing the KMT China-centric policies and identity of the past, such a policy shift would hardly be tolerated by the KMT, and especially by the PRC. This common opposition to the DPP's non-recognition of the One-China Policy thus turns the former bitter enemies, the KMT and the CCP, into strange bedfellows—despite each of them deceptively claiming to represent both China and Taiwan—an intriguing example of how a white lie can serve a useful political purpose for both the KMT and the CCP.

This dilemma of the current DPP government prompts me to examine, in the next section, Martha Nussbaum's ideas of generosity and justice in order to handle anger and resentment; I believe this is the best way forward in achieving truth and reconciliation involving past grievances and wrongdoings. To resolve any dilemma, we need to think morally, with future generations in mind.

Morality / Cinquain 2012

Morality
Inter-generations
Gratitude, obligation, reciprocity
Duties to the dead and the unborn
Personhood

10.2. Anger, Truth, and Reconciliation

> . . . the world has been propelled, to a large extent, by rage and retribution, but let us create something better, in ourselves and in our political culture. Let's not be the way the world is right now. (Nussbaum, 2016, p. 247)

THERE IS SO MUCH INJUSTICE IN THIS WORLD, MAKING ME ANGRY AND indignant at times. Anger, like pain, is a natural, emotional defense mechanism, signaling a perception of wrongdoing that someone has been treated badly and unfairly. Research shows, moreover, that anger and hostility reinforce each other, especially for aggressive people (Tiedens, 2001). It is critical, therefore, to keep anger in check, and the American Psychological Association, on its website (http://www.apa.org/helpcenter/controlling-anger.aspx), lists the following strategies for controlling ager: relax, don't dwell, change the way you think, focus on breathing, use imagery, improve your communication skills, get active, and recognize and avoid your triggers.

Since anger tends to cloud judgment, probably the most productive strategy among all is to change the way we think and act, to always focus on building a better future for all concerned rather than on retribution and payback. That is the central message of Martha Nassbaum's (2016) remarkable book, *Anger and Forgiveness: Resentment, Generosity, Justice*. By debunking the myths of inevitability that anger is "hardwired in human nature," "entails an inhuman, extreme, and unloving type of detachment," and is "good, powerful and manly," she urges us to pursue "non-anger." She went as far as saying: "If this book achieves anything, I hope it achieves that sort of square-one reorientation, getting its reader to see clearly the irrationality and stupidity of anger" (p. 249).

I think Nussbaum overstated her case, though, since, as I stated earlier, anger is an appropriate response to the perception of wrongdoing. What I object to postmodernism and third-wave feminism is their tendencies to endorse moral relativism—that anything goes, so they are not angry at social injustices and not voicing any objections against them. Anger is not "irrational and stupid": we need it like we need the sensation of pain, since it is a curse without anger. As Dr. Ingo Kurth of the Institute of Human Genetics in Aschen, Germany explains: "We fear pain, but in developmental terms from being a child to being a young adult, pain is incredibly important to the process of learning how to modulate your physical activity without doing damage to your bodies, and in determining how much risk you take" (Cox, 2017). Anger too is important to the process of learning how to deal with social injustices without clouding our clear thinking and acting stupidly. As the director Stephen Campanelli of the film, *Indian Horse*, based on Wagamese's novel with the same title, says, the film is not only meant to expose the dark legacy of Canada's residential school system and its enduring effects, it's also a call to action:

> Our biggest goal for this movie is to keep the conversation going. To be able to give people an opinion to say, "Wow, I can't believe this happened. How can I help? Let's have a call to action. Let's do something about this. Let's get

mad. Let's call the government, or whatever we can do to help this go on." (Van Evra, 2018)

We should, therefore, keep our cool and control our anger just like we control our pain, without eliminating it altogether.

How should we then manage our anger? According to Nussbaum, a natural reaction is to seek the payback, but this does not make sense since punishing the wrongdoer does not undo the fact that the harm is already done; striking back to reduce the wrongdoer's social status is also worthless, since it does not improve one's own status, and status itself is not something we should value as an ideal anyway. Nussbaum illustrates her points eloquently by citing a story of Nelson Mandela, which denounces both the payback and the status error while he interacted with a white Afrikaner warder, Viktor Vorster. It happened when Mandela was still a prisoner prior to his official release. On the question of how the dishes would be done, Mandela stated:

> I took it upon myself to break the tension and a possible resentment on his part that he has to serve a prisoner by cooking and then washing dishes, and I offered to wash dishes and he refused. . . . He says that this is his work. I said, "No, we must share it." Although he insisted, and he was genuine, but I forced him, literally forced him, to allow me to do the dishes, and we established a very good relationship. (Nussbaum 2016, p. 245)

Nussbaum concludes: "Injustice should be greeted with protest and careful, courageous strategic action. But the end goal must remain always in view: as [Martin Luther] King said so simply: 'A world where men and women can live together.' Building such a world takes intelligence, control, and a spirit of generosity" (p. 249).

The message is clear: It is the spirit of generosity and respect for others—even for the political opponents—that is likely to produce friendship and cooperation. That is the legacy of Nelson Mandela, who successfully steered the course of post-apartheid South Africa after being imprisoned for 27 years. All of us can learn a great deal from Mandela. How can that spirit and philosophy applied to the dilemma facing Taiwan?

As discussed in Section 10.1, Taiwan's current DPP government is facing an extremely delicate political situation with the KMT at home, and with the CCP (Chinese Communist Party) in China. To realize their dream of further developing Taiwan into a sovereign, prosperous, democratic country, the DPP should, first of all, treat the KMT generously and with respect, so as to gain the cooperation required to advance their common goals—implementing policies and measures to improve the quality of life for the people of Taiwan. To that end, it is of critical importance to highlight and pursue the common goals cooperatively, since that is the best way to get things done by minimizing resentment and resistance. Sure, there are many disagreements and conflicts of interest between the two parties, such as: the issues of truth and reconciliation, and the compensation of the victims of the White Terror; the appraisal of the assets of the KMT; the education and cultural policies; and the relationship with China; etc. In pushing for reforms, however, the DPP should respect the legitimate concerns of the KMT. As Nussbaum states:

> Progress is impeded by the other party's defensiveness and anxious self-protection. Anger, consequently, does nothing to move matters forward: it just increases the other party's anxiety and self-defensiveness. A gentle and cheerful approach, by contrast, can gradually weaken defenses until the whole idea of self-defense is given up. (p. 230)

This is particularly the case with respect to truth and reconciliation:

> A nation that moves forward needs both trust and mutual respect. It seems that truth is very important for trust, but it also seems that a certain way of positioning the truth jeopardizes respect, hence reconciliation. By offering

amnesty, South Africa wisely took the process out of the retributivist framework that it might so easily have inhabited, facilitating attitudes of trust and emotions of national solidarity. (p. 243)

If the goal of transitional justice is "to pursue true social reconciliation," as stated in President Tsai's inaugural address in 2016, then it is imperative that the DPP treat the KMT with generosity and respect, and, at the same time, serving justice without retribution. Offering unconditional amnesty to wrongdoers to get at the truth is a way to minimize retribution.

Cooperating with the KMT is also important for the DPP to improve its relation with the CCP. Having lost the Mainland China to the CCP in the civil war in 1949, the KMT become a *de facto* government only for Taiwan and surrounding islands until the opposition DPP took power in 2000-2008 and also in 2016. After nearly 70 years of separation from Mainland China, the KMT's identity is more with Taiwan than with China despite its close historical roots in Mainland China. However, the KMT has never denounce its claim of sovereignty over all of China, and in 1992, the then native-Taiwanese KMT president, Lee Teng-hui, initiated contacts with the CCP, resulting in the so-called "1992 Consensus" (Quora Contributor, 2014):

- Both sides agree that there is only one Chinese nation comprising all of Mainland China, Taiwan, Penghu, and the offshore islands.
- Under this Chinese nation, there are two states.
- Both sides agree to disagree on the definition of control of these two states.
- Thus, "both sides agreed that the other side existed, but they would disagree about everything else." That is, the interpretation of "One China" is left to each party.

The DPP's position, on the other hand, is that Taiwan is Taiwan, and not part of China—a position China strongly objects. Now, China loves to assert jurisdiction over Taiwan and not recognize the *de facto* existence of a state on the other side of the Taiwan Strait, thus applying all sorts of retaliatory measures against the DPP government to limit Taiwan's international space—including blocking Taiwan's participation in the World Health Assembly in 2017 and cancelling the 2019 East Asian Youth Game in Taichung, Taiwan. Predictably, these measures further angered and alienated the Taiwanese, especially the young people, as mentioned earlier. The blocking of Taiwan's participation in international health organizations is particularly ill-conceived and unethical, since "diseases have no borders" and could have serious health consequences globally.

I think all three parties, the DPP, the KMT, and the CCP, could benefit from Mandela's teachings: be respectful and generous to the opponents. The 1992 Consensus can be a flexible document, so perhaps it is possible to accommodate the aspirations of all parties involved. Perhaps within this "Chinese Nation," the statehood and sovereignty of the Taiwanese government (ROC or Republic of China) can be recognized explicitly by the CCP and internationally, for the ROC to also become a member of the United Nations (UN)—as the former Soviet Union had three seats in the UN. Within this Chinese Nation, it could be guaranteed that both the DPP and the KMT could carry out their political agenda of either the Taiwan-centric or China-centric cultural and economic policies, depending on which party is in power in Taiwan. China would have Taiwan as part of the Chinese Nation, and all three parties could work cooperatively toward peace and prosperity—without regarding others as threats—politically, economically, culturally, environmentally, or militarily. Unlike Hong Kong, Taiwan (or the ROC) is a *de facto* independent state, so it is possible that "One Country, Two Systems" has different interpretations for Hong Kong and Taiwan, guaranteeing *de jure* independence for Taiwan and the status quo across the Taiwan Straits under the One-China Policy. As the former DPP president, Chen Shui-bian had agreed to such an arrangement, perhaps the DPP could initiate the dialogue first with the KMT, followed by the KMT approaching the CCP to negotiate an overall understanding and consensus—agreeable to all three parties.

It should be noted that reconciliations among peoples, as at the personal level, are one of the most urgent tasks facing all of us throughout the world—in the United States, India and South Africa, for example, as Nussbaum's book attests. Just as Taiwan has been struggling to erase Chiang Kai-shek's authoritarian legacy by enacting a law in 2017 to rename streets, schools, etc., in his honour and to remove his statues, Canada too has been embroiled in the bitter controversy about the glum, racist legacy of Indian residential schools, and in August, 2018 Victoria has become the first city in Canada to remove the statue of John A. Macdonald, the nation's first prime minister and the architect of that system, from the steps of its city hall.

It is only through generosity and respect for others that we could hope for just reconciliations, and to achieve peace with ourselves and with others. Yesterday's heroes can become today's villains. We need to be angry at injustices, but at the same time, we must also focus on working toward rational strategies, to join hands with others to ensure injustices are not repeated and cherished goals are achieved. As stated in the Truth and Reconciliation Committee of Canada's (2015) Final Report:

> Getting to the truth was hard, but getting to reconcili-
> ation will be harder . . . Reconciliation requires that a
> new vision, based on a commitment to mutual respect,
> be developed . . . Reconciliation is not an Aboriginal
> problem; it is a Canadian one. Virtually all aspects of
> Canadian society may need to be reconsidered. (p. VI)

Similarly, reconciliation in Taiwan is not just a DPP problem; it also involves the KMT and the CCP, and all aspects of Taiwanese and Chinese society may need to be reconsidered in order to ensure peace and prosperity and avoid war and misery for all parties involved. Let's give peace a chance to succeed!

Give Peace a Chance to Succeed / Analyzed Rhyme / 2009

I am angry with war's perpetrators
    For causing unspeakable miseries
To innocent women, men, and children
    Through organized violence, rapes, and terrors

I'm mad at war's insensitivity,
    A total waste of precious resources.
Patriotism is a lame pretence
    For such a crime against humanity

Worshiping hyper-masculinity
    Perpetuates the mindless violence
We must elevate femininity
    For society's peace and prosperity

War's an avoidable calamity
    And peace on earth is a most cherished need
Let's deplore male superiority
    So as to give peace a chance to succeed

10.3. Open Versus Closed Societies

> Anybody who has ever lived under another form of government—that is, under a dictatorship which cannot be removed without bloodshed—will know that a democracy, imperfect though it is, is worth fighting for and, I believe, worth dying for. (Popper, 1988, p. 25)

AMONG ALL THE THINKERS, THE ONE INFLUENCED ME THE MOST IS perhaps Karl Popper (1902–1994). I obtained a pirated copy of his *The*

Open Society and its Enemies (1950/1945) while I was studying philosophy in Taiwan in the late 1950s, and also his *The Logic of Scientific Discovery* (1961/1934) while studying philosophy at the University of Minnesota in the early 1960s. I still remember Popper in person, who was invited to Herbert Feigl's Philosophy of Science class at the University of Minnesota to talk about quantum mechanics, Heisenberg's uncertainty principle, the Copenhagen interpretation, the meaning of objectivity as inter-subjectivity, etc. Popper (1963) further elaborated his theory of the growth of scientific knowledge in his book, *Conjectures and Refutations* (1963), that all scientific theories are by nature conjectures and inherently refutable. While it is logically impossible to conclusively verify and confirm a scientific theory or a universal proposition, a single counterexample could conclusively falsify it. If a theory has withstood the most rigorous testing for a long period of time, then, according to Popper, instead of stating that it has been verified, we should recognize that the theory has attained a high degree of corroboration and may be provisionally accepted, until it is falsified.

To Popper, this way of thinking is just an extension of common sense, although it has been challenged with the publication of Thomas Kuhn's (1970) *The Structure of Scientific Revolutions*. When I was studying mathematics and statistics at the University of Toronto, Kuhn's book was a huge hit among historians of science. Instead of steady, cumulative, progress as seen in a "normal science" phase, anomalies start to appear, and usually, such anomalies are resolved—either by uncovering the error in the observation or experiment, or by incremental changes to the accepted theory or intellectual framework, which Kuhn called the paradigm. If, however, there comes a point when such anomalies cannot be resolved, then the paradigm itself may be questioned, and the discipline enters a period of crisis. The crisis ends when a new paradigm emerges to successfully account for such anomalies, thus replacing the old paradigm.

Looking back now, I think the theories as formulated by Popper and Kuhn are really complementary: while Popper's focus is on the epistemology and truth in science, Kuhn's is on the sociology of science. In fact, paradigm shifts are likely based on Popper's framework of conjectures and refutations, to reject old paradigms in favour of the new in order to account for anomalies. When I was engaged in the statistical analysis of issues in heart disease, I relied mainly on Popper's framework of testing conjectured hypotheses for refutations or corroborations. On the other hand, I am currently advocating a paradigm of cooperation for promoting health equity, hoping that a shift would occur in its favour away from the hegemonic, competition paradigm. To some extent, these two paradigms are "incommensurable," since they are based on different value systems: equity is valued in the cooperation paradigm, whereas freedom trumps all other values in the competition paradigm. One of the anomalies in our competitive world is social inequality: since the problem is accentuated with the competition paradigm, the solution is to bring in the cooperation paradigm to engineer a paradigm shift, as we have advocated (Chang & Fraser, 2017).

The most remarkable aspect of Popper's philosophy, however, is his unified worldview. Perhaps this has a great deal to do with his wide variety of interests and exposures to different subjects, such as music, cabinet making, primary and secondary school teaching, social and political issues, before completing a doctoral dissertation on the methodological problem on cognitive psychology at the University of Vienna. This focus on scientific methods became his lifelong preoccupation, and the annexation of Austria by Nazi Germany in 1938 prompted Popper to extend his interest from the philosophy of science to social and political philosophy. In 1945, just before the end of WWII, his book, *Open Society and Its Enemies*, was published.

In that book, he launches a determined and spirited attack on what he called historicism—historic determinism that prophesizes the course of historical events according to some inherent historical laws. In his opinion, such a deterministic doctrine, as contained in the writings from Plato to Hegel to Marx, is socially dangerous, since it is closely related to holism—the view that human social groupings are greater than the sum of their members—and inevitably leads to totalitarianism and authoritarianism with centralized government control of the individual and the imposition of large-scale social planning—which is inherently ill-conceived and inevitably disastrous. Extending his ideas of "conjectures and refutations" to political history, Popper advocates an open society involving "piecemeal social engineering"—i.e., through ongoing public participation to critically evaluate the consequences of the implementation of government policies, which can then be abandoned or modified in the light of such scrutiny. Furthermore, as Thornton (2005, Section 6) stated in his article on Popper,

> in such a society, the rights of the individual to criticise administrative policies will be formally safeguarded and upheld, undesirable policies will be eliminated in a manner analogous to the elimination of falsified scientific theories, and differences between people on social policy will be resolved by critical discussion and argument rather than by force.

Popper (1988) revisited *The Open Society* and clarifies his "more realistic theory" of democracy, which is to reformulate the old question "Who should rule?" as, "how is the state to be constituted so that bad rulers can be got rid of without bloodshed, without violence?" His answer: any of the modern so-called democracies, "for they all adopt what is the simplest solution to the new problem—that is, the principle that the government can be dismissed by a majority vote"

By saying this is the best system, Popper does not say the majority vote will always or even usually right, he only says that "this very imperfect procedure is the best so far invented." He also says, as I quote him at the beginning of this section:

> Anybody who has ever lived under another form of government—that is, under a dictatorship which cannot be removed without bloodshed—will know that a democracy, imperfect though it is, is worth fighting for and, I believe, worth dying for.

And he reasons as follows:

> And we do not base our choice on the goodness of democracy, which may be doubtful, but solely on the evilness of a dictatorship, which is certain. Not only because the dictator is bound to make bad use of his power, but because a dictator, even if he were benevolent, would rob all others of their responsibility, and thus of their human rights and duties.

How apt for Popper to say that a dictator is "bound to make bad use of his power"—corroborated by the news in March 2018 that China's National People's Congress removed the term limit on Xi Jinping's presidency, so he may hold China's top posts for life! Popper is also wise not to base our choice on the goodness of democracy, since things can and does go wrong sometimes as shown by the title of Stephen Walt's 2017 article: "Trump isn't sure if democracy is better than autocracy. America's president is voluntarily abdicating one of the country's biggest strategic advantages." Having lived under a dictatorship, though, I am wholeheartedly convinced of the superiority of democracy over authoritarianism. Democracy can be bad or inefficient sometimes, as has been happening all over the world throughout history, but we can get rid of a bad government sooner or later under a democracy but not as easily under a dictatorship—as witnessed in Taiwan's history since WWII.

Similarly, it's possible for us to live authentically and magnanimously under a democracy, but not necessarily under a dictatorship. That's why I admire Popper and his vision of an open society. Although he had great admiration for Friedrich Hayek's libertarian economics—which led to neoliberalism—Popper continued to value socialism, equality, and state interventions through piecemeal social engineering to protect the economically weak from the economically strong—the philosophy of social democracy. I like what Popper (1974) wrote in his intellectual autobiography, *Unended Quest*: "For nothing could be better than living a modest, simple, and free life in an egalitarian society," despite his eventual conclusion that socialism was "no more than a beautiful dream," and the dream is undone by the conflict between freedom and equality. Popper may be right, although I'd still like to keep my dream of "a free and equal society" alive, because equality and freedom, like the yin and the yang, are indispensable for living an authentic and magnanimous life.

Popper's reluctance about defending the positive virtues of democracy is understandable. For democracy to succeed, one key ingredient, often missing in real politics, is truth-telling—to engage in rational debates among the candidates regarding the relative merits of their election platforms and policies—rather than resorting to mean-spirited personal attacks, negative ads, fearmongering, etc., to deceive the voters, such as the notorious Donald Trump campaign for the presidency in the United States in 2016, and the Doug Ford campaign for the premier of Ontario in 2018. I was so upset about Stephen Harper's Canadian federal campaign in 2011 that I wrote the following poem while fully convinced, as a statistician, that political lies are much worse than statistical ones:

Lies, Damn Lies, and Politics / Pantoum Puzzle / 2011

Lies, damn lies, and politics
Negative ads, fearmongering
For the Tories to get a majority
That's what politics is about

Negative ads, fearmongering
These are untrue and mean-spirited
That's what politics is about
These politics of exclusion

These are untrue and mean-spirited
They demonize one's opponents
These politics of exclusion —
A sure way to divide our people

They demonize one's opponents
It's a shameful and unworthy way
A sure way to divide our people
By deceit rather than truth-telling

It's a shameful and unworthy way
For the Tories to get a majority
By deceit rather than truth-telling
Lies, damn lies, and politics

11.

Concluding Remarks

WHAT IS IT ALL ABOUT? OUR WORLDVIEW IS DETERMINED BY A SERIES OF epistemological questions, the first of which is: does life have a purpose? While some philosophers such as existentialists do not see any purpose in life and therefore must create one for oneself, a more defensible position, in my view, is Aristotelian, that human life has a purpose: it aims at survival and flourishing, to seek meaning and attain earthly happiness. To that end, all of us should develop and use the given abilities to the fullest extent to flourish and be happy.

A key component of human flourishing, as I understand it, is love, without which life withers. Love, on the other hand, relates to the rationality of truth, the morality of goodness, and the aesthetics of beauty. Since human potentials can be contradictory, and their development may foster or impede the achievement of good life, individually and collectively, we need the three interrelated desiderata of truth, goodness, and beauty to guide our choices of what potentials (e.g., generosity, empathy) to nourish and actualize, and what other potentials (e.g., envy, hate) to transcend or suppress. This is what morality is about, the rational choice of what actions to take to facilitate the achievement of personal and collective well-being.

Now, there are many ways to attain human flourishing, depending on the external environment. Steven Pinker, in his book *Enlightenment Now* (2018), characterizes it in this way:

We are born into a pitiless universe, facing steep odds against life-enabling order and in constant jeopardy of falling apart. We are shaped by a force that is ruthlessly competitive. We are made from crooked timber, vulnerable to illusions, self-centredness, and at times astounding stupidity. (p. 452)

Therefore, we needed to be fiercely competitive in order to survive and flourish. On the other hand, Pinker adds:

Yet human nature has also been blessed with resources that open a space for a kind of redemption . . . We have an instinct for language, allowing us to share the fruits of our experience and ingenuity. We are deepened with the capacity for sympathy and ingenuity—for pity, imagination, compassion, commiseration. (pp. 452–453)

Indeed, it is the capacity for cooperation, based on sympathy, ingenuity, compassion, and commiseration, etc., that enabled us to survive and flourish while other hominid species all vanished. According to Christopher Kukk (2017), human evolution should be characterized as "survival of the kindest," rather than "survival of the fittest". (pp. 10-14) I maintain that, in an increasingly interconnected world, the future of human survival crucially and increasingly depends on our ability to cooperate, and to forego destructive competition. Competition, if avoidable, should be seen as a vice rather than a virtue, since it does not help in the flourishing of the losers of competition. Even the winners, they may not enjoy a good life. This is because competition is ultimately destructive not only socially, but increasingly also ecologically. In the twenty-first century, we should cooperate to pursue together the goals of "good life" for all, consisting not only of liberty and equality, but also sustainability.

In his book, *When Breath Becomes Air* (2016), the thirty-six-year-old author, Kalanithi worked extraordinarily hard to become a chief resident in neurosurgery at Stanford—just months away from completing the most gruesome training in all medical fields—when he was diagnosed with terminal cancer. He also did award-winning research on gene therapy, and was a gifted writer. The book tells a story of his journey to become a doctor, and then as a patient and also as a husband to Lucy, also a medical doctor. Bill Gates (2017) wrote a review, "This book left me in tears," highly recommending it. He said, "I thoroughly enjoyed Kalanithi's stories about his surgical training. I've always admired doctors. They have to make impossibly hard decisions, and so much of their work has life-and-death implications".

Kalanithi, of course, is a superhero, a hard worker and high achiever, and a role model, serving as an inspiration to all of us in this competitive world. As a high achiever himself, Bill Gates naturally appreciated Kalanithi's talents and work ethic. But, I have been wondering, as Kalanithi had spent all his life searching for meaning, is this the kind of life he was longing for? As medical residents in Canada and United States often spend 80–100 hours per week, and up to 24–28 hours per single shift, such working hours are far from ideal, as compared to a maximum of 48 hours as is the norm in Europe. Since doctors' incomes are already much higher than most other professionals, wouldn't it be more ideal if we trained more doctors with lower but decent incomes than fewer doctors with very high incomes? I think we can all have a better and more meaningful life if we build a more cooperative and just society so everyone can flourish and excel without sacrificing their health and/or dignity. Interestingly, Catherine Clifford (2018) reported, "In Canada, more than 500 doctors and residents, as well as over 150 medical students, have signed a public letter protesting their own pay raises." The letter said:

> We, Quebec doctors who believe in a strong public system, oppose the recent salary increases negotiated by our medical federation.
>
> These increases are all the more shocking because our nurses, clerks and other professionals face very difficult working conditions, while our patients live with the lack of access to required services because of the drastic cuts

in recent years and the centralization of power in the Ministry of Health.

The only thing that seems to be immune to the cuts is our remuneration.

To me, these 500 doctors and residents and 150 medical students are equally admirable as Dr. Kalanithi, if not more so. They sense the injustice in the government's treatment of health care workers, empathize with them, and rebel against an unfair system. They want to defend the ideal of our public health care system. They are our heroes, and I salute them. As Bill Gates is touched by Dr. Kalanithi's stories, I am touched by the story of these doctors, residents, and students. They make me proud of Canada, where I find, in their protest, love, truth, goodness, and beauty—and meaning—to make this world less idiotic.

And, surprise, surprise, working too much as Dr. Kalanithi did is bad for economy and environment! For example, according to Peeples (2012), the sociologist at Boston College, Juliet Schor has found that a reduction of 10% in working hours could trim carbon footprints by 15% due to decreased consumption of goods and energy. Moreover, shorter working hours such as fewer than 35 hours per week from Monday to Thursday in the Netherlands—which has spread to Germany and France among other countries—leads to more productivity per hour, lower unemployment rates, and better family life in these countries. However, shorter work hours is less feasible if income disparities are great, because working less could mean less income and real hardship for those already living on a tight budget.

Without question, we need a good strategy based more on equity and cooperation to make our lives happier, healthier, more beautiful, more sustainable, and more meaningful. Yes, let's keep dreaming beautiful dreams, to make life more meaningful and beautiful.

A Utopian Dream / Espinela / 2016

Utopia makes life meaningful
Charting the way for us to tread
Toward a better world we need
To make life much more beautiful

Dystopia! Many are fearful
That greed tramples goodwill
To make utopian dreams unreal
So, make such dreams humanistic
Respectfully democratic
Without ideological overkill

Utopia needs not be a mirage
If we can be more altruistic

Postscript

I HAD A MAJOR ACCIDENT WHEN I WAS WORKING ON THE LAST CHAPTER of this manuscript. I stated in the manuscript that I took pride in graceful ageing, but now that I hurt myself so badly, do I change my mind about life, and, in particular, on graceful ageing? What do I think now?

It was a fluke accident on the last day of Edmonton's long winter on April 12, 2018. The weather had been nice and warm for a number of days before so I had been riding my bike everywhere although there was still snow and ice on the lawn and back alleys. I attended the last class of the course "Culture and Identity in Taiwan" on that day, and was happily pedalling home around 3:30 in the afternoon. When I came to the back alley leading to my backyard, I made a fatal turn into it. The two car tracks were more or less dry, and I thought I could navigate on these tracks, but somehow the front tire hit the ice and slipped. When I went down, I tried to support myself with my left hand, which also landed on the ice and slipped. I must have twisted my arm to let my shoulder hit the ground, for it to be dislocated and fractured. I was in excruciating pain, lying on the ground, and couldn't move at all. Just then I heard the voices of a man and a woman.

"Are you okay?"

"Can you get up?"

"I can't," I replied.

"I'm Stefan. I have some first aid experience. I'll get a sling for you," the man, my neighbour, said. He went home to get a piece of beige cloth, and then he put my arm into it and tied it around my neck to make a sling. Seeing that I couldn't even stand up, he put my bike away in my backyard, got his car, helped me into it, gathered my backpack, and drove me to the University Hospital emergency department just a couple blocks away.

At the hospital ER, they froze my shoulder, gave me a strong pain killer, fentanyl, took the X-rays, and before I knew it, the doctors had reset my shoulder to restore the glenohumeral alignment while I wasn't conscious. That evening, I was assigned to a bed in the surgical unit in room 3F4 to wait for surgery to fix the fractures, for which I had to wait for four more days. All the procedures were done superbly, and I was impressed with the quality of care I received from the hospital staff, including the physiological and the occupational therapy staff at the time of discharge. They also referred me to home care, and a home care case manager came to set up home visits on Monday, Wednesday, and Friday, to help me change the dressing on my wound if needed, and putting on a sling after the shower, etc., which I couldn't do myself.

For the brachial plexus assessment, I was given a phone number for me to phone and set up an appointment after discharge, although my surgeon's instruction was to set up an appointment prior to discharge. A few days later, I received a letter from the Glenrose Electromyography (EMG) Clinic stating that there was a three- to four-month waiting list. Two weeks after the surgery on April 30, I had an appointment with my surgeon Dr. Bury and to remove the stitches, I told him about the wait time. He said it was ridiculous and he would fix it. Soon after, I received a phone call from Glenrose for an appointment on May 7.

I learned a lot from this experience. One thing the University Hospital really needs to improve is patient management. I shared the room with three other patients, and their behaviour was despicable. Pain management was a problem for all of us, including me, but they yelled and screamed day and night, cursing at the nursing staff, wouldn't listen to the nurses explaining that physicians were responsible for pain management, and for changing the medications and dosing if appropriate. One patient was incontinent, making a mess every now and then, so he constantly yelled for help, day and night, to clean up the mess and also to get him up and do physiotherapy, ignoring the nurses' advice not to disturb other people's sleep in the middle of the night. Another gentleman patient had the TV on all the time, and he spoke loudly—on the phone, to his visitors, and with the other patients—regardless of the hour and against the advice of the nurses. The third patient had been in pain all the time, constantly yelling at nurses, and was very abusive. The nurses were powerless, but hospital management should be made aware of this, and take action to correct this situation from happening again and again. What's happening to manners, courtesy, and civility in this world?

Another area that requires improvement is surgical scheduling from the patient perspective. I went to the hospital on April 12, and had the surgery done on April 16. I waited on April 13–15 without knowing which date my surgery was to be performed, and on April 14 and 15, as soon as I was told there would be no surgery that day I was given a day pass to go home and come back early the next day, so I took advantage of it and slept at home while the hospital bed was reserved for me. I think in this day and age it should be able to practice more "patient-centred care," to schedule based on the priority and estimated length of each operation, allowing for unexpected emergent operations, and let patients know the likely date of surgery! Instead, the nurses on the unit were told about the operation only one hour before the surgery to get us ready and wheel us to the operating room. Does it really have to be this way? I wonder.

So, my loss is also my gain, in understanding what's going on at the University of Alberta Hospital, the health care system, and society at large. As I was writing this, I did take my time as a patient, and as a former quality assurance professional, to file patient feedback to Quality Improvement at Alberta Health Services. Quality improvement is everybody's responsibility, though not everybody's priority. If nobody takes the responsibility, the system is less likely to change for the better. In the quality improvement literature, we used to say, "Every error is a treasure." It motivates change for improvement. Let's keep hoping and dreaming!

But the root problem is in our culture. I am on the board of a seniors centre in Edmonton, and we had to deal with similar complaints about the centre residents abusing the centre staff, thinking their membership at the centre entitled them to use the centre as they please. So the issue of abusive patients is much broader and deeper, well entrenched in our culture.

Going back to the question of graceful ageing, Dr. Vivien Brown (2017) has the following four secrets:

1. Keep learning something new.
2. Embrace the real you.
3. Allow the relations to change and grow.
4. Always try your best.

I think these are wonderful prescriptions, and I will continue to preach the same even though my left arm can no longer function normally as before, temporarily or permanently, due to brachial plexus nerve injuries. After a couple months of physiotherapy and acupuncture, most muscles have recovered somewhat, although the deltoid, the biceps, and the triceps muscles have not. I still have one good arm, though, to do most of the activities I used to do before. However, it has been a challenge to do things with one hand instead of two, as it required learning new routines to get things done. I still can type, for example, but one-handed typing is much slower with more mistakes than two-handed typing. When I tried to use the left hand to help, it was cumbersome and hard on my shoulder, so I gave up. Without a sufficient degree of recovery, therefore, I would miss doing things like riding my bike, although, luckily, I still can play tennis, although not at 100%! Life is becoming a little more challenging for me, but my handicap is nothing in comparison to those of lots of other people I witness on the street—in wheelchairs, with walking sticks, all by themselves. Besides, I can do more reading, writing, painting, walking, and hiking, etc. Life is still full of potential even with diminished capabilities. So, let me keep at it and keep learning new ways of doing things, embracing myself to allow the relations to change and grow, and keep trying to do my best.

To plan for the summer, I looked up the 2018 summer school at the University of Alberta, and registered for a course, Late-Century Canadian Texts: Reading and Thinking Models of Care. In order to go to the class, I tried my bicycle and lo and behold, I was able to ride fairly confidently even with my weak left arm. So I started to ride my bike again after three to four months of physical therapy—against the advice of my physiotherapist! As well, I could start typing with both hands!

Despite all the problems with myself and in the world, therefore, my life goes on pretty much as usual—although a full recovery will take many more months or even years, if it ever will—and I feel immensely grateful to my neighbour who rescued me, to the health care professionals who treated me superbly, to my family and friends who lent me their support, to the Canadian health care system that has provided excellent facilities and covered all the expenses, and to the Canadian education and social welfare systems that allow me to continue learning and thriving. Therefore, I remain extremely grateful and hopeful, as expressed in a poem I wrote in 2011:

Why I'm Grateful / Glose / 2011

I'm grateful my family loves me
I'm grateful my family isn't poor
I'm grateful I can go to school
and get a good education
I'm grateful we don't live in a war

I'm grateful to all who care(d) for me
My mother, father, brother, and sisters
Who nurtured me, and sent me overseas
To study and prosper, and be free
My favourite teachers and writers
Who inspired and enriched my soul
My delightful son and daughter
Who share(d) our sorrows and laughter
I'm thankful for my loved ones, one and all
I am grateful my family loves me

I'm grateful for our family tradition
That demanded all our members paid
Tribute to higher education
When I experienced destitution
As a needy student, they came to my aid
Now that financial crises befall
All around us, we are not afraid
Because secure foundations have been laid
And my children are thriving overall
I'm grateful my family isn't poor

I am grateful that I am still well
And live in an inspiring environment
Although ageism against our personnel
Impelled me to bid my workplace farewell
Retirement brings novel excitement
It frees me to chase my alluring dream
Classrooms are no longer a torment
Rather a fine place for enlightenment
To improve my knowledge and self-esteem
I'm grateful I can go (back) to school
and get a good education

Thanks to those who unmask war's cruelty
I'm against its false rationalization
It's a crime against humanity
For those thriving on macho mentality
Like aggression and exploitation

Oppression and militarism
It's a despicable institution
Capable of horrific destruction
Having realized its absurdism
I'm grateful we don't live in a war

References

Acevedo, B. P., & Aron, A. (2009). Does a long-term relationship kill romantic love? *Review of General Psychology, 13*(1), 59–65. doi:10.1037/a0014226.

Adamson, P. (2018). Wittgenstein & the war. *Philosophy Now, 124*, 41.

Admin (2016, June 2). Artist feature: who is Xiao Lu? How To Talk About Art History. Retrieved from http://www.howtotalkaboutarthistory.com/artist-feature/artist-feature-who-is-xiao-lu/.

Anderson, R. (2016, September 6). The ugly truth about online dating. Are we sacrificing love for convenience? *Psychology Today*. Retrieved from https://www.psychologytoday.com/ca/blog/the-mating-game/201609/the-ugly-truth-about-online-dating.

Anonymous (2018, February 6). Increasing pipeline capacity—without building new pipelines. *Oil Sands Magazine*. Retrieved from https://www.oilsandsmagazine.com/news/2018/2/6/increasing-pipeline-capacity-without-building-new-pipelines-partial-upgrading-fractal-systems.

Arendt, H. (1964). *Eichmann in Jerusalem: A report on the banality of evil.* New York, NY: Viking.

Barak, S. (2008, April 22). Stephen Hawking says NASA should budget for interstellar travel. *The Inquirer*. Retrieved from https://www.theinquirer.net/inquirer/news/1024968/stephen-hawking-nasa-budget-interstellar-travel.

Beaudet, P. (2009). Globalization and development. In P. Haslam, J. Schafer, and P. Beaudet (Eds.), *Introduction to international development: Approaches, actors, and issues* (pp. 107-124). Don Mills, Ontario: Oxford University Press.

Belck, J. (1967). *The Faith of Helen Keller: The Life of a Great Woman, with Selections from Her Writings.* Kansus City, Missouri: Hallmark Cards, p. 55. Retrieved from http://www.archive.org/stream/onfaithhelen/onfaithhelen_djvu.txt.

Bell, D. A. (2008). *China's new Confucianism: Politics and everyday life in a changing society.* Princeton, NJ: Princeton University Press.

Borgonjon, D. (2017). Can We Talk about *Dialogue?* A Pre-script to Art and China after 1989. MCLC Resource Center, The Ohio State University. Retrieved from http://u.osu.edu/mclc/online-series/borgonjon/.

Botta, M., & Abbasi, A. (2015). Armed conflict versus global sustainable development as functions of social change. *Journal of Future Studies, 19*(4), 51–72.

Brody, R. (2013, March 31). Hannah Arendt (film). *The New Yorker.* Retrieved from https://www.newyorker.com/culture/richard-brody/hannah-arendt-and-the-glorification-of-thinking.

Brown, V. (2017). *A Woman's Guide to Healthy Aging: 7 Proven Ways to Keep You Vibrant.* Toronto: Barlow Publishing.

Burton, N. (2017, March 12). What's the difference between friendship and love? *Psychology Today.* Retrieved from https://www.psychologytoday.com/ca/blog/hide-and-seek/201703/whats-the-difference-between-friendship-and-love.

Butler, J. (1999). *Gender Trouble. Ferminism and the Subversion of Identity.* New York, NY: Routledge.

Butler, J. (2012). *Parting Ways. Jewishness and the Critique of Zionism.* New York: Columbia University Press.

Camus, A. (1991/1955). *The myth of Sisyphus and other essays* (reissue ed., J. O'Brian, Trans.). New York, NY: Vintage.

Capra, F. (1999) *The Tao of physics. An exploration of the parallels between modern physics and Eastern mysticism.* Boulder, CO: Shambhala Publications.

Capra, F. & Jakobsen, O.D. (2017). A conceptual framework for ecological economics based on systemic principles of life. *International Journal of Social Economics*, 44(6), 831-844, Retrieved from https://doi.org/10.1108/IJSE-05-2016-0136.

Carpenter, T. G. (February 20, 2018). Will the U.S. go to war with China over Taiwan? *The American Conservative.* Retrieved from https://www.theamericanconservative.com/articles/will-the-u-s-go-to-war-with-china-over-taiwan/.

Chang, W.-C., & Fraser, J. (2017). Cooperate! A paradigm shift for health equity. *International Journal for Equity in Health*, *16*(12). doi:10.1186/s12939-016-0508-4.

Chiung Yao (2017, March 14). Queen of romance novels wants simple send-off after death, *The Straits Times*.

Chua, A. (2011, January 8). Why Chinese mothers are superior. *The Wall Street Journal*. Retrieved from https://www.wsj.com/articles/SB10001424052748704111504576059713528698754.

Clifford, C. (March 6, 2018). Over 500 Canadian doctors protest raises, say they're being paid too much (yes, too much). *CNBC: Make It.* Retrieved from https://www.cnbc.com/make-it/.

Clancy, C. (2017, September 29). Debate over future of the oilsands has changed, says Indigenous activist. *Calgary Herald*. Retrieved from https://calgaryherald.com/business/energy/debate-over-future-of-the-oilsands-has-changed-says-indigenous-activist.

Cox, D. (April 27, 2017). The curse of the people who never feel pain. *BBC Future*. Retrieved from http://www.bbc.com/future/story/20170426-the-people-who-never-feel-any-pain.

Daly, H. (2005, September). Economics in a Full World. *Scientific American*, 293(3), SPECIAL ISSUE: Crossroads for Planet Earth, 100 107.

Davies, C. (2008). Becoming sissy : a response to David McInnes. In B. Davies (Ed.), *Judith Butler in Conversation : Analyzing the Texts and Talk of Everyday Life* (pp. 117-133). Abingdon, UK: Routledge.

Dawkins, R. (1995). *River out of Eden: A Darwinian view of life.* London: Weidenfeld & Nicolson.

de Bary, W. T., & Bloom, I. (1999). *Sources of Chinese tradition: From earliest times to 1600* (2nd ed., Vol. 1). New York, NY: Columbia University Press. Retrieved from https://books.google.ca/books/about/Sources_of_Chinese_Tradition.html?id=TQN9nwkkXGsC.

de Beauvoir, S. (1989). *The second sex.* New York, NY: Vintage Books.

Defalco, A. (2016). Introduction: Literature, care, and Canada. In A. Defalco. *Imagining care: Responsibility, dependency, and Canadian literature* (pp. 3–26). Toronto: University of Toronto Press.

De Souza. M. & Meyer, C. (2018, August 30). Court quashes Trudeau's approval of Trans Mountain pipeline. *Canada's National Observer.*

Dewey, J. (2011/1934). "Art as experience." In D. Goldblatt & L. Brown, *A reader in philosophy of the arts,* (3rd ed.). Upper Saddle River, NJ: Prentice Hall.

Diamond, J. (2005). *Collapse: How societies choose to fail or succeed.* New York, NY: Viking Books.

Earp, B. (2012). Love and other drugs. *Philosophy Now, 91*(July/August), 14–17.

Eisler, R. (2007). Our great creative challenge: rethinking human nature—and recreating society. In R. Richards (Ed.), *Everyday creativity and new views of human nature: Psychological, social, and spiritual perspectives* (pp. 261–285). Washington, DC: American Psychological Association.

Elson, D. (2000) Socializing markets, not market socialism. *Socialist Register, 36.*

Etcoff, N. (2000). *Survival of the prettiest.* New York, NY: Knopf Doubleday Publishing.

Ezra, M. (2007). The Eichmann polemics: Hannah Arendt and her critics. *Dissent*, (Democratiya 9, Summer 2007).

Figueres, C., Schellnhuber, H. J., Whiteman, G., et al. (2017). Three years to safeguard our climate. *Nature*, 546: 593–595.

Filar, R. (2013, July 30). Willing the Impossible: An Interview with Judith Butler. *Berfrois*.

FlorCruz, M. (2014, March 24). Taiwan student protests escalate: economic trade agreement with Beijing reflects annexation fears. *International Business Times*.

Forrest, B. (2000). Methodological naturalism and philosophical naturalism: clarifying the connection. *Philo*, *3*(2), 7–29.

Frankl, V. (1963). *Man's search for meaning*. Boston, MA: Beacon Press.

Friedman, T. (2005). *The world is flat*. New York, NY: Farrar, Straus and Giroux.

Fry, D. (2005). *The human potential for peace: An anthropological challenge to assumptions about war and violence*. New York, NY: Oxford University Press.

Fukuyama, F. (1989, Summer). The end of history? *The National Interest*.

Fukuyama, F. (1992). *The End of History and the Last Man*. London, UK: Penguin.

Gates, B. (2017, March 7). This book left me in tears. *Gatesnotes*. Retrieved from https://www.gatesnotes.com/Books/When-Breath-Becomes-Air

Galtung, J. (2004). *Peace by Peaceful means. Building Peace Through Harmonious Diversity. The Security Approach and the Peace Approach; & What Could Peace Between Washington and Al Qaeda/Iraq Look Like? Some Points for Presidential Candidates to Consider*. Retrieved from https://doc.uments.com/d-peace-by-peaceful-means.pdf.

Geisner, I. M., Mallett, K., & Kilmer, J. R. (2012). An examination of depressive symptoms and drinking patterns in first year college students. *Issues in Mental Health Nursing, 33*(5), 280-287. doi: 10.3109/01612840.2011.653036.

Gilligan, C. (1993). *In a different voice: Psychological theory and women's development*, (2nd ed.). Cambridge, MA: Harvard University Press.

Gilly, B. (2008). Legitimany and Institutional Change. The Case of China. *Comparative Political Studies*, 41(3), 259-284.

Grange, J. (2001). Dao, technology, and American naturalism. *Philosophy East & West, 51*(3), 363–377.

Griffin, R.S. (n.d.). On "Cloud 9". DOCBOX. Retrieved from https://religiondocbox.com/Atheism_and_Agnosticism/68606768-On-cloud-9-robert-s-griffin.html.

Guignon, C. (2008). Authenticity. *Philosophy Compass*, 3(2), 277–290.

Hardin, G. (1968). The tragedy of the commons. *Science, 162*(3859), 1243–1248.

Hauptli, B., & Passmore, J. (1995). *The reasonableness of reason.* Chicago, IL: Open Court Publishing.

Hayatli, Z. (2018). The philosophy of war. *Philosophy Now, 124*, 6–9.

Hillman, B. (2008, June 1). Rethinking China's Tibet policy. *The Asia-Pacific Journal, 6*(6).

Housseini, K. (2007). *A Thousand Splendid Suns.* New York, NY: Riverhead Books.

Hugh, D. (2018). *Canada's energy outlook: Current realities and implications for a carbon-constrained future.* Ottawa, ON: Canadian Centre for Policy Alternatives.

Hume, D. (1960/1888). *A treatise on human nature*, (L. A. Selby-Biggle, Ed.). Oxford: The Clarendon Press.

Imamkhodjaeva, O. (2018). Non-violent voices. *Philosophy Now, 124*(February/March), 14–16.

Institute for Economics and Peace. (2016). *The economic value of peace: Measuring the global economic impact of violence and conflict.* Author. Retrieved from http://economicsandpeace.org/wp-content/uploads/2016/12/The-Economic-Value-of-Peace-2016-WEB.pdf.

Jenkins, A. (2017, March 10). Bill Gates says 'this Book Left Me in Tears'. *Fortune.* Retrieved from http://fortune.com/2017/03/10/bill-gates-paul-kalanithi-when-breath-becomes-air/.

Kalanithi, P. (2016). *When breath becomes air.* New York, NY: Random House.

Kamboureli, S. (2007). The limits of the ethical turn: Troping towards the other, Yann Martel, and self. *University of Toronto Quarterly, 76*(3), 937–961.

Kelly, M. (2012). *Owning Our Future. The Emerging Ownership Revolution. Journeys to a Generative Economy.* Penguin Random House Canada. Retrieved from https://www.bkconnection.com/static/Owning_Our_Future_EXCERPT.pdf.

Kessel, B. (2001). "Sexuality in the older person." *Age and Ageing, 30*(2), 121–124.

King, I. (2014). Moral Laws of the Jungle. *Philosophy Now, 100* (January/February), 20–22.

King, T. (2012). *The inconvenient Indian.* Minneapolis, MN: University of Minnesota Press.

Kim, R. (2016, June 1). With great fanfare, but limited results. *Quora.* Retrieved from https://www.quora.com/profile/Richard-Kim-15.

Kinoshita, F. (2016, May 31). How were Korean and Chinese (Taiwan) names converted to Japanese during the colonialism period? *Quora.* Retrieved from https://www.quora.com/How-were-Korean-and-Chinese-Taiwan-names-converted-to-Japanese-during-the-colonialism-period.

Kukk, C. L. (2017). *The compassionate achiever: How helping others fuels success.* San Francisco, CA: HarperOne.

Kwilecki, S., & Wilson, L. (2003, May 1). Feminist Follies: Facing Facts At Fifty. *Women in Higher Education, 12,* 25-27.

Kyōko, H. (August 30, 2013). Taiwan's complicated love affair with Japan. *Nippon.com.* Retrieved from https://www.nippon.com/en/in-depth/a02201/.

Lai, L. (2001). Corrupted lineage: Narrative in the gaps of history. *West Coast Line, 34*(3),40–53.

Lau, E. (1989). *Runway: Diary of a Street Kid.* Toronto: HarperCollins Publishers Ltd.

Li, A. (1986). *The butcher's wife and other stories* (H. Goldblatt & E. Yeung, Eds. & Translators). Boston, MA: Cheng & Tsui Company.

Lin, Y. (1998). *The importance of living.* New York, NY: HarperCollins.

Lind, J. (2009). The perils of apology: What Japan shouldn't learn from Germany. *Foreign Affairs, 88*(3), 132–146.

Lindau, S. T., Schumm, L. P. Laumann, E. O., Levinson, W., O'Muircheartaigh, C. A., & Waite, L. J. (2007). A study of sexuality and health among older adults in the United States. *New England Journal of Medicine, 357*(8), 762-774. doi:10.1056/NEJMoa067423.

Lorenz, A. (2005, March 7). The Chinese miracle will end soon. *SPIEGEL Online.*

Lyons, S. (2014). On happiness. *Philosophy Now, 100* (January/February), 28–31.

Magee, B. (2016). *Ultimate questions.* Princeton, NJ: Princeton University Press.

Marano, H. E. (2009, July 1). Jealousy: Love's destroyer. *Psychology Today.* Retrieved from https://www.psychologytoday.com/.

Marks, J. (2016). *Hard atheism and the ethics of desire: An Alternative to morality.* Basingstoke, UK: Palgrave Macmillan.

McGowan, K. (2014, March 6). The second coming of Sigmund Freud. *Discover.*

McGreal, S. A. (2012, September 5). Reason versus faith? The interplay of intuition and rationality in supernatural belief. *Psychology Today*.

Meagher, M. (2009). Jenny Saville and a feminist aesthetics of disgust. *Hypatia* 18(4), 23-42.

Midgley, M. (2010). *The solitary self: Darwin and the selfish gene*. Durham, UK: Acumen.

Milojević, I. (1999). The Cost of Past-Oriented Thinking. *Metafuture*. Retrieved from http://www.metafuture.org/the-cost-of-past-oriented-thinking-1999/.

Moeller, P. (2012, May 1). 10 Ways Older People Withdraw from Life. *U.S. News*. Retrieved from https://money.usnews.com/money/blogs/the-best-life/2012/05/01/10-ways-older-people-withdraw-from-life.

Moore, A. & Gibbons, D. (1986-1987). *Watchman*. Burbank, CA: DC Comics.

Moran, M. (2014, January 29). Global elites finally admit income inequality is a problem. *Salon*. Retrieved from https://www.salon.com/2014/01/29/the_super_rich_from_their_alpine_resort_inequality_is_a_serious_issue_parnter/.

Morgan, G. (2017, December 21). Canada's first refinery in 30 years could rescue battered oil producers. *Financial Post*. Retrieved from https://business.financialpost.com/commodities/energy/a-new-refinery-in-alberta-has-come-to-the-rescue-of-battered-oil-producers-so-why-is-its-ceo-sad.

Morris, D. (2009, February 21). Can jumbo elephants really paint? Intrigued by stories, naturalist Desmond Morris set out to find the truth. *Daily Mail*. Retrieved from http://www.dailymail.co.uk/sciencetech/article-1151283/Can-jumbo-elephants-really-paint--Intrigued-stories-naturalist-Desmond-Morris-set-truth.html

Nussbaum, M. (1992). Human functioning and social justice: In defense of Aristotelian essentialism. *Political Theory*, *20*(2), 202–246. doi:10.1177/0090591792020002002.

Nussbaum, M. (1994, October 1). Patriotism and cosmopolitanism. *Boston Review*.

Nussbaum, M. (2016). *Anger and Forgiveness : Resentment, Generosity, Justice*. New York, NY: Oxford University Press.

Nerlich, G. (2013). J. J. C. Smart, 1920-2012. *Philosophy Now, 94* (January/February), 41.

Nin, A. (1969). *The Diary of Anais Nin*, Volume 1: 1931-1934. St. Charles, IL: Houghton Mifflin Harcout.

O'Flynn, P. (2011, October/November). Spinning narratives, spinning selves. *Café Philosophy*.

Oredsson, E. (2016, June 2). Artist feature: Who is Xiao Lu? *How to Talk About Art History*.

Parfit, D., & Scheffler, S. (2011). *On what matters* (Vol. 1). Oxford, UK: Oxford University Press.

Peeples, L. (2012, February 24). Work Less, Help Economy And Environment. *The Huffington Post*. Retrieved from https://www.huffingtonpost.ca/entry/work-less-economy-environment_n_1299792.

Pinker, Steven (2018). *Enlightenment now*. New York, NY: Viking.

Pinker, Susan (2013). The Longevity Puzzle. *CBC Radio*. Retrieved from https://www.cbc.ca/radio/ideas/the-longevity-puzzle-1.2913255.

Pinker, Susan (2014). *The Village Effect. How Face-To-Face Contact Can Make Us Healthier and Happier*. Toronto: Random House Canada.

Popova, M. (2014, June 3). Leo Tolstoy on Finding Meaning in a Meaningless World. *BrainPickings*.

Popper, K. (1950). *The open society and its enemies*. London, UK: Routledge.

Popper, K. (1961). *The logic of scientific discovery*. London, UK: Hutchinson & Co. Ltd.

Popper, K. (1963). *Conjectures and refutations*. London, UK: Routledge.

Popper, K. (1974). *Unended quest.* Chicago, IL: The Library of Living Philosophers, Inc.

Popper, K. (1988, April 23). From the archives: The open society and its enemies revisited. Retrieved from https://www.economist.com/democracy-in-america/2016/01/31/from-the-archives-the-open-society-and-its-enemies-revisited.

Quora Contributor (2014, December 26). Why is the 1992 Consensus so important to Beijing and Taipei? *Quora.* Retrieved from https://slate.com/human-interest/2014/12/1992-consensus-why-is-the-agreement-important-to-beijing-and-taipei.html.

Ramzy, A. (2014, March 23). Anger grows in Taiwan against deal with China. *The New York Times.* Retrieved from https://www.nytimes.com/2014/03/24/world/asia/anger-grows-in-taiwan-against-deal-with-china.html.

Rees, W. (2010). Globalization, eco-footprints and the increasingly unsustainable entanglement of nations. In S. Bastinaoni (Ed.), *The State of the Art in Ecological Footprint Theory and Applications*, Footprint Forum 2010, Academic Conference Short Communications, Global Footprint Network, pp. 1–2.

Rees, W., & Wackernagel, M. (1996). Urban ecological footprints: why cities cannot be sustainable—and why they are a key to sustainability. *Environmental Impact Assessment Review, 16*, 223–248.

Ricci, N. (2012). *The origin of species.* Toronto: Anchor Canada.

Rigger, S. (2014). *Why Taiwan matters: Small island, global powerhouse.* Lanham, MD: Rowman & Littlefield.

Roberts, M. (2011). Let's abolish "art." *Philosophy Now, 84* (May/June), 31-32.

Rowen, I., & Rowen, J. (2017). Taiwan's truth and reconciliation committee: The geopolitics of transitional justice in a contested state. *International Journal of Transitional Justice, 11*(1), 92–112.

Ryan, S. Y. (2013). *Green Island.* New York, NY: Penguin.

Saad, G. (2010, January 22). Pornography: Beneficial or detrimental? It turns out that pornography is good for you. *Psychology Today*.

Said, E. (1978). *Orientalism*. New York, NY: Pantheon.

Sahlberg, P. (2012). A model lesson: Finland shows us what equal opportunity looks like. *American Educator*, *36*(1), 20-27.

Sari, Y. (2014). Hannah Arendt (film). *Philosophy Now*, *100* (January/ February), 42-43.

Sartre, J.-P. (2007/1945). *Existentialism is a Humanism*. Hew Haven, CT: Yale University Press.

Schumacher, E. F. (1999/1973). *Small is beautiful: Economics as if people mattered*. Dublin: Hartley & Marks.

Schweickart, D. (2002). *After capitalism*. Lanham, MD: Rowman & Littlefield.

Seifert, K. (2013, November 1). We are not created equal. *Psychology Today*.

Shattuck T.L. (2017, February 27). Taiwan's White Terror: remembering the 228 Incident. *Foreign Policy Research*. Retrieved from https://www.fpri. org/article/2017/02/taiwans-white-terror-remembering-228-incident/.

Sher, L. (2004). Depression and alcoholism. *QJM: An International Journal of Medicine*, *97*(4), 237–240. doi:10.1093/qjmed/hch045.

Snyder, C. (2008). What is Third-Wave Feminism? A New Directions Essay. *Signs: Journal of Women in Culture and Society*, *34*(1), 175–96.

Sorokan, S.T., Finlay, J.C., Jefferies, A.L., et al. (2015). Newborn male circumcision. Canadian Paediatric Society position statement. *Paediatric Child Health*, *20*(6), 311-315.

Springer, K. (2012, April 01). The 'Naked Face Project': Two Months, Sans Beauty Products. *Time*. Retrieved from http://newsfeed.time.com/2012/04/01/the-naked-face-project-two-months-sans-beauty-products/.

Steffen, W., Rockstrom, J., Richardson, K., et al. (2018). Trajectories of the Earth system in the Anthropocene. *PNAS* 115(33), 8252–8259.

Stiglitz, J., & Bilmes, L. (2010, September 5). The true cost of the Iraq war: $3 trillion and beyond. *The Washington Post*. Retrieved from http://www.washingtonpost.com/wp-dyn/content/article/2010/09/03/AR2010090302200.html.

Strange, S. (1996). *The retreat of the state: The diffusion of power in the world economy*. Cambridge, UK: Cambridge University Press.

Summers, S. (2010). "*Twilight* is so anti-feminist that I want to cry:" *Twilight* fans finding and defining feminism on the World Wide Web. *Computers and Composition*, 27(4), 315-323.

Talaga, T. (2017). *Seven fallen feathers*. Toronto, ON: House of Anansi Press.

Taylor, C. (1994). The politics of recognition. In A. Gutmann (Ed.), *Multiculturalism and the politics of recognition* (pp. 25-73). Princeton: Princeton University Press.

Thim, M., & Matsuka, M. (2014, May 15). The odd couple: Japan and Taiwan's unlikely friendship. *The Diplomat*.

Thornton, S. (2005). Karl Popper. In E. Zalta (Ed.) *Stanford Encyclopedia of Philosophy*. Retrieved from https://plato.stanford.edu/entries/popper/

Tiedens, L.Z. (2001). The effect of anger on the hostile inferences of aggressive and nonaggressive people: specific emotions, cognitive processing, and chronic accessibility. *Motivation and Emotion*, 25(3), 233-251.

Tirman, J. (2009, January 29). Bush's war totals. *The Nation*.

Tolstoy, L. (1879–1880). *A Confession*. Retrieved from http://rintintin.colorado.edu/~vancecd/phil150/Tolstoy.pdf.

Tsai, I-w (2016, May 20). Full text of President Tsai's inaugural address. *Focus Taiwan*. Retrieved from http://focustaiwan.tw/news/aipl/201605200008.aspx.

Truth and Reconciliation Commission of Canada. (2015). *Honouring the Truth, Reconciling for the Future. Summary of the Final Report of the Truth and Reconciliation Commission of Canada*. Author. Retrieved from http://www.trc.ca/websites/trcinstitution/File/2015/Findings/Exec_Summary_2015_05_31_web_o.pdf.

Tumblr (2010, April 23). *Posters For Good.* Retrieved from https://posters-for-good.tumblr.com/post/542977597/if-you-have-food-in-your-fridge-clothes-on-your.

United Nations Educational, Scientific and Cultural Organization (2017). *School violence and bullying: Global status report.* Paris, FR: Author. Retrieved from http://unesdoc.unesco.org/images/0024/002469/246970e.pdf.

United States Conference of Catholic Bishops (1993, November 17). *Centrality of Conscience.* Retrieved from http://www.usccb.org/issues-and-action/human-life-and-dignity/war-and-peace/excerpts-from-the-harvest-of-justice-is-sown-in-peace-centrality-of-conscience-1993-11.cfm.

Van Evra, J. (2018, April 12). Indian Horse: 10 things about the groundbreaking new Canadian film. *CBC.* Retrieved from https://www.cbc.ca/radio/q/blog/indian-horse-10-things-about-the-groundbreaking-new-canadian-film-1.4616397.

Wagamese, R. (2012). *Indian Horse.* Madeira Park, BC, Canada: Douglas and McIntyre Ltd.

Walt, S. M. (2017, November 13). Trump isn't sure if democracy is better than autocracy. America's president is voluntarily abdicating one of the country's biggest strategic advantages. *Foreign Policy.* Retrieved from https://foreignpolicy.com/2017/11/13/trump-isnt-sure-if-democracy-is-better-than-autocracy/.

Wasserstrom, J. (2014, April 11). Taiwan's Sunflower Protests: A Q&A with Shelley Rigger. *Dissent.* Retrieved from https://www.dissentmagazine.org/online_articles/taiwans-sunflower-protests-a-qa-with-shelley-rigger.

Well, T. (2017, July 25). Why more women are happily going without makeup. Research explains the psychology of going barefaced. *Psychology Today.* Retrieved from https://www.psychologytoday.com/ca/blog/the-clarity/201707/why-more-women-are-happily-going-without-makeup.

Wen, P. (2014, May 30). 25 years on, artist remembers 'first gunshots of Tiananmen'. *The Sydney Morning Herald.*

White, M. K. (2014). Soaring income gaps: China in comparative perspective. *Daedalus, 143*(2), 39–52. doi: 10.1162/DAED_a_00271.

Wittgenstein,. L. (1961/1921). *Tractatus Logico-Philosophicus* (D.F. Pears & B.F. McGuinness, trans.). Bungay, Suffolk, UK: Routledge & Kegan Paul Ltd.

Wood, G. (2011, April 15). Secret fears of the super-rich. *The Atlantic.*

World Health Organization (2015a). *Alcohol* (fact sheet). Retrieved from http://www.who.int/news-room/fact-sheets/detail/alcohol.

World Health Organization (2015b). *Global status report on road safety 2015.* Retrieved from http://www.who.int/violence_injury_prevention/road_safety_status/2015/GSRRS2015_Summary_EN_final2.pdf?ua=1.

World Health Organization (2016, April 13). Investing in treatment for depression and anxiety leads to fourfold return—UN report, *UN News.* Retrieved from https://news.un.org/en/story/2016/04/526622-investing-treatment-depression-and-anxiety-leads-four-fold-return-un-report.

World Health Organization (2017). *Violence against women* (fact sheet). Retrieved from http://www.who.int/mediacentre/factsheets/fs239/en/.

Wright, A. (2018, March 1). 30 countries with the most billionaires, 2018. *Geoworld Magazine.*

Wu, H. (2004). Daoist wisdom and popular wisdom: a sociolinguistic analysis of the philosophical maxims in the *Daode Jing* and their proverbial equivalents. In V. Shen & W. Oxtoby (Eds.), *Wisdom in China and the West: Chinese philosophical studies, XXII,* (pp. 303-328). Washington, D.C.: The Council for Research in Values and Philosophy.

Wu, Z. (1944). The Doctor's Mother. In J. S. M. Lau & H. Goldblatt (Eds.), *Columbia Anthology of Modern Chinese Literature* (2nd ed., pp. 184-194), New York: Columbia University Press.

Wylie, K., & Frcpsych, M. D. (2009). A global survey of sexual behaviours. *Journal of Family and Reproductive Health, 3*(2), 39–49.

Xiao, L. (2010). *Dialogue.* Hong Kong University Press.

Yang, J. (2015, February 9). For a vision of common, comprehensive, cooperative and sustainable security. *China Daily.*

Yang, O. (2017). Walking through the 228 Incident: 10 facts about 228. *Outreach for Taiwan,* 2/28. Retrieved from https://international.the-newslens.com/article/62328.

Zhang, Y., & Sloan, F. A. (2014). Depression, alcohol dependence and abuse, and drinking and driving behaviour. *Journal of Behavioral Health, 3*(4), 212–219.

Index

INDEX

Please note that the italicized "*f*" after a page reference indicates a figure and the italicized "*n*" a footnote.

A

Abbasi, A., 188

Aboriginal peoples: *see also* First Nations peoples; Austronesians (in Taiwan), 196; collective rights of, 123–124; land as central to, 110-111; pipeline construction and, 111–113; racism against, 110; self-government and, 112; word warrior advocate for rights of, 116, 116*n*

About Schmidt (movie), 153

Acevedo, B.P., 14

acid rain, 170

acupuncture, xi, xiii, 4, 33, 34, 226

Adamson, Peter, 25, 158

Adkin, Laurie, 185

aesthetics, 77, 217; development in West of, 77; of health, 97; as multidimensional experience, 78; study/knowledge of beauty in Chinese, 77; surgical procedures, 95

Afghanistan: war in, 55

African Union, 117

After Capitalism (Schweickart), 152

ageing: gender and sexual activity in, 161–162; genetics and, 155; graceful, 151–153, 156; lifespan and, 155; loss of social connections in, 154; physical activity in, 154, 155, 156; pornography and, 165; sense of purpose in, 155; sexual activity and, 160–162; symptoms, 151

ageism, 228

aggression, 126, 228

agnosticism, 23; active, 24

agoraphobia, 25

Alberta: economy of, 179–181; pipelines, 111–113, 169; tar sands, 110–111, 169

alcoholism, 8; costs of, 188–189

alienation, 102, 153

al-Janabi, Rafid Ahmed Alwan (*a.k.a.* Curveball), 50

Allen, Elizabeth Akers, 12

All Together (movie), 161

altruism, 221

Alzheimer's disease, 154

American dream, the, 191

American Psychological Association, 203

anarchism, 130

Anderson, Hans, 178

Anderson, R., 162

Confucianism, 51, 52*f*, 53; authoritarian and hierarchical aspects of, 105; just war theory and, 53–54, 56
Confucius, 3, 7, 77, 130
Confucius Institutes, 53
Conrad, Alfred Haskell, 126
consciousness, 29
conservatism, 152
Conservative Party,113, 173, 180, 215, 216
cooperatives, 152–153
cosmology, 31
Cox, D., 204
creation, 22–23; art as, 91; myths, 35
critical thinking, 148
Cross-Straight Services Trade Agreement (CSSTA), 57
Cruz, Nikolas Jacob, 46
CSSTA. *See* Cross-Straight Services Trade Agreement (CSSTA)
cultural genocide, 114
cultural relativism, 102
culture(s), 20; black identity, 102; as conditioner of beauty, 96; differences between Eastern and Western, 120; environmental sustainability and, 169–171; equal worth for all, 123; failure of once-mighty, 179; feminism and, 126; French Quebec, 123; gender relations' changes, 138; intelligent designer variations in, 22; mainstream Canadian, 102; marginalization of minority, 123; multiculturalism and, 103–104; Orientalism, 109–110; post-feminist, 130–131; sustainable global, 190; terrible practices of, 95; of violence and war, 49; violent, 143; Western, 135; xenophobic, 109
Cummings, E.E., 12
cupping, 33
cyberbullying, 189

D
Dadaism, 90
Dalai Lama, 64
Daly, Herman, 185, 186
Damasio, Antonio, 30
Daode Jing. See Tao Te Ching (a.k.a. Daode Jing)(Laozi)
Dartmouth College, New Hampshire, 116*n*, 198
Darwin, Charles, 35
Darwinism, 35
Darwish, Mahmoud, 148
Davidson College, North Carolina, 175
Davies, Cristyn, 106
Dawkins, Richard, 2, 3, 35
Dean, James, 192
death: celebration of, 158–159; death instinct, 59, 61;

Ma, Ying-jeou, 58
Macdonald, John A., 209
MacEwan University, xiii, 4, 33, 91
Maclean's magazine, 144
Made in Bangladesh? (tv documentary), 66
Magee, Bryan, 23, 24
magnanimous living, 194
Mandela, Nelson, 205, 206, 208
Man's Search for Meaning (Frankl), 2
Marano, Hara Estroff, 13
Marks, Joel, 35
Marshall, Claire, 83
Marx, Karl, 212
masculinity, 4; active psychosocial traits, 129; left brain and, 129; as yang power, 126, 127, 129
Maslow, Abraham, 45
match.com, 162
materialism, 21
Matsuka, M., 197
May, Elizabeth, 112
May, Theresa, 103
Mayo Clinic, 154
McGowan, Kat, 30
McGreal, Scott, 39
Meagher, Michelle, 77, 130
memes, cultural, 3
Mencius, 51, 53
mental harassment, 189
metaphysical naturalism, 23
metaphysics, 26
methodological naturalism, 23
Meyer, Stephenie, 131
Mid-East conflicts, 56
Midgley, Mary, 2, 35, 36, 47
militarism, 105, 228; costs of, 187–188
militarization, 49
Mill, John Stuart, 178
Milojevic, I., 189
mind-body identity, 29-31
mind *vs.* matter, 21
minimum wages, 68, 69, 70
60 Minutes (tv series), 82, 85
Misericordia Hospital, Edmonton, 95
misrecognition, 121–122
Moeller, P., 154

qigong, 33
Qing Ming tomb-sweeping festival, 18
Qiu, Miaojin, 8, 92
quantitative *vs.* qualitative, 4
queer activism, 147
Quora Contributor, 207

R
racism, 102–110; against Aboriginal peoples, 110; in Canada, 103, 105-106
Ramzy, A., 58
Rand, Ayn, 45
rationalism, 105
rationality, 32, 37
rational system of thought, 39
Reagan, Ronald, 66
realism, 152
reality: beauty and, 78; common-sense view of, 20–21; countless aspects of, 23–24; as distinct from fiction, 21–22; logical pictures of, 26; as mental constructs or simulations, 21, 22; social constructivism ideas of, 26; underlying language are propositions describing, 26
reason, 37, 38; justifying of by reason, 39; reasonableness of, 38–40; /rationality vs. emotion/intuition, 4
Reason, Age of, 22
Rebel Without a Cause (movie), 192
recognition: politics of, 121–124; related to honour and dignity, 122–123; related to identity and authenticity, 122
reconciliation, 208–209
Rees, William, 182, 183
religions, 22; *see also* individual religions; extremism, 24; faith and, 37; irrationality of, 24; myths, 22; purpose of relieving human suffering, 24
renewables, 181
repatriation, 107
Resentment, 204
retirement, 151, 153–154, 228
Ricci, Nino, 26, 27
Rich, Adrienne, 126, 127
Rigger, Shelley, 175
Rihanna (Fenty, Robyn Rihanna), 144
Riot Grrrl bands, 131
Road to Serfdom, The (Hayek), 200
road traffic injuries, 189
Roberts, Mark, 84
romanticism, 105
Room of One's Own, A (Woolf), 105
Rowen, Ian, 202

Williams, Jody, 144
Wilson, Loretta, 134, 135, 137, 138, 139
Winterson, Jeanette, 7
Wittgenstein, Ludwig, 23, 25, 26, 84, 158
Wolf, Naomi, 79
Women in Higher Education, 134
women's rights, 42
Wood, Graeme, 69
Woolf, Virginia, 3, 8, 105, 127, 129
world: artificial, 20; citizenship, 176; mental (psychological), 20; physical, 20
World Animal Protection, 83
World Economic Forum (WEF), 67
World Health Assembly, 208
World Health Organization, 188, 189, 195
World Is Flat, The (Friedman), 54, 170
worldview, 212
World War II. *See* Second World War (World War II)
Wu, Helen, 32
Wu, Zhuoliu, 196
wu-wei (non-action), 34, 84
Wylie, Kevan, 160

X
xenophobia, 108, 109
Xi, Jinping, 214
Xiao, Lu, 86, 87–88, 87*f,* 89

Y
Yale University, 120
Yang, Jiechi, 63
Yang, O., xii
Yellow Emperor's Classic of Internal Medicine, The, 155
Yin, Hai-kuang, 199, 200, 200*f,* 201
yin and yang, xi, xiii, 4, 33, 74, 126, 127, 128, 129

Z
Zhang, Y., 188
Zhang, Zhijun, 55
Zika virus, 158
Zionism, 147

Printed in the USA
CPSIA information can be obtained
at www.ICGtesting.com
JSHW082031041123
51231JS00001B/35